W9-AAY-591

The Legal Guide to Costa Rica

Fifth Edition

———————————— Roger A. Petersen

Attorney at Law

©COPYRIGHT   2009

Fifth Edition

1st Edition 1994
2nd Edition 1997
3rd Edition 2002
4th Edition 2005
5th Edition 2009

©**All Rights Reserved**. No part of this publication may be reproduced in any form or by any means, including photocopying, without prior written permission of the copyright holder.

ISBN 978-0-9715815-4-8

For ordering information visit:

www.costaricalaw.com

E-mail: **info@costaricalaw.com**

Published and Distributed by Amerilatin Consultores, S.A., San Jose, Costa Rica
Apartado 643 Centro Colon, San José, Costa Rica

Layout & Design
Gisela Sanchez T.
www.giselasanchez.com
e-mail: sancheztinoco@gmail.com

Table of Contents

Figures

APPENDIX

PREFACE

Costa Rica has undergone significant changes since the first edition of The Legal Guide to Costa Rica was published in 1994. At that time Costa Rica was often overlooked as a retirement and investment destination. That certainly has changed as news about living in Costa Rica spread like wildfire to the point where it topped the list of top international retirement destinations in the world. The affordable life style that Costa Rica offered to many retirees has become a challenge as its popularity sparked a Real Estate boom that began in 2004 sending property prices through the roof in many popular areas, specifically coastal areas. Most of the property purchasers in Costa Rica came from the US and the unraveling of the housing market there will impact the Costa Rican real estate market as well. How deep and how long it will affect Costa Rica is anybodys guess. As such, now more then ever you need reliable information to help you make informed choices when embarking on your Costa Rican venture.

The difference in cultural attitudes, work ethic and business practices will certainly be different than what you are accustomed to in your home country. For example if you always attempt to look for the common sense and logical path in Costa Rica you may find yourself frustrated. The system often opeates in a chaotic and unplanned manner. But then again that is also part of the attraction of Costa Rica. When you are in Costa Rica you will often hear the expression "Pura Vida" which is literally translated into "Pure Life" which means a state of mind and an attitude of living life to the fullest. That attitude is entrenched in Costa Rican culture. If you enjoy the country and its people without trying to "change" it then your experience will be much more enjoyable.

Over the years I have found that those expats that gather information and make informed decisions and surround themselves with good advice are the ones that have the best experiences in Costa Rica. I wrote the Legal Guide to Costa Rica to provide newcomers with easy to understand information about many of the areas of local law that they would encounter when they move to or invest in Costa Rica. Each chapter of the book is divided into specific areas of the law and the Appendix contains examples of the most common forms of legal documents that you will encounter in Costa Rica.

I hope you find the information helpful and that you have an enjoyable and successful venture in Costa Rica, whatever it may be.

CHAPTER 1

COSTA RICA: THE CIVIL LAW SYSTEM

1. WHAT IS A CIVIL LAW SYSTEM

The civil law system derives from the system of jurisprudence held and administered in the Roman Empire, which developed the idea of compiling its written laws into codes. The earliest and most elaborate codification of these laws was found in the Code of Justinian which was developed in 533 A.D. The Code of Justinian was the inspiration for the development of three of the most influential modern legal codes, the French (Napoleonic), German and Swiss.

Under the civil law system, the "code" is a written codification of all the various topics and subdivisions of the law set forth by the legislature. This system of law is used throughout Latin America including Costa Rica. The basis of all Latin American codes was the French Napoleonic Code.

Typically, a civil code will address different areas of the law by subdividing them into specific legal areas such as: the law of property, the law of succession, the law of obligations, the law of persons, and commercial laws.

1.1 CIVIL LAW VS. COMMON LAW

Unlike Costa Rica, which has a civil law system, the United States functions as a "common law" country? Common law in the United States was derived from case law originally developed in England. The Common law relies on the case law that is generated by the court system instead of the legislative enactments typically relied upon in civil law countries.

Interestingly, the differences between both systems have been reduced over the years, as we see a wider use of codification of laws in the United States in the form of federal and state statutes. Meanwhile, countries such as Costa Rica begin to publish and organize their case law, known locally as Jurisprudencia, in an effort to develop precedent for similar cases.

However, in Costa Rica the decisions of the appellate court are not necessarily binding on the lower court. Only the decisions of the Constitutional Chamber of the Supreme Court are mandatory and binding on all lower courts in Costa Rica.

2. THE DEVELOPMENT OF COSTA RICAN LAW

Costa Rica acquired its independence from Spain in 1821 and ratified its first Constitution in 1825. Despite its independence from Spain and the creation of a Supreme Court of Justice, the Costa Rican legal system was dependent on Spanish law to administer justice. As such, Costa Rican courts adhered to the principles and resolutions of the law of Spain. This procedure endured until 1841 when Costa Rica began to develop its own legal framework by borrowing from the legal codes of other countries. For instance, the first civil code adopted by Costa Rica was in large part a copy of the French civil code and the criminal code was identical to that of Spain.

Throughout the late 1800's and the early 1900's, Costa Rica developed new legal codes and revised its existing ones. The modern codes of Costa Rica are heavily influenced by those of France, Spain, Chile, Mexico and Argentina. The bulk of Costa Rican law can be found in the following codes:

(1) The Civil Code

The Civil Code (*Codigo Civil*) is the codification of all the laws governing persons, property, succession and obligations. The Costa Rican Civil Code currently in force was first adopted on January 1, 1888 and amended by Law No. 7020 on January 6, 1986.

(2) The Commercial Code

The Commercial Code of Costa Rica (*Codigo de Comercio*) provides the legal framework for all commercial transactions. This includes corporations, negotiable instruments, banking and bankruptcy. The Commercial Code was passed by the legislature as Law No. 3284 on September 19, 1964.

(3) The Labor Code

The Costa Rican Labor Code (*Codigo de Trabajo*) regulates all rights and obligations of employees and employers and provides for the organization and jurisdiction of Labor Tribunals to handle labor disputes. Although social legislation was passed in the early 1900's, the first labor code was passed in 1943 and is heavily influenced by legislation from Mexico, Chile, Colombia, Venezuela, and Argentina.

(4) The Family Code

The Family Code (*Codigo de Familia*) establishes the legal rights and obligations for marriage, divorce, paternity, guardianship and adoption. The Family Code was first adopted by the legislature by Law No. 5476 on September 21, 1973.

(5) The Code of Civil Procedure

The Costa Rican Code of Civil Procedure (*Codigo Procesal Civil*) governs the practice and procedure that needs to be followed when appearing before the civil courts of Costa Rica. The Code of Civil Procedure currently in effect was introduced in 1989.

(6) The Code of Criminal Procedure

The Costa Rican Code of Criminal Procedure (*Codigo Procesal Penal*) sets forth the procedures to be followed in the Costa Rican criminal courts. The current code models the German criminal procedural code and was implemented in 1998.

(7) The Penal Code (*Codigo Penal*) sets forth all the acts and or omissions, which constitute a criminal offense and thus are punishable by law. The current code was passed by the Legislature as Law No. 4573 on May 4, 1970.

3. THE STRUCTURE OF COSTA RICAN GOVERNMENT

3.1 THE EXECUTIVE BRANCH

The Executive branch of the government is made up of the President of the Republic who is elected through a general election, held every four years. The President appoints two vice-presidents and twenty cabinet officers who each head one of the following Ministries:

(1) Ministry of Economy, Industry & Commerce, (2) Ministry of Foreign Trade, (3) Ministry of Foreign Affairs, (4) Ministry of Health, (5) Ministry of Public Security, (6) Ministry of Justice (7) Ministry of Finance, (8) Ministry of the Presidency, (9) Ministry of Labor and Welfare, (10) Ministry of Information and Communications, (11) Ministry of Public Works and Transportation, (12) Ministry of National Planning and Economic Policy, (13) Ministry of Housing and Human Services, (14) Ministry of Agriculture, (15) Ministry of Energy, Mines, and Natural Resources, (16) Ministry of Public Education, (17) Ministry of Government and Police, (18) Ministry of Culture, Youth and Sports (19) Ministry of Science and Technology, (20) Ministry of Women's Issues.

In order to contact any of these Ministries and other key government offices refer to Appendix 1 which contains pertinent telephone numbers and addresses. The internet address for the office of the president is www.casapres.go.cr

3.2 THE LEGISLATIVE BRANCH

The Legislative Branch is a unicameral congress which consists of fifty-seven Deputies who are elected every four years. The deputies are elected by province and may not be re-elected successively. Each province is allocated a specific number of deputies in proportion to the population of the province.

The Legislature has two ordinary sessions, one that runs from May 1- July 31 and the other from September 1- November 30. The Legislature requires a two thirds quorum for a session and has the power to enact and amend laws, approve or reject international agreements and public treaties, and the appointment of judges. The website for the Costa Rican Legislature is www.asamblea.go.cr

A. The Legislative Commissions

Within the Legislature there are several commissions which are made up of deputies of the legislature and are responsible for reviewing proposed laws. These commissions can either be Permanent Commissions, Special Commissions or Investigatory Commissions. The Permanent Commission is responsible for evaluating proposed laws. There are six Permanent Commissions which are: (1) Agricultural and

Natural Resources, (2) Economic Affairs, (3) Government and Administration, (4) Budgeting and Taxation, (5) Judicial Affairs and (6) Social Affairs. Depending on the subject matter of the proposed law, it will be assigned to one of the six permanent commissions for evaluation. There are also special and investigatory commissions that are charged with specific duties. At the present time there are ten special commissions:

(1) Constitutional Consulting, (2) Control of Public Spending, (3) Honorary Citizens, (4) Narcotics, (5) Drafting, (6) International Relations, (7) Environment, (8) Women's Issues, (9) Juveniles and (10) Appointments.

The members of the commissions whether permanent or special are named by the President of the Legislative Assembly. They are appointed to the commission for one-year terms but may continue to be re-appointed to the same commission.

B. How a Law is Made

A proposed law, referred to locally as Proyecto de Ley may be filed with the administrative branch of the Legislature by any of the deputies of the Legislature or the executive branch. Once received, the administrative office notifies the President of the National Legislature of the proposed law.

The President assigns the project to one of the permanent legislative commissions who will review the proposed law. Before the bill is sent to the Commission it is sent to the Archive Department where a bill number is assigned to it and recorded in the legislative entry book. A copy of the proposed bill is also sent to the National Printing Office so that bill can be published in the official newspaper, *La Gaceta*. Once the Archive Department completes this phase, the bill is sent to the Permanent Commission to which it was assigned for evaluation. The Commission must wait until the bill has been officially published before the Commission can vote on it. If approved by the Commission, the bill is then placed on the Legislative agenda for debate. If rejected, the file is sent back to the Archive Department.

On the Legislative floor the bill is introduced for a first debate session. If approved in the first debate, it is returned to the respective commission who will review and prepare the final draft of the future law. The final text is submitted to the plenary session for a second debate. If approved, the file is forwarded to the Parliamentary Services Department where the text is edited and then forwarded to the President for signature. The President may veto the bill and return it to the Legislature with his objections. If approved by the President he signs it and the text of the law is published in its final version in the official newspaper La Gaceta. Generally, new laws become applicable once published in La Gaceta. The electronic version of La Gaceta is published on-line daily and can be viewed at www.gaceta.go.cr.

3.3 THE JUDICIAL BRANCH

Judicial power in Costa Rica is vested in the Supreme Court of Justice. The Supreme Court is the court of last resort since the Costa Rican legal structure is composed of trial and appellate courts. The jurisdiction of a Costa Rican court is explained below and illustrated in Figure A.

A. The Trial and Lower Courts

Any litigated issue in Costa Rica will either be litigated before a Trial Court (*Juzgado*) or one of the lower courts with proper jurisdiction over the amount and the subject matter of the dispute.

The majority of litigation in Costa Rica proceeds through the trial court system known as *Juzgados*. These are either civil or criminal.

(a) Civil Matters

Civil matters are distributed according to the amount in controversy and the legal specialty involved. The major subsections include matters of (I) General Civil Jurisdiction; (ii) Labor Law, (iii) Administrative and Tax Law; (iv) Family Law; and (v) Agrarian Law.

(b) Criminal Court (*Penal*)

The Criminal Court is known as the Juzgado Penal and its jurisdiction is limited to criminal matters. There is also a Juvenile Criminal Court (*Juzgado Penal Juvenil*) and a Domestic Violence Court (*Juzgado de Violencia Domestica*).

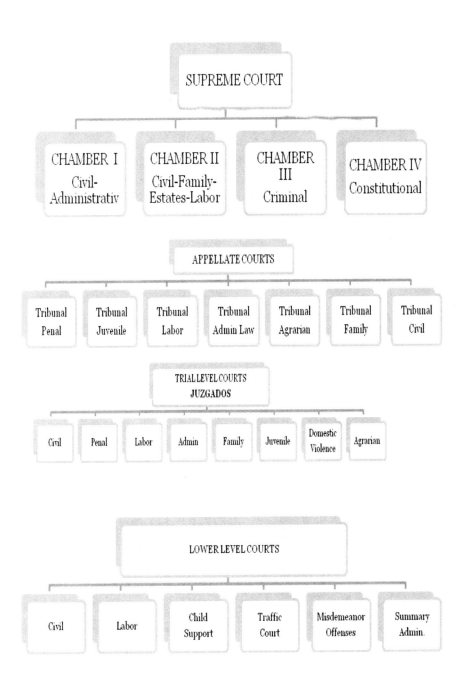

Figure A   The Costa Rican Court Structure

(1) The Lower Courts

The Small Claims Court (*Juzgado de Menor Cuantia*) is a court of small claims. The jurisdiction of the Small Claims Court is limited to the particular territory in which it sits as well as the monetary value of the controversy involved. By law, the Small Claims Court has exclusive jurisdiction of all matters related to the Landlord-Tenancy Law regardless of the amount involved.

These courts also have jurisdiction over misdemeanor criminal offenses (*Contravenciones*) which are committed within their territory and child support enforcement (*Pensiones Alimenticias*).

(2) Labor Court

All matters related to the Costa Rican Labor Code must be litigated before a Labor Court with proper jurisdiction over the parties. The Labor Courts are specialized courts that only hear labor cases.

(3) Administrative Court

Any litigation where a government entity, either national or municipal is involved will be litigated before the Administrative Court (*Juzgado Contencioso Administrativo*).

(4) Traffic Court

The jurisdiction of Traffic Court (*Juzgados de Transito*) is limited to cases involving traffic accidents and infractions of the traffic laws. These are by far the most congested of all the courts in Costa Rica. It is quite common for a traffic related case to take upwards of two years to wind itself through traffic court.

B. The Appellate Courts

The Appellate Courts are known as Tribunales Superiores and they have jurisdiction over decisions rendered by a lower court that have a right to an appeal. Generally, each Appellate Court hears cases within their designated specialty, which are Civil, Criminal, Administrative, Family, Labor, and Agrarian.

C. The Supreme Court

The Costa Rican Supreme Court is located in the capital city of San Jose and is divided into four chambers. Each chamber, numbered I through IV, has jurisdiction over specific legal topics.

(1)   First Chamber (*Sala Primera - I*)

The First Chamber is made up of seven Magistrates. This chamber has jurisdiction over all administrative matters and civil suits of general jurisdiction. The First Chamber also has jurisdiction when a decision of one Court conflicts with that of another Court.

(2)   Second Chamber (*Sala Segunda-II*)

The Second Chamber is made up of five Magistrates. This chamber has appellate jurisdiction over all matters related to family law, estates, and labor law. It also has jurisdiction over conflicts of power that may arise between judicial authorities and administrative authorities.

(3)   Third Chamber (*Sala Tercera - III*)

The Third Chamber is made up of five Magistrates. This chamber has jurisdiction over all criminal matters.

(4)   Fourth Chamber (*Sala Cuarta- IV*)

The Fourth Chamber is also referred to as the Constitutional Chamber since its jurisdiction is limited to interpreting the Costa Rican Constitution and violation of constitutional rights.

3.4 LOCAL GOVERNMENT

Costa Rica is divided into seven provinces: (1) San Jose, (2) Alajuela, (3) Heredia, (4) Cartago, (5) Guanacaste, (6) Limon, and (7) Puntarenas. These seven provinces are in turn divided into eighty one cantons which are further divided into four hundred and sixty three districts. (See Appendix 3, The Political Subdivision of Costa Rica).

The trend in the past couple of years has been to allow more autonomy to the local municipal government and thus decentralization from the national government. The Municipal government consists of a body of commissioners called Regidores, and a Mayor called Alcalde. The commissioners and the mayor are elected by popular vote. The number of commissioners varies from municipal government from five to thirteen depending on the population of the municipal area where they will serve.

The election for commissioners is held simultaneously with the Presidential elections every four years in February. The municipal government is regulated by the Municipal Code, Law number 7794 of 1998 (*Codigo Municipal*).

4. THE CONSTITUTION

The framework for the development of a Constitution for Costa Rica began in 1823 when the representatives of all the Central American countries met and jointly drafted the Constitution of the Federal Republic of Central America. The Central American Constitution was modeled after the Constitution of the United States. Soon after, the individual Central American countries began to promulgate their own constitutions. Costa Rica passed its first constitution on January 25, 1825 which created three separate branches of government: the Legislative, Executive and Judicial. Several Constitutions would follow over the years as Costa Rica struggled with political upheaval and dictatorships.

Constitutional maturity and stability came about at the conclusion of the 1948 revolution, with the passage of the Political Constitution of the Republic of Costa Rica (*Constitución Politica de la República de Costa Rica*) on November 7, 1949. This Constitution remains in effect to this day.

In addition to implementing a separation of powers, the Costa Rican Constitution is characterized for the individual rights and social guarantees provided to its citizens.

4.1 PROTECTION OF INDIVIDUAL RIGHTS

The Costa Rican Constitution sets forth specific guarantees to preserve the right of the individual to freely transit and be secure in their persons, homes and documents.

A. Search and Seizure

According to the Constitution, the home and other private residence of the inhabitants of Costa Rica may not be violated without a court order issued by a judge with proper jurisdiction or to prevent the commission of a crime. The same applies to private documents and written and oral communications.

B. The Right to Assemble and Petition the Government

The citizens have the right to freely assemble for legal purposes and may not be forced to form part of any association. Also, the right to petition the government whether collectively as a group or individual is guaranteed by the Constitution.

C. Freedom of Speech and Right to Information

The Constitution guarantees freedom of speech by stating that all persons may communicate their thoughts by words or in writing without prior censorship. However, it does indicate that those that abuse these rights may be liable. This refers to the limitations set forth in the Costa Rican Penal Code for defamation and slander.

The international press has often criticized Costa Rica because it feels that the defamation and slander laws currently in place and the manner in which they are interpreted by the courts are a limitation on freedom of the press.

The Constitution also guarantees private citizens the right to access information from government offices that are of public interest and not classified as secrets of state.

D. Equal Protection Under the Law

The Constitution prohibits any type of discrimination and states that all persons are equal under the law.

4.2 SOCIAL GUARANTEES

The Constitution of Costa Rica sets forth several guarantees which are aimed at the general well-being of the citizens. These constitutional rights protect the right to the family, right to work, right to housing, and freedom of religion.

5. THE NATIONAL REGISTRY

One of the most vital entities in Costa Rica is the National Registry (*Registro Nacional*) which is under the direction of the Ministry of Justice. This institution plays an integral part in the Costa Rican legal system because it is responsible for receiving and recording all documents that relate to tangible and intangible property, security interests, negotiable instruments, mortgages, powers of attorney, corporate documents and any other document which by law must be recorded to put third parties on notice.

Many transactions in Costa Rica must be filed in the National Registry in order to have legal effect and enforcement and it is in the National Registry where all this information is consolidated.

The National Registry came into existence in its present form in 1975 by Law No. 5695 *(Ley de Creación del Registro Nacional)* and it has exclusive national jurisdiction so that the filing of all documents in Costa Rica are centralized within this entity. The National Registry is located in the capital city of San Jose and is subdivided into specialized sections. The Property Section of the National Registry *(Registro de la Propiedad)* contains all deeds and interests that relate to real property. All recorded properties are assigned a title number known as Folio Real. The Property Registry then keeps track of all documents and instruments that are recorded against that particular title number. The property indexes can generally be searched by title number or by owner name and the National Registry will issue official certificates of title which list all information including liens and annotations recorded against the property. The general public may access the National Registry database via the internet at www.registronacional.go.cr and conduct searches on all records filed in the National Registry.

All documents relating to the capacity of individuals must be filed in the "persons" section of the National Registry. This includes all documents which modify the civil capacity of persons, all testamentary documents, powers of attorney and marital agreements. The Mercantile Section of the National Registry records all documents which relate to commercial transactions, including all matters related to corporate formation and modifications. All title and liens to vehicles and water-craft are recorded in the Movable Property Section (*Bienes Muebles)* of the National Registry. Figure B illustrates the Costa Rican National Registry System.

PROPERTY SECTION
- Deeds
- Mortgages
- Liens
- Easements
- Condominiums
- Instruments Affecting Real Estate

MERCANTILE SECTION
- Corporations
- Partnerships
- Commercial Transactions
- Any Instrument Affecting Commercial Entities

PERSONS SECTION
- Powers of Attorney
- Testamentary Instruments
- Pre-Marital Agreements
- Any Instrument Affecting the Legal Capacity of Persons

INTELECTUAL PROPERTY SECTION
- Trademark Registration
- Patents
- Copyright Registration

Figure B.   The National Registry of Costa Rica

6. THE CIVIL REGISTRY.

The Civil Registry of Costa Rica was established in 1887. The purpose of the Civil Registry is to document the civil and electoral information of the citizens of Costa Rica. As such the Civil Registry is the office where birth, marriage and death certificates are recorded.

Every citizen of Costa Rica must have a national identity card known as the Cedula. This card is also the citizen voting registration card which authorizes them to vote in national and local elections. Figure C details the different branches of the Civil Registry.

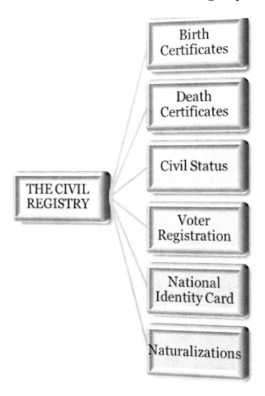

Figure C. The Civil Registry of Costa Rica

CHAPTER 2

THE RULES OF COURT PROCEDURE

1. CIVIL PRACTICE AND PROCEDURE

In Costa Rica, the Code of Civil Procedure governs the function and operation of the Costa Rican courts and the procedures that must be followed for conducting litigation. Unlike the adversary system that is characteristic of the United States and U.K., in Costa Rica, litigation is governed from beginning to end by a trial judge. The trial judge may interrogate witnesses and order the production of evidence so that they can narrow the legal issues that need to be resolved. Unlike oral hearings generally used in the United States, Costa Rican procedural rules require written, formal declarations to be filed in court which in turn is ruled upon in writing by the presiding Judge. There are several proposals currently being debated to introduce oral hearings in the judicial process in order to expedite the judicial process. I would expect to see more incorporation or oral proceedings in the process in the years to come.

Costa Rica does not have a Jury based system and all judicial decisions are generally made by a panel of judges.

1.1 JURISDICTION

In general terms, a Costa Rican judge will have jurisdiction over cases where the defendant is domiciled in Costa Rica; where an obligation has to be performed within Costa Rica and where the claim is based upon an act or omission which occurred within Costa Rica. Which particular court within Costa Rica will hear the case depends on the subject matter involved and the amount in controversy and the province where either of the parties resides or the controversy arose.

A. Subject Matter Jurisdiction and Amount in Controversy

The case load among the civil division of the courts is distributed according to the subject matter and the amount in controversy. The civil courts known as Juzgados, are divided into General Civil; Administrative; Labor; Agrarian; Family; and Juvenile Courts. The Civil Courts have exclusive jurisdiction over: (1) Matters in which the amount in controversy is greater than the limit established by the Supreme Court. (2) Appeals which come up from the small claims courts. (3) Disputes over jurisdiction between two lower territorial courts. (4) Any other civil matter as provided under the law.

The Small Claim Courts known as *Juzgados de Menor Cuantia* have exclusive jurisdiction over: (1) Civil matters where the amount in controversy is below the jurisdictional amount established by the Supreme Court. (2) These Courts also retain exclusive jurisdiction over landlord-tenant actions without regard to the monetary amount involved. (3) All matters related to consignment of payments.

B. Territorial Jurisdiction

Where a case will actually be heard depends on the location of the subject matter of the lawsuit; the place of residence of the defendant or the place where the act or omission occurred.

1.2 LITIGATION

When a lawsuit is filed in Costa Rica it can proceed under three different procedural tracks: ordinary, abbreviated and summary procedures. Which procedure applies depends on the subject matter of the controversy.

A. Ordinary Procedure

Cases that do not fall into the abbreviated or summary category must proceed under the ordinary litigation track. The civil lawsuit is initiated by filing a complaint in the court with proper jurisdiction to hear the case. The complaint must contain the following: (1) The name of the parties to the action; (2) the facts which give rise to the dispute; (3) the legal basis for the complaint; (4) a breakdown of the damages alleged; (5) any evidence which forms the basis for the complaint must be attached to it as well as the names of any witnesses; (6) an address where to receive notice and service of process.

Once a complaint is filed, the defendant must be notified that a lawsuit has been initiated against them. This notice of the lawsuit is done by serving the defendant personally with a copy of the complaint along with a summons, which requires that an answer be filed. Generally, service of process is carried out by a court process server (*notificador*) that works within the court where the complaint was filed. Each court in Costa Rica has their own full time process server that works directly for the judicial branch and is in charge of processing service of summons and physically carrying out the service within their jurisdictional territory. It is very common practice and most of the times necessary for the party that files the lawsuit to do all the preliminary work to locate the individual to be served. Once located, it is recommended that the party initiating the action or their Attorney coordinate service with the court process server. Since the majority of process servers do not have transportation this means picking them up at the courthouse and driving them to the location. It can take several trips back and forth with the process server before you actually complete service. The law allows service at the contractual domicile stipulated by the parties in a contract and when corporate entities are involved service is made upon the legal representative or at the legal domicile of the corporation. Under certain circumstances, the law allows court appointed public notaries to carry out service of process or service by publication.

The Civil Code requires that the initial summons and complaint be served at the defendant's residence by leaving a copy with any person over the age of fifteen. Upon receipt of the summons and complaint the defendant has thirty days (30) in which to file an answer to the complaint. The answer must either admit or deny the allegations contained in the complaint and have attached to it all the evidence and list of witnesses which will contradict the defendant's allegations. Failure to respond to the complaint within thirty (30) days will result in all the allegations contained in the complaint being accepted as true and a continuation of the civil action against the defaulting defendant in their absence. In the answer the defendant may assert any affirmative defenses and file a countersuit if applicable. Also at this time the defendant may file any motions challenging jurisdiction, service of process, or other procedural matters related to the lawsuit. If the defendant answers the complaint within the time frame allowed then the proceedings move into the evidence gathering phase.

Once the introductory pleading stages have been completed, the court will open the evidence gathering phase for a period of forty (40) days. During this time period the plaintiff gathers evidence to prove the truth of the allegations contained in the complaint and the defendant gathers his to counter those allegations. The Code of Civil Procedure allows a party to a lawsuit to prove their allegations by proffering any of the following: (1) testimony of the parties; (2) testimony of the witnesses; (3) documents and reports; (4) judicial notice; (5) scientific evidence; (6) expert testimony and (7) presumptions. At any time during the course of the proceedings the judge at the request of either of the parties, or on their own initiative may order them to appear in court to answer interrogatories related to the cause of action.

The method for questioning a party to a lawsuit about facts related to the cause of action is regulated by the Code of Civil Procedure. The most common way that this is handled in Costa Rica is that the Court will set a date for the taking of the testimony of the Defendant to the lawsuit. Prior to the date set, the Plaintiff to the lawsuit will prepare written interrogatories, no more than twenty questions are allowed, which are then placed in a sealed envelope and filed with the court prior to or on the date of the scheduled hearing. At the hearing which is presided by the Judge, the envelope filed with the court containing the questions to be asked of the Defendant are opened by the Judge and it is the Judge not the Attorney who asks the questions. The Judge may also rule on their own initiative that one or more of the questions contained in the interrogatory are not relevant and may reject them. The Attorney may ask for a clarification or reserve the right to follow up questions. The presiding Judge who asks the interrogatory questions must also make a record of the question and the answer and they generally do this by typing it themselves into their word processor in the presence of all the parties.

There are no court reporters in the Costa Rican judicial system to transcribe testimony. Instead, it is the responsibility of the presiding Judge to ask the questions, gather the answers and then make a record of it. All the testimony gathered at that hearing is then read back to the parties present and their Attorneys who all must agree and sign the transcription certifying that its content is accurate.

The taking of the testimony of the witnesses does not require written interrogatories but follows similar formalities. When either party indicates a witness to be used in support of their position they must set forth the exact items to which they will testify. When the witness is called to testify, it is the Judge who will present the questions to the witness and transcribe their answers for the record. The Attorney has the right to ask follow-up questions to the witness but only at the end of their testimony. In other words, the Attorney cannot interrupt the witness to ask for a clarification and instead must wait for the entire testimony to finish and then ask for the clarification.

If one of the parties to the lawsuit or witnesses does not speak Spanish the law requires that a court appointed interpreter be assigned to translate both the questions being asked and the answers being provided.

Depending on the cause of action of the lawsuit other common forms of evidence used in Costa Rica are a judicial inspection of the site and the naming of an expert to render an opinion as to a particular subject matter within the lawsuit. In Costa Rica, the Attorney for either of the parties does not hire the experts. Instead, the Court maintains a list of "experts" on various subject matters. If an expert opinion is required or requested by either party to the lawsuit then the Court will randomly select the name of the next expert on the list. The party that requested the expert will then be notified by the Court that he must deposit with the Court Registry in advance the fees and expenses to cover the professional services of the expert.

This system of evidence gathering is different from the expansive discovery process that is available in the United States legal system. In that legal system, the judiciary delegates to the Attorneys the entire task of evidence gathering. It is the Attorneys who gather the evidence, take deposition testimony of parties and witnesses obtain discovery of records and documents and hire experts to support their position. In comparison to that system, the hands of the Attorney in Costa Rica are tied. However, the current system in Costa Rica wastes valuable judicial resources by tying up Judges with evidence gathering tasks which should be used for trying the cases and reducing the tremendous case backlog that exists in the Costa Rican judicial system. It is not uncommon for an ordinary lawsuit to drag on for ten years.

After the taking of evidence, the court proceeds to rule on the admissibility of the evidence provided and gives all parties to the lawsuit ten days to present the court with their final statements and conclusions.

These are written briefs that are filed with the Court and it is the opportunity for each party to summarize the facts of the case and set forth their legal arguments to support their position. After the ten days have elapsed, the court closes the taking of further testimony or evidence. The judge then evaluates the evidence and the argument made and enters a final judgment. A final judgment rendered by a trial court (*Juzgado*) may be appealed to the Appellate Court (*Tribunal Superior Civil*).

B. The Abbreviated Procedure

The Costa Rican Code of Civil Procedure provides that certain types of cases may proceed to an abbreviated as opposed to the ordinary procedure. Only the following causes of action may proceed according to the abbreviated procedure: marital dissolution actions, paternity, legitimization, interdiction, disputes related to rental contracts, request for accounting, shareholder resolutions, easements and sales at public auction. The abbreviated process shortens some of the time frames applicable to the ordinary procedure in half but in practice the difference between an ordinary and an abbreviated process are minimal.

C. The Summary Process

The Summary Process does make a significant difference regarding the time it takes for a case to wind through the judicial system from the filing of the complaint to a final judgment. However, the Summary Process is only available for the following causes of action: Landlord-Tenant evictions and rental increases, collection proceedings based upon executory financial instruments, injunctions, false claim to legal right or obligations due, restitution, controversies involving joint ownership of property or condominiums, guaranty, and possession of personal property. In the Summary Process the time to answer the complaint is five days and the period established for evidence gathering is also shortened to expedite the process. Most importantly the rulings that may be appealed are limited thus reducing the number of appeals and the time required for those appeals to be resolved.

Those causes of action which are not specifically named in Articles 420 for Abbreviated Procedure or Article 432 for Summary Procedure of the Costa Rican Procedural Code must proceed pursuant to the "ordinary" civil process.

In most instances, civil litigation in Costa Rica can become a lengthy and tedious process. This is due to a combination of factors and one of which is insufficient or inefficient use of available funding of the Judicial Branch. The lack of funds and inefficient use of the funds available prevents the proper staffing of the courts to handle the case load which results in delays in the processing of lawsuits.

The lack of an oral process to expeditiously dispose of the numerous pretrial motions filed between the parties is a drain on the judicial resources that are available. Since motions must be filed in writing and then ruled upon in writing by the presiding Judge and the ruling served upon both parties before the proceedings can continue results in extended delays.

It is also common practice in Costa Rican litigation for defense counsel to drag out the lawsuit as much as possible by appealing every ruling possible in effect, stalling the procedure pending the appellate resolutions. Sanctions against Attorneys for filing frivolous motions or misrepresenting factual issues in their pleadings are rarely, if ever punished. This in turn fosters this type of behavior among litigants to the complete detriment of the judicial process and erodes the public's perception and confidence in the judicial system.

The fact that many Judges are named as "temporary" (*Interinos*) as opposed to "permanent" (*Propietarios*) employment positions results in Judges who are hesitant to rule and make final decisions. This happens because as long as they are in "temporary" status their employment can be terminated and they are afraid to lose their job. In a country with over sixteen thousand Attorneys, employment within the judicial court system is a coveted and well paid position by Costa Rican standards.

These factors combined with the fact that the Costa Rican system does not provide for punitive damages and forces the losing party to pay the costs and attorney's fees of the prevailing party make litigation in Costa Rica an extremely tedious and frustrating experience which should be avoided, unless it becomes absolutely indispensable. Voltaire summed up the impact of lawsuits as follows: "I was never ruined but twice: once when I lost a lawsuit, and once when I won one".

2. MEDIATION AND ARBITRATION

Since litigation within the Costa Rican judicial system is a tedious and lengthy process mediation and arbitration can be a viable alternative.

Costa Rica passed its Alternative Dispute Resolution Law (*Ley Sobre Resolución Alterna de Conflictos y Promocion de la Paz Social*) in 1997 and as a result of this law there are now alternatives to litigation. The law allows the creation of privately operated mediation and arbitration centers that comply with the requirements set forth in the law. Selecting the arbitrator that will oversee the arbitration is the most important factor in alternative dispute resolution since the credibility, professionalism and independence of the arbitrator will determine the success of the proceeding.

2.1 MEDIATION

In mediation which is generally referred to as conciliation (*conciliación*) in Costa Rica a neutral third person acts as an intermediary in a dispute between two parties. Many judicial systems in developed nations have implemented mandatory mediation within their judicial proceedings to dispose of cases before they go to trial. However, in those countries that implement this system they generally have private-sector professional mediation centers that are specialized in dispute resolution. In Costa Rica, although the Code of Civil Procedure establishes a mediation procedure it is voluntary. It is generally the Judge who also must act as the mediator. In its current form the mediation system is not as effective as it could be if the parties were obligated to mediate in good faith before professional independent mediators.

2.2 ARBITRATION

Arbitration is a voluntary mechanism by which parties submit their dispute to a neutral third party. Arbitration is a private matter and the parties must agree to arbitration generally by inserting a clause in the contract stipulating that any dispute will be subject to arbitration. In Costa Rica all matters related to Arbitration are governed by the Alternative Dispute Resolution Law (*Ley Sobre Resolución Alterna de Conflictos y Promocion de la Paz Social*). The law allows for matters to be arbitrated if the parties have agreed to arbitration in writing. The law does not require a specific formality other than it be agreed to "in writing". However, it is recommended that the arbitration clause be as specific as possible to avoid interpretation problems. Once the arbitration clause is invoked and the matter is assigned to the arbitrators specified in the arbitration clause it will proceed until the arbitrators issue their ruling. The Arbitration award is binding upon the parties in the same manner as a Judgment issued by a court of law. In Costa Rica, there is no right to appeal an arbitration award and the parties may only request an addition or clarification of the arbitration award so long as it does not alter the essence of the award. Costa Rican judges have consistently upheld Arbitration clauses refusing to hear cases which have a legally binding arbitration clause in the agreement.

Once the arbitration award is final, it becomes executory meaning that the prevailing party may request the Court to enforce and execute the award.

In Costa Rica, the arbitration centers are of an institutional nature. This means that they are organized by Chambers or Associations as opposed to individuals. The most commonly used arbitration centers in Costa Rica are:

(1) The Costa Rican Chamber of Commerce (*Camara de Comercio*) which operates the Centro de Conciliación y Arbitraje and their web site is http://www.camara-comercio.com/centro_de_conciliacion_y_arbitraje.php.

For conciliation proceedings the center charges $40 per session and the professional fees of the Administrative Fee Schedule – Chamber of Commerce -CCA mediator is $50 per hour.

For arbitration the center charges an initial deposit of $150. The fees for the arbitrators are based upon a percentage of the amount in dispute as set forth in the following chart.

CCA – Chamber of Commerce

AMOUNT	ADMINISTRATIVE FEE
$ 1 a $ 25.000	2% Minimum of $ 300
$ 25.000 a $ 50.000	$ 500 + 1% over excess of $ 25.000
$ 50.001 a $ 100.000	$ 750 + 1% over the excess $ 50.001
$ 100.001 a $ 200.000	$ 1.250 + 1.25% over the excess $ 100.001
$ 200.001 a $ 1.000.000	$ 2.500 +1.25% over the excess $ 200.001
$ 1.000.001 a $ 2.500.000	$ 6.500 + 0.2% over the excess $ 2.500.001
$ 2.500.001 a $ 5.000.000	$ 9.500 + 0.1% over the excess $ 2.500.001
$ 5.000.001 or more	$ 12.000 + 0.1% over the excess $ 5.000.001

(2) The American-Costa Rican Chamber of Commerce (AMCHAM) operates the Centro Internacional de Conciliación y Arbitraje. Their center has a web page with information on the services offered at www.amcham.co.cr./information/cica/. The fee schedules for mediation and arbitration are set forth below:

Conciliation Fees

Initial Payment	US$ 150
Administrative Fee	US$ 500.00
Conciliator´s fee	US $100.00 per hour. If more than 3 conciliators are used the fee is US $80.00 per hour for each one

CICA Arbitration Rates

Initial Payment Administrative Fees Services	US $150.00
The rate does not include: translations, experts fees, copies, couriers, faxes, internationals calls, recording and transcriptions of hearings .	1% of the amount Mínimum US$ 150.00 Máximum US$ 12.500.00
Arbitrator Fee	This rate is based upon the following amounts: • Up to $10.000= $500 • From $10.001 to $50.000 = $500 + 2% of the excess of $10.000 • From $50.001 to $200.000 = $1.300 + 1% of the excess over $50.000 • From $200.00 to $500.000 =$2.800 + 0.6% of the excess over $200.000 • From $500.000 and more = $4.600 + 0.5% over what exceeds $500.000

(3) The Costa Rican Chamber of Realtors *(Camara Costarricense de Bienes Raices)* sponsors the Real Estate Alternative Dispute Resolution Center *(Centro de Resolucion de Conflictos en Materia de Propiedad)* which specializes in resolving disputes involving real estate transactions.

The Architect and Engineering Association *(Colegio Federado de Ingenieros y Arquitectos de Costa Rica)* also has an Alternative Dispute Resolution Center *(Centro de Resolucion de Conflictos - CRC)* This conciliation center specializes in disputes which relate to real estate transactions. Their web site is http://www.cfia.or.cr/crc.htm which sets out the regulations and fees.

3.   INTERNATIONAL LITIGATION

There are instances when a party from a foreign country wants a judgment which was issued in that country to be enforced in Costa Rica. The Costa Rican Code of Civil Procedure, Articles 705-708 states that the recognition of all foreign rulings, judgments, orders and other pronunciation of foreign courts must be requested before the First Chamber of the Costa Rican Supreme Court. The process is known locally as an *Exequatur* proceeding.

3.1   AN EXEQUATUR PROCEEDING

In order to file an Exequatur petition before the Supreme Court it is necessary that all documentation on which the petition will be based be authenticated by a Costa Rican Embassy or Consulate from the country where the documents were issued. The documents must be filed with the Ministry of Foreign Relations in Costa Rica for further authentication and translated into Spanish by an official translator approved by the Ministry of Foreign Relations. In evaluating the recognition proceeding the Supreme Court will evaluate the following: (1) That the defendant was properly notified of the lawsuit and final judgment was entered against them. This is to ensure that the due process provisions of the Costa Rican Constitution are not violated; (2) That the foreign judgment or ruling does not interfere with the exclusive jurisdiction of the Costa Rican courts; (3) That at the time the petition is made there is no case pending in Costa Rica nor judgment issued in Costa Rica related to the same cause of action as the foreign proceeding; (4) That the ruling or judgment sought to be enforced in Costa

Rica must be final and executory; (5) That the ruling or judgment is not contrary to Costa Rican public order. This means that it is not contrary to the principles and values reflective of Costa Rican society. If the foreign judgment adheres to the criteria set forth above the petition will be granted, otherwise it will be rejected.

A review of the case filings before the First Chamber of the Supreme Court reveal that from 1991-2001 there were a total of 668 requests for Exequatur presented. Of the total cases presented the vast majority, 87% of them are related to family law issues such as recognition of foreign divorce decrees, child custody, paternity and adoptions. The remaining cases are related to wills and estate proceedings (7%) and general civil cases (6%). The requests for recognition came from 32 different countries but the vast majority, 58% came from the United States, followed by Nicaragua, Germany and Canada.

3.2 LETTER ROGATORY

Unlike the Exequatur proceeding which is a request for recognition of a foreign ruling or judgment, the Letter Rogatory (*Carta Rogatoria*) is a request for judicial assistance by one court to another. In the absence of any treaty agreement, the Letter Rogatory is the most common method of obtaining assistance from a foreign court. The Letter Rogatory generally comes through diplomatic channels. In Costa Rica, the Letter Rogatory is ruled upon by the First Chamber of the Supreme Court. If granted, the Costa Rican Supreme Court will order the corresponding local court to carry out the request. According to the filings of the First Chamber of the Supreme Court for the years 1994-2001 there were 336 Letter Rogatory requests filed.

Of those requests, 47% were for criminal matters, 35% for civil law matters and 18% for family law matters. The Letter Rogatory request came from 30 different countries. The majority of them came from Panama, Spain, Germany, United States, Argentina and Colombia.

CHAPTER 3

THE CRIMINAL JUSTICE SYSTEM

The criminal justice system in Costa Rica is made up of the body of laws which dictates what types of acts or offenses constitute a crime and the procedural system used by the government to charge and prosecute those offenses. The two most important sources of information for criminal law in Costa Rica are the Penal Code (*Código Penal)* and the Code of Criminal Procedure (*Código Procesal Penal)*. The first, codifies the bulk of all the acts or omissions established by law that constitute a criminal offense and the second sets forth the procedures for charging and prosecuting a crime through the criminal court system. In addition to the procedural aspect, this section will also discuss the criminal offenses as set forth in the Penal Code as well as the major offenses which are not contained in the Penal Code but constitute criminal offenses of laws passed by the legislature subsequent to the adoption of the Penal Code.

1. THE PENAL CODE

In Costa Rica, what constitutes a crime is anything that the legislature has defined as such. The bulk of offenses which are defined as crimes are codified in the Costa Rican Penal Code (*Código Penal,* Law 4573 of May 4, 1970). Other laws passed by the legislature may contain criminal penalties attached to them and although they are not codified in the Penal Code they constitute criminal offenses. The Penal Code divides offenses according to the gravity of the offense. A crime is either a felony (*delito)* punishable by imprisonment or a misdemeanor (*contravencion)* punishable by a monetary fine.

1.1 CRIMINAL OFFENSES

The Penal Code breaks down the criminal offenses into the following sixteen categories:

1. Offenses Against Human Life. These are criminal offenses that result in bodily injury or death. In this section you have all degrees of homicide as well as negligence which results in bodily injury. The concept of negligence requires some further discussion because in most cases it is treated as a criminal rather than a civil matter. In common law, there is generally a line drawn between "civil negligence" which is conduct that constitutes an unjustified foreseeable risk of causing harm and "criminal negligence" which constitutes a gross deviation from the standard of care imposed upon the individual that caused the harm. In common law, the courts define this conduct as "recklessness" or "gross negligence".

In Costa Rica, any act which results in bodily injury is a criminal offense known locally as "*lesiones*" which translated into English means "injury".

The degree of the criminal offense that the person will be charged with will depend on the gravity of the injury caused. The Penal Code divides these into (a) Gross injury: Which occurs if the act or omission to act caused permanent disability to work, deformation of the face, loss of sensation or loss of use of any body organ or limb. The penalty is a prison sentence from 3 to 10 years. (b) Grave Injury: If the act or omission to act resulted in a persistent deterioration of health, weakened sensation or use of any body organ or limb. The penalty is a prison sentence from 1 to 6 years. (c) Light Injury: Is that act or omission to act which caused injury to the body or health of the individual which resulted in an incapacity for work of more than 10 days but no greater than one month. The penalty is a prison sentence from 3 months to 1 year or a fine of up to 50 days. Other offenses that constitute a crime against human life include Duels, Aggression with firearms, Abandonment and Abortion.

2. Offenses Against Honor: Under Costa Rican law, acts which injure the honor and reputation of another can constitute a criminal offense. The two main causes of action under the Penal Code are for defamation and slander. Defamation occurs when an individual discredits the honor and integrity of another to third parties while slander results when one falsely attributes to another person the commission of a criminal act.

The international press associations have criticized this portion of the criminal code which has resulted in large judgments being levied against the print media in several high profile cases. The press feels that the law as applied is an infringement on the right of free speech.

3. Sex Offenses: Sexual conduct which constitutes criminal offenses in Costa Rica are: (a) Rape which in Costa Rica constitutes having "carnal knowledge" with violence or intimidation or when the victim lacks the mental capacity to resist or the victim is under the age of twelve. This charge can result in a prison sentence from 5 to 18 years depending on the aggravating factors involved in the commission of the offense. (b) Statutory Rape: The law states that having "carnal knowledge" either oral, anal or vaginal with a person of any sex that is older than 12 years old and younger than 15 years of age even with their consent is sanctioned with a prison sentence of 2 to 6 years. Likewise, those that pay a minor of any gender or promise an economic benefit to the minor in exchange for sex or erotic acts can face a prison sentence of 4 to 10 years. (c) Sexual Abuse can be charged for sexually abusive acts even when no sexual intercourse occurred. This charge can carry a sentence of 3 to 10 years. (d) Sexual corruption of a minor. A charge of sexual corruption occurs when a person promotes the corruption of a person under the age of 16 with perverse or excessive acts even if the victim consents. The sexual abuse and corruption offenses were modified by Law No. 8002 on June 2, 2000 to provide greater penalties against the sexual abuse of children and the elderly. These tougher sanctions were adopted in response to promoters advertising "sex tours" in Costa Rica. The new law imposes prison sentences from 3 to 10 years. (e) Pimping. Those who profit from or facilitate prostitution can be charged with pimping which carries a prison sentence of 2 to 10 years. (f) Sodomy. Having "carnal knowledge" with a minor under the age of 17 but older than 12 carries a 1 to 3 year prison sentence.

4. Offenses Against the Family: These are offenses which affect the unity of the family and marriage and they range in offenses from simulated matrimony to consigning false information in a marriage or birth certificate. Also included, as a criminal offense in Costa Rica is failure to provide support, defined as the means necessary for subsistence to one's children or elderly parents. This offense carries a fine of 15 days or prison sentence from 1 month to 2 years.

5. Offenses Against Liberty: This section of the Penal Code is divided into crimes against individual liberty which include kidnapping and unlawful detention offenses which can carry prison sentences of 6 to 25 years. Interfering with the free determination of the individual by way of threats or intimidation is also classified as a criminal offense.

6. Offenses Against Privacy: This section of the Penal Code establishes the rights of privacy which the citizens of Costa Rica have regarding communications, mail, telephone, and their dwelling. Article 196 of the Penal Code establishes the penalties for violation of secrets which it describes as unlawfully opening or interfering with the content of a letter or any other telegraphic, cablegraphic or telephonic communication which is destined to another person or makes unlawful use of a recording machine. The penalty for interfering with any of the above is from 60 to 100 day fine or 6 months to 1 year in prison. To keep pace with computer technology, Law 8148 of 2001 created Article 196 Bis which punishes with 6 months to 2 years in prison those that interfere or access private communications such as messages, data, or images through electronic or computer means. Other offenses within this section include (a) Recording Communications. The law imposes a fine of 30 to 60 days or 1 month to 6 months in prison to those who tape record the communications of others not destined for the public without their consent or to those who by technical means listen in on the private manifestations of others.(b) Postal and Telecommunication Employees. The law imposes a prison sentence of 9 months to 3 years to the postal and telecommunication employees who abusing their position take custody of a letter, telegram, cablegram or other piece of correspondence or interferes with its content and communicates it or delivers it to a person other than the intended recipient. (c) Disclosure of Secrets. The law imposes a fine of 30 to 100 days or prison from 1 month to 1 year to any person who without just cause, divulges information obtained due to his position, employment, occupation or profession which constitutes a secret and which if divulged could result in damages. (d) Trespass and Illegal Entry. The law prohibits third parties from entering into the dwelling or business place of another against the willingness of the occupant. If the person entering is a public official or government agent who does so without a warrant and in violation of the formalities established by law then he can be charged with illegal entry and face a prison sentence of 6 months to 3 years. (e) Violation of Electronic Communications. The law imposes prison terms of 6 months to 3 years to those that access, modify, alter, suppress, intercept, interferes or uses electronic communications destined to another person without their consent.

7. Offenses Against Property: The Penal Code divides the crimes against property into six distinct sections and those are (a) Theft. This offense usually consists of the unauthorized possession or use of property of another for personal gain. Whether the theft is carried out with or without violence becomes an aggravation of the offense. (b) Robbery. This is an aggravated theft and generally involves the use of violence, force or intimidation. The penalty can range from 6 months to 15 years depending on the circumstances and the amounts involved. (c) Extortion which carries penalties that range from 2 to 12 years in prison. (d) Fraud. The Penal Code defines fraud as obtaining a financial benefit from one person by concealing or creating false representations that are relied upon by that person to their detriment. The offense is punishable by prison sentence which can range from 2 months to 3 years. Other offenses included within this section include (e) Fraudulent Transfer which occurs when a person enters into a contract, transaction or judicial pleadings which are simulated and done with the intent of depriving another of their intended benefit. (f) Fraud with Check. This occurs when the payment made for goods and services is made with a check that has insufficient funds. (g) Fraudulent Administration and Unlawful Detainer. The crime of fraudulent administration mostly arises in the context of corporate entities and is used to charge an administrator of a crime which involves corporate assets. Unlawful Detainer is charged when there is a legal obligation to return an item or property and the holder wrongfully refuses to do so. (h) Appropriation. This occurs when an individual disposes another individual of their rightful possession and enjoyment of property using violence, threats, or deceit. This crime carries a prison sentence of 6 months to 3 years.

8. Financial Crimes. The actual translation of this section of the Penal Code is crimes against the good faith of business transactions which I have abbreviated as financial crimes and these include (a.) Fraudulent bankruptcy or insolvency which is charged when it is suspected that a bankruptcy or business insolvency has been done with the intent to hinder outstanding creditors. (b.) Usury which according to Costa Rican law occurs when one takes advantage of the necessity or inexperience of another for pecuniary gain which is evidently disproportionate with the amount of the loan or to provide collateral which is clearly extortive. The crime carries a penalty of 6 months to 2 years in prison or 20 to 80 day fine. The Consumer Protection law doubles the penalty when the victim of Usury is a consumer as defined in the Consumer Protection Law. (c.) Offenses against public confidence. These prohibit concealment of facts or false manifestations regarding the sale of public bonds or corporate stock and providing false financial statements. Also included in this section is the bad check statute, which provides from 6 months to 3 years in prison or 60 to 100 day fines to those who write bad checks. (d.) Securities Manipulation. The law regulating the public securities market created two criminal offenses related to the securities market. The first prohibits the manipulation of any security traded on the Costa Rican stock exchange to obtain a financial benefit. The second prohibits trading insider information on securities traded in the Costa Rican stock exchange to obtain a financial benefit. The law establishes a penalty of 3 to 8 years for these offenses.

9. Offenses Against Public Security. This section of the Penal Code sets forth offenses which constitute a threat to public welfare such as use of bombs and explosives, interfering with any means of public transportation, interfering with power plants, communications or public services, and which carry a sentence of up to 10 years in prison. Also included in this section are crimes against piracy and acts which threaten public health such as altering or contaminating food supply or medicines all of which can carry a prison sentence of up to 15 years.

10. Offenses Against Public Order: These offenses involve threats against public order, namely rioting, illegal association, and inciting rebellion. These offenses carry prison sentence from 1 month to 6 years in prison.

11. Offenses Against National Security: These offenses are divided into: (1) Treason which the code defines as taking up arms against the nation or providing assistance to its enemies, (2) Offenses which interfere with the peace and dignity of the nation such as hostile acts, revealing national secrets, espionage and sabotage.

12. Offenses Against Political Power and Constitutional Order. These offenses are aimed at preserving the constitutional order and the framework established within it for the peaceful transition of political power. Specific offenses included in this section include rebellion, sedition, and defacing national symbols.

13. Offenses Against Public Officials. A person can be charged with the offenses in this chapter of the Penal Code for interfering with a public official or court orders. The main offenses in this chapter are

(a) Disobedience of an order from a public official in the exercise of their official capacity, which carries a prison sentence of 15 days to 1 year. (b) Threatening a public official is punishable by imprisonment of 1 month to 2 years in prison. (c) Perjury can be charged for manifesting untruthful statements under oath which carries a prison sentence of 3 months to 2 years.

14. Offenses Against the Administration of Justice. These are acts that interfere with the administration of justice. (a) Perjury and Witness tampering. False statements made under oath, known as perjury or offering false witnesses can result in prison sentence that ranges from 6 months to 5 years. Tampering with witnesses in a judicial proceeding carries a sentence of 6 months to 3 years. (b) False Accusations. The comparable common law offense to this would be malicious prosecution which occurs when an individual accuses another of committing a criminal offense knowing that the person is innocent or creates false material evidence against that person. This offense carries a prison sentence of 1 to 6 years. (c) Concealment of Evidence. Any individual that assists another in concealing or altering the evidence of a crime or with criminal investigation can be charged with this offense which carries a prison sentence of 6 months to 2 years. (d) Evading confinement. These are offenses charged when the individual escapes or evades a judicially imposed confinement or imprisonment and carries an additional sentence of up to 2 years in prison.

15. Offenses By Public Officials. This chapter focuses on offenses, which are chargeable against public officials who abuse their public office either by abusing the authority conferred upon them or realizing financial gain from their public position. (a) Abuse of Authority. Costa Rica places great emphasis on individual liberty and as such it is the ability to charge a public official with abuse of authority that keeps the check and balances between the individual and the government. Evidence of this is the recent amendment made to Article 11 of the Costa Rican Constitution which now reads as follows: "Public Officials are simple depositories of authority. They are obligated to fulfill the obligations imposed on them by law and may not take upon themselves more authority than conferred by law. Public Officials must swear under oath to abide and comply with the Constitution and the law. Failure to abide with these responsibilities shall result in a criminal offense. The Penal Code imposes a prison sentence of up to 2 years for the crime of abuse of authority. (b) Corruption of Public Officials.

These offenses can be charged against public officials who receive payments as bribes related to acts or omissions inherent to their public position. It also involves financial offenses carried out by Public Officials against public funds under their administration. These offenses carry prison sentences from 6 months to 12 years.

16. Offenses Against Public Faith. These offenses are charged against individuals who alter, modify, or falsify in any manner public documents and carry prison sentences up to 6 years. Also included within this section of the Penal Code are offenses related to falsifying currency and government seals.

17. Offenses Against Human Rights. The main provision of this section is to prohibit any discrimination based upon race, sex, age, religion, political, social or economic standing. The penalties are monetary fines which range from 20 to 60 days.

1.2 MISDEMEANOR CRIMINAL OFFENSES

Book III of the Penal Code, sets forth all misdemeanor type offenses which do not result in a prison sentence but result in monetary fines. For many years Costa Rica has had a very lax view at enforcement of misdemeanor offenses. The main reason for this is that the Constitution prohibits any individual from being imprisoned for monetary obligations. Since a misdemeanor offense only imposes a monetary obligation, nonpayment of that monetary obligation according to the Constitutional Court could not result in imprisonment. To overcome this hurdle the Penal Code provision was modified in 2002 to allow the judges to sentence an individual who has not paid the monetary fine to prison, if they have the ability to pay the fine, or to do community service work to discount the sentence if they cannot pay the fine imposed.

1.3 JUVENILE CRIMINAL OFFENSES

When a crime is committed by a juvenile the procedure that is followed to adjudicate the guilt or innocence depends on the age of the offender. If the child is under the age of twelve then jurisdiction over the child lies with the Child Welfare Agency (Patronato Nacional de La Infancia). If the offender is between the ages of twelve and seventeen he falls under the jurisdiction and application of the Juvenile Criminal Justice Law (Ley de Justicia Penal Juvenil). The age of majority in Costa Rica is eighteen.

2. OTHER SOURCES OF CRIMINAL LAW

Although the Penal Code contains the bulk of the criminal offenses chargeable under Costa Rican law, many laws have been enacted after the adoption of the Penal Code and those laws also contain criminal sanctions. In this section I will discuss the most relevant legislation that has been adopted and which contain criminal sanctions punishable by imprisonment.

2.1 ENVIRONMENTAL LEGISLATION:

(1) The Forestry Law: The Costa Rican Forestry Law provides criminal penalties resulting in prison of 3 months to 3 years for those who invade and occupy an area which has been designated as a conservation or protected area. The same penalty applies for those who illegally harvest trees from protected forestry zones and those who transport the trees. The law even includes a provision that authorizes the government to seize any and all machinery and tools used in the illegal cutting of trees. Intentionally or negligently causing a forest fire in Costa Rican can result in a prison sentence of up to three years.

(2) Law of Water: The laws that govern the use and protection of water reserves are known as the Water Law. The law provides prison sentences of 3 months to 1 year for those who toss garbage, metals and substances which contaminate the public water sources.

(3) Fitosanitary Law: The Fitosanitary Law. The law imposes a prison sentence of up to 3 years for those who violate the quarantine requirements established in this law or import vegetables, biological control agents or other organisms for agricultural use which are prohibited by law.

(4) The Public Health Law: The Costa Rican Public Law, provides for a prison sentence of 6 months to 3 years to those who illegally practice medicine, dentistry, pharmacy, veterinary and clinical chemistry and microbiology. From 6 years to 12 years to those who cultivate, coca, marihuana or any other plant or seeds of similar effect and whose possession or traffic has been declared illegal or restricted by the Ministry of Public Security.

(5) Customs Law: The Customs Law governs all the procedures for importing products into Costa Rica including the payment of import duties. The Customs Law imposes a prison sentence of up to 3 years for those individuals who contraband and elude customs controls in the importation or exportation of merchandise from Costa Rica. The same sentence can be imposed upon those who have in their possession false customs' identification or seals.

2.2 CONSUMER PROTECTION LAW

The Consumer Protection Law provides that failure to abide by resolutions or orders from the Consumer Protection Commission shall result in the criminal offense of contempt as defined in the Penal Code.

2.3 DRUG ENFORCEMENT LEGISLATION.

Law No. 7786 addresses almost every aspect of drug-related offenses in Costa Rica. This law borrows heavily from United States legislation on the matter, introducing concepts such as undercover agent, informant, drug intelligence unit, seizures, forfeiture and money laundering to Costa Rican law enforcement. The law creates the Joint Intelligence Center (*Centro de Inteligencia Conjunto Antidrogas*) which is part of the Executive branch of the government and whose purpose is to fight illegal drug trafficking and connected illegal activities. In passing this legislation, the legislators introduced substantial regulations for Costa Rican financial and banking institutions. Article 16 of the law requires that all financial institutions in Costa Rica abide by the following dispositions in an effort to avoid laundering of drug proceeds: (1) Prohibits numbered or anonymous bank accounts; (2) Requires the registration and verification of the identity of all bank customers; (3) Requires banks to maintain records on the beneficiaries of bank accounts and to keep said records in storage for up to five years; (4) Requires banks to keep records of the identity of clients, account records commercial correspondence and financial transactions of customers for a period of five years. The law also makes it mandatory for all financial institutions to comply with judicial requests for information relative to any information or documentation in their custody and which is subject of investigation pursuant to this law. The law also imposes affirmative duties upon financial institutions. It requires them to fill out a form and report any and all cash transactions of ten thousand dollars or more and that they report any and all "suspicious" financial activity. In the past, Costa Rican penal law protected bank secrecy by prohibiting officials from divulging confidential information. This new legislation creates an exception to that confidentiality by relieving of any criminal, civil or administrative liability the financial institutions, their officers, owners, directors or employees for divulging said information in good faith. The law also introduces the concept of "asset seizure" to Costa Rica. The law states that all tangible or intangible property, vehicles, instruments, equipment, money or other objects that are used in the commission of an offense punished by this law shall be seized and forfeited. The forfeited assets are allocated 55% to the Center for Drug Prevention and 45% are allocated to the Drug Intelligence Unit. Violations of the drug laws can carry a prison sentence of up to 15 years.

2.4 TAX LAW

Until 1995 all offenses related to Costa Rican tax laws carried only administrative monetary fines. The Tax Justice Law of 1995 introduced criminal penalties into the tax system. Some of the relevant provisions of that law as it relates to offenses which can result in imprisonment are: (1) Inducing the tax authorities into error by altering, simulating or concealing truthful information with the intent of obtaining a financial benefit to the detriment of the public treasury. This offense carries a possible sentence of 2 to 5 years depending on the monetary amount involved. (2) Collecting applicable taxes and failing to turn those over to the public treasury within the required time frame also carries a sentence of up to 5 years imprisonment. (3) Those who deny, conceal or provide incomplete or false information regarding their financial or economic relation with third parties as it relates to tax implications can be sanctioned with imprisonment of 1 to 3 years. (4) Concealing or destroying accounting books, goods, documents, computerized systems or programs relevant to a tax investigation carries a sentence of 1 to 3 years.

2.5 CUSTOMS LAW

The Customs Law (*Ley General de Aduanas*) regulates the entry and exit into the country of all merchandise, vehicles and transportation. Violation of the Customs Law can under certain circumstances result in imprisonment. The law provides for a sentence of 1 to 3 years imprisonment for those that intentionally elude or evade the payment of customs duties.

2.6 DOMESTIC VIOLENCE LAW

The Law of Against Domestic Violence (*Ley de Violencia Domestica*), law number 7586 of October 4, 1996 regulates the procedures required to protect the victims of domestic violence. The law imposes an affirmative duty on the police to intervene in situations of domestic violence and to detain the aggressor if necessary. The victims of domestic violence may petition the court for an order of protection against an aggressor.

3. CRIMINAL PRACTICE AND PROCEDURE

The Costa Rican Code of Criminal Procedure (*Código Procesal Penal*) has been in effect since 1996 and was modeled after the German, Italian and Spanish procedural system. The law transfers all investigative functions previously carried out by a Judge of Instruction directly to prosecutors (fiscal) in the Costa Rican Public Ministry. The prosecutor carries the burden of investigating, charging and prosecuting all criminal offenses.

Proponents of the new Code of Criminal Procedure believed it would result in a more efficient overhaul of the criminal justice system in Costa Rica. The reality has been to the contrary and rather than expediting criminal prosecutions it actually increased the timeframe for completing investigations and getting cases to trial. Prosecutors are assigned large case loads and more responsibilities, but little support staff. For example, in the Fraud Division of the Prosecutors' Office, it is not uncommon for one prosecutor to have more than one hundred active files at one time. The reality in Costa Rica is that if you file a criminal complaint you better hire your own Attorney to actually investigate, gather the necessary evidence and interact with the Prosecutor; otherwise, depending on the type of case involved it will go nowhere. Every month dozens of criminal cases are dismissed because the Prosecutors' Office could not get them to trial before the statute of limitations for the offense expired.

3.1 THE PARTIES IN THE CRIMINAL JUSTICE SYSTEM

A. THE POLICE FORCES

Costa Rica has several independent police departments each charged with different duties. The largest police contingency, the Fuerza Publica is under the control of the Ministry of Police and Public Security *(Ministerio de Seguridad Publica)*. They are responsible for the protection of national sovereignty, citizen security, crime prevention and response. The most typical example of this is the patrol officer that patrols the streets in metropolitan San Jose.

In the capital city of San Jose the structure of the police department is based upon a community based police unit that would be more in tune with events that are happening in the community where they are assigned. To that end eighteen different police units patrol eighteen specific areas within metropolitan San Jose. These police units are known locally as Deltas. See Figure D for contact information for the Judicial Investigation Bureau and the Community Police Patrol for selected areas.

JUDICIAL INVESTIGATION BUREAU (O.I.J)

Criminal Complaint Filings 2295-3639
Criminal Investigations..2295-3399
Evidence Gathering Unit 2285-3925
Homicide 2.295-3860
Property Crimes 2295-3306
Drug Unit 2295-3859
Sexual Crimes Unit 2295-3317
Fraud Unit...2295-3830
Juvenile Unit..2295-3319
Misc Crimes Unit 2295-3319
Criminal Archives 2295-3040

COMMUNITY POLICE UNITS (Deltas)

D-1 San Jose Central Downtown 2233-4194
D-3 Desamparados 2250-0822
D-5 Montes de Oca 2225-6050
D-6 Curridabat 2225-0162
D-8 Pavas...2231-2697
D-12 Moravia 2235-8785
D-15 Sabana Park Area 2296-7319
D-18 Escazú 2228-1274

Other police units that are part of the Ministry of Police and Public Security include the Immigration Police (*Policia de Inmigracion y Extranjeria*) which is responsible for enforcing Costa Rican immigration laws; the Border Police (*Policia de Fronteras*) which are in charge of patrolling the borders; Drug Enforcement Police (*Polica del Control de Drogas*) which are specialized in policing drug related offenses and the Tourism Police (*Policia Turistica*) which are posted in popular tourism destinations and charged with protecting Tourists in Costa Rica.

Some local municipal governments have created their own municipal police force *(Policia Municipal)* which is under the administration of the local municipal government. This police force only has jurisdiction within their territorial limit.

The police force that conducts criminal investigations is the Judicial Investigation Bureau (*Organismo de Investigación Judicial*) which is under the direct control of the Ministry of Justice. The Code of Criminal Procedure stipulates that the judicial police (O.I.J) shall work under the direction and control of the prosecutor to (1) Investigate all public crimes; (2) prevent the commission of crimes; (3) individualize the participants and perpetrators of criminal offenses; (4) gather all evidence necessary to substantiate a criminal indictment; (5) carry out all other functions stipulated by law. If you are a victim of a crime it will be the Judicial Investigation Bureau that will be charged with investigating your complaint.

The Ministry of the Treasury also has its own police force, the Fiscal Police *(Policia Fiscal)* to investigate violations of Costa Rica's tax and customs laws and the Executive Branch (President) has under its direction the Directorate of Intelligence and National Security (DIS).
When you drive a vehicle on the Costa Rican roads then you will be under the jurisdiction of the Transit Police (*Policia de Transito*). This police force is under the direction of the Ministry of Public Works (M.O.P.T.) and they are responsible for the enforcement of Costa Rican traffic laws. The officer is referred to locally as oficial de transito or trafico.

A. THE PROSECUTOR

When the government charges an individual with a criminal offense it does so through the Public Ministry (*Ministerio Público*) represented by a Prosecutor (*Fiscal*). The Public Ministry is the prosecutorial branch of the criminal justice system. The Public Ministry has prosecutorial offices (*Fiscalias*) throughout Costa Rica since they are divided by territory for jurisdictional purposes. Within each territorial office there may be specialized units or divisions that deal with a particular subject matter of the criminal offense involved. In San Jose, some of the specialized departments within the prosecutor's office include: (1) Robbery Unit, (2) Assault Unit, (3) Fraud Unit, (4) Vehicle Theft Unit, (5) Narcotics Unit, (6) Sexual Offenses and Domestic Violence Unit, (7) Economic Crimes, Corruption and Tax Unit, (8) Juvenile Crimes Unit, (9) Environmental Unit.

B. THE ACCUSED

Those under investigation in Costa Rica for the commission of a crime have the same basic rights that they do in any other democratic judicial system. In the criminal process the accused (*imputado*) is any individual who has been singled out as the possible perpetrator of a criminal offense.

However, under the Costa Rican system, all those accused shall be presumed innocent until they have been adjudicated guilty by the trial court and there has been a final judgment rendered in that proceeding. Any suspect in a criminal proceeding has the right (1) to know the charges against him; (2) to communicate with any person, group, or association the fact that he is being detained; (3) to a Public Defender if they so choose; (4) to refrain from rendering a statement or if he wishes to render a statement to request that his Attorney be present.

If the accused is arrested he may not be detained for more than 24 hours before he is brought before a Judge for a hearing. If the Prosecutor deems that the Accused is either a flight risk because he may leave the country or that he may hamper an ongoing criminal investigation he may request that the Judge hold the accused in jail as a preventive measure. Depending on the seriousness of the offense the Judge may order the preventive detention of the accused. The preventive detention measures can last up to one year depending on the severity of the underlying offense. This means that in Costa Rica an accused could remain in jail under preventive detention for a year or more without being adjudicated guilty of any offense.

C. THE VICTIM

In the Costa Rican criminal justice system the victim is able to take an active role in the prosecution of a criminal offense. The victim has the right to participate in the criminal proceeding and must be notified about any court rulings that conclude the criminal case and they have a right to appeal any findings which dismiss a criminal charge. The victim, their heirs or beneficiaries may file a civil action for restitution and damages within the criminal case that is being prosecuted against the accused. This civil complaint known locally as *Accion Civil Resarcitoria* is heard by the criminal judge in the same criminal proceeding. The Court will rule on the civil complaint and enter a finding as to the amount of monetary restitution and damages.

3.2 THE CRIMINAL COMPLAINT

The criminal complaint which is called a *Denuncia* in Costa Rica is the method by which the "State" is put on notice of the possible commission of a criminal offense. This act, in theory, imposes upon the Public Ministry the obligation to initiate a criminal investigation into the allegations contained in the complaint. In Costa Rica, crimes are placed into three categories each of which has a distinct procedural manner of prosecution. (1) Public Offenses: These are offenses which are mandatory for the state to pursue even if the victim has no interest in pursuing the offense. The prosecution of these offenses can begin at the insistence of the prosecutor and police and it is not necessary to have a formal complaint filed by a victim. (2) Semi Public Offenses: Although these are offenses are in the public interest to pursue, the discretion of whether to pursue them or not is left to the victim who must file a formal criminal complaint to initiate the prosecution of the offense. In this category we have some of the sexual offenses, negligence resulting in injury, threats, abandonment, illegal taking of property and other property related offenses. (3) Private Criminal Offense: These are offenses that can only be prosecuted based upon an official criminal complaint being filed by the victim. If the victim does not file the criminal complaint then no action will be taken by the State. The typical offenses that fall in this category are defamation, slander, and unfair trade practices.

The criminal complaint *(Denuncia)* can be filed in writing or orally. Depending on the situation and the type of crime charged it is preferred that the criminal complaint be filed in writing setting forth the facts alleged to constitute the criminal offense, the alleged perpetrator of the offense and indicating any witness to the commission of the offense along with the location of any evidence. If possible, the complaint can set forth the criminal laws that are alleged to have been violated, but this is only essential in complex criminal matters and after consulting a criminal attorney to assist in the drafting of the criminal complaint. By doing so, you are providing the Prosecutor that will be assigned to the case a good starting block for conducting their investigation. If it is done orally, the law enforcement official that takes your statement will make an official record in writing of what is stated.

Once the prosecutor has gathered evidence and interrogated witnesses it will serve a summons to appear upon the accused, if the accused is not already in pre-trial detention. Since the Costa Rican Constitution presumes that one is innocent until proven guilty, pre-trial detention will only occur when there is provable evidence that a crime has been committed and in Costa Rica such detention is regarded as the exception rather than the rule. The Constitutional Court has ruled that "detention of an individual should only occur if there are no other means to guarantee appearance of the suspect in Court. As such, there was an overwhelming tendency to release the suspects on their own recognizance. This practice was strongly criticized by the media after several high profile "white collar" defendants involved in multi-million dollar fraud cases simply posted bail and fled the country. As a result, the pendulum has gone to the other extreme. Judges are much more aggressive in ordering suspects detained and jailed in preventive prison in high profile cases. The most common grounds for substantiating preventive prison are to prevent the flight of the suspect and prevent the suspect from destroying or altering evidence or tampering with witness during a criminal investigation.

The Constitution also requires that the police notify a Prosecutor within six hours of the time of detention of a suspect so that the suspect can invoke their right of defense. Further rulings from the Constitutional Court require that a suspect which is held in police custody must be brought before a Judge no later than 24 hours after being detained. Failure to abide by these time frames can result in the automatic release of a suspect from custody. Unfortunately it happens all too often and that is why we see offenders on the street the very next day after they have been arrested.

Once the Prosecutor completes the gathering of evidence and has taken the statement of the accused, they will decide if there is sufficient evidence to warrant a formal indictment or if the charges should be dismissed. If the Prosecutor decides to go forward, he must draft a formal indictment (*acusación*) which is then filed in the Criminal Court requesting a trial for the offenses charged. The basis for the indictment must be submitted to a Judge in a Preliminary Hearing.

3.3 THE PRELIMINARY PROCEDURE PHASE

The Code of Criminal Procedure establishes a safeguard against possible prosecutorial misconduct or malicious prosecution by establishing a preliminary hearing in which the prosecutor must file the indictment and all the evidence against the defendant to justify the criminal case proceeding to trial. During this phase, which is ruled upon by the Judge, the Prosecutor can request that the case be elevated to trial for the offenses charged in the indictment or he can request that the charges against the accused be dismissed. The defense can also appear in this phase of the proceeding to request the dismissal of the charges against the accused. If the Prosecutor indicts, he will have to file a formal indictment with the Judge, who will in turn schedule a preliminary hearing which will be attended by the Prosecutor and the Defense Counsel of the accused. Prior to the hearing, the parties to the proceeding are given the opportunity to review all the procedures and evidence gathered by the Prosecutor through the date of the preliminary hearing. During this preparatory phase the Judge will also rule on all evidentiary matters as well as issues related to arrest and pretrial detention. If the Judge determines that it is overwhelmingly evident that no criminal offense has occurred or could not have been committed by the accused or if it is barred by the statute of limitations for the offense, then the Judge may order that the file be permanently closed. When this occurs the judge enters an order dismissing the case either permanently or provisionally. Such a ruling is known as Sobreseimiento which means dismissal. The provisional dismissal can be issued for one year period and grants the Prosecutor that period of time to gather additional evidence.

If after one year no request is filed with the court to reopen the proceedings then the automatic dismissal of the case will be entered. On the other hand, if the judge approves the indictment, he will then issue a ruling stating that the accused must stand trial for the offenses charged and the criminal proceedings pass to a second stage known as the Intermediary Phase.

3.4 THE INTERMEDIARY PROCEDURE AND TRIAL PHASE

This phase has two purposes; the first one is an attempt to resolve the criminal indictment prior to trial but if that fails, the focus turns to steering the case toward the established trial date by narrowing the issues, when applicable, which will be tried. The Judge at the intermediate level which may or may not be the same Judge that ruled in the Preparatory Phase may also dismiss the case for cause as indicated above. The Code of Criminal Procedure establishes an Abbreviated Procedure which allows the Defendant to enter a guilty plea for the offenses charged. If the accused enters a guilty plea during this phase of the proceeding he is guaranteed to serve only 1/3 of the minimum sentence established for that offense.

As such, if an offense is punishable by three years in prison but the accused pleads guilty to the offense he will only have to serve a one year sentence. In order to proceed, the accused must admit guilt and consent to the application of the abbreviated procedure. The Prosecutor and the accuser must agree to the abbreviated procedure. During this phase, the Prosecutor may also request the Judge to grant immunity to one of the accused in exchange for their cooperation and testimony against some of the other accused.

The Code of Criminal Procedure also introduces into the Costa Rican criminal justice system the option, depending on the offense charged, for the victim and the accused to meet at a conciliation proceeding to conciliate and resolve the accusations before a trial date is set. The law allows the parties to settle misdemeanors and criminal offenses which are either semi-public actions or public actions and those crimes where a suspended sentence is allowed. If the parties agree, the case is simply dismissed. Given the back log of criminal cases in the Costa Rican judicial system Prosecutors are very open to conciliation as a way to dispose of their heavy case load.

If any of the methods to dispose of the case are not accepted during this phase then the Judge will issue a formal ruling declaring the trial phase open and a date will be set for the public trial of the accused.

The trial itself is public and both the prosecution and the defense must orally set forth their arguments. After both sides have rested by setting forth their case, the three judge panel immediately retires to chambers for secret deliberations. When the panel completes the deliberation they issue a verdict in the case. The verdict must specifically set forth the basis for the court's decision and the legal principles which were applied and read in open court. The final stage of the criminal trial is sentencing. Here, the judge or tribunal president establishes the penalty for the offense committed and notifies the Public Ministry and the defendant. If there are no legal objections to sentencing, it is automatically executed. The decision of the Criminal Court may be appealed to a Superior Tribunal which in turn can be appealed to the Third Chamber of the Supreme Court which hears only criminal appeals.

3.5 CIVIL ACTION IN THE CRIMINAL CASE

Costa Rican law allows victims of a crime, their heirs or beneficiaries to file a civil action for restitution and damages against the criminal defendant. This civil complaint (*Accion Civil Resarcitoria*) is filed in the Criminal Tribunal where the criminal case is being heard. If the defendant is found guilty of the underlying criminal offense, the tribunal will enter a finding as to the amount of monetary damages set forth in the civil complaint.

3.6 STATUTE OF LIMITATIONS IN CRIMINAL CASES

The statute of limitations is a legal disposition which dictates the term by which legal action must be undertaken. If legal action is brought after the statute of limitations has expired the Judge can dismiss the case and the accused cannot be charged with that same offense.

The statute of limitations is governed by the Code of Criminal Procedure. That Code provides that the statute of limitations for offenses which carry a prison sentence shall be a term equal to the maximum sentence provided for that offense but under no circumstance might the term exceed ten years or be less than three years. Those criminal offenses which do not carry a prison sentence have a statute of limitations of two years.

As such, assume an individual is a suspect of a simple robbery which carries a maximum prison sentence of three years. Under the guidelines established in the Code of Criminal Procedure the statute of limitations for that offense would be three years. However, the Code of Criminal Procedure also provides that the statute of limitations is cut in half and begins to run again when the accused is formally called in before a prosecutor to render a statement as to the charges levied against him. This means that in the example above, once the simple robbery suspect formally appears to answer the charges against him the statute of limitations is cut in half from 3 years to 1 1/2 years and the only manner to stop the running of the statute of limitations once it has been cut in half is to have a final judgment entered. In many cases, the timeframe for actually getting a case to trial is greater than the statute of limitations provided by law and as such many offenses end up getting dismissed because the Prosecutor is unable to bring it to trial before the statute of limitations runs out.

4. EXTRADITION

Extradition is the procedure by which one nation requests that a fugitive from justice from that nation and located in another country be returned to stand trial for the offenses charged in that nation. Generally extradition is a matter of international legal assistance among nations and is governed by treaties. Specifically, the Costa Rican Constitution provides that extradition shall be regulated by law or by international treaties. In Costa Rica, the government has entered into bilateral extradition treaties with the following countries: Spain, China, Mexico, Belgium, Italy, Nicaragua, Colombia, and the United States. Costa Rica is also a signatory on the Inter-American Convention on Extradition which it ratified in March of the year 2000. This means that the Inter-America convention treaty can be used as the basis for extradition among the signatory countries.

In the absence of a treaty agreement the extradition request will be governed by the Extradition Law of Costa Rica which was enacted in 1971. The extradition laws apply only to foreign citizens located in Costa Rica. The law specifically provides that citizens of Costa Rica may not be extradited to a foreign country.

4.1 EXTRADITION PROCEDURE UNDER
THE EXTRADITION LAW

This procedure is followed by those countries that wish to have one of their citizens extradited from Costa Rica to stand trial for a criminal offense carried out in their country of origin. Under this law, Costa Rica will not grant the request for extradition if the following issues are present: (1) If the individual sought is a Costa Rican citizen. (2) If the individual sought is currently on trial in Costa Rica for the same offenses as those set forth in the extradition request. Or, if the individual has been acquitted, pardoned or served time for the same offenses for which extradition is sought. (3) If the individual sought is standing trial or has been convicted in Costa Rica of an intentional or negligent act which resulted in bodily injury. However, once the sentence is served or if he is acquitted of those charges then the extradition request will be allowed to proceed. (4) If the offense which is the basis for the extradition request is not an offense according to Costa Rican law then the extradition will not be allowed. If the offense is punishable under Costa Rican law, the statute of limitations specified for that particular offense must not have run out for the extradition to proceed. (5) The criminal offense which is the basis for the extradition request must carry a term of imprisonment of no less than one year. (6) If the crime was not committed within the country that is requesting the extradition then the petition will not be allowed. (7) If the crimes are political or politically connected. (8) If the criminal offense carries the death penalty then Costa Rica will not authorize the extradition. The extradition will be granted if the requesting country agrees that it will not apply the death penalty to the offender. (9) If Costa Rica has given political asylum then any extradition request against that person will be rejected.

If the requesting party has been able to satisfy the requirements set forth above then it may proceed with the extradition request. The requesting party can petition the Costa Rican government to detain the individual prior to formally filing the extradition request. The process shall follow the steps through the appropriate diplomatic channels. It will start by submitting a formal request to detain the individual. The request for detention must be filed with the Legal Office of the Ministry of Foreign Relations whom in turn will notify the relevant authority to carry out the arrest. The petition for detention must prove that there is either an adjudication of guilt or an arrest warrant for the individual that is sought. The requesting party must also certify that they will file the formal extradition request no later than ten days (10) from the date on which the individual is taken into custody in Costa Rica. Failure by the requesting party to comply the time limits will result in the release of the individual held in custody. The formal extradition procedure begins when the requesting party files the petition through the Ministry of Foreign Relations of Costa Rica. This is the government ministry in Costa Rica in charge of receiving and processing extradition requests from foreign governments. The petition must contain the following: (1) Documentary proof in the form of a judgment or arrest warrant on the individual for which extradition is sought. (2) A certified copy of the court file where the individual was tried or the relevant portions thereof which substantiate the culpability of the individual sought. (3) Information which clearly identifies the individual sought. (4) The legal conclusions from the judgment which sets forth the criminal offense, the crime attributed to the individual sought, the applicable punishment for the offense and the statute of limitations for the offense.

Once the request is received the Ministry of Foreign Relations files it with the Prosecutor's Office of the Ministry of Public Security who will appoint a Prosecutor to represent the government in the extradition procedure. The individual against whom extradition is sought has the right to appoint a private Attorney to represent him during the process. If he cannot afford a private Attorney the court will then assign a Public Defender to represent him. Once formally served with the extradition petition the individual has twenty days in which to present his case opposing the extradition petition. If he does not want to oppose the extradition he can submit to a voluntary extradition and he will be turned over to the requesting party. If not, the extradition process continues until the criminal court rules upon the petition. If the extradition request is denied then the individual is set free. If the request is granted then the individual sought is turned over to the police authorities of the requesting party. The original ruling by the criminal court either granting or denying the extradition may be appealed before the criminal appellate court. Its ruling will be conclusive on the matter.

4.2   EXTRADITION PROCEDURE PURSUANT TO AN EXTRADITION TREATY.

If the requesting party has an extradition treaty with Costa Rica, the process will follow the steps in accordance with the procedures set forth in the specific treaty. In some instances, the limitations imposed by the Extradition Law can be waived if so stipulated in an Extradition Treaty by the contracting countries. In order to compare the procedures between the Extradition Law discussed above and an Extradition Treaty we will analyze the Extradition Treaty between the Republic of Costa Rica and the United States of America.

The United States-Costa Rica Extradition Treaty was originally signed on December 4, 1982 but was not ratified by the Costa Rican government until 1991 and effective as of October 11, 1991. Despite its ratification the treaty was challenged on constitutional grounds in Costa Rica and was tied up in litigation until the Supreme Court of Costa Rica validated its application in December of 1996.

The essence of the treaty is that the contracting parties agree to extradite to each other persons found in the territory of one of the contracting parties who have been charged with, are being tried for, or have been found guilty of an extraditable offense. The extraditable offenses specified in the treaty are as follows: (1) An offense shall be an extraditable offense if it may be punished under the laws of both contracting parties by deprivation of liberty for a maximum period of more than one year or by any greater punishment. (2) An offense shall also be extraditable if it consists of an attempt to commit or participate in the commission of any offense. (3) Extradition shall also be granted for illicit association, as provided by the laws of Costa Rica, and for conspiracy as provided by the laws of the United States of America, to commit any such offense. (4) An offense shall be extraditable: (a) Whether or not the laws of the contracting parties place the offense within the same category of offenses or denominate the offense by the same terminology; or (b) Whether or not the offense is one for which United States federal law requires, for the purpose of establishing jurisdiction in a United States federal court, proof of interstate transportation, or use of, or effect on mails or other facilities affecting interstate or foreign commerce. Since Costa Rica objects to the death penalty as a form of punishment, the treaty carries forth the restriction contained in the Extradition Law which refuses extradition for offenses punishable by death. However, if the Requesting State furnishes assurances that the death penalty will not be imposed and the Requested State considers those assurances sufficient or, if imposed, shall not be executed then the extradition may proceed. Other limitations set forth within the treaty are that: (1) Extradition shall not be granted when the person sought is being tried; has been convicted, acquitted, or pardoned; or has served the sentence imposed by the Requested State for the same offense arising out of the same acts for which extradition is requested.

(2) The Requested State shall undertake all available legal measures to suspend proceedings for the naturalization of the person sought until a decision is made on the request for extradition and, if that request is granted, until that person is surrendered. (3) If the Requested State refuses extradition on the basis of nationality, it shall, at the request of the Requesting State, submit the case to its competent authorities for prosecution.

In order to initiate an Extradition procedure pursuant to the treaty the Requesting State must make the request through a diplomatic agent. The treaty requires that the Extradition request clearly provide the identity of the person sought and the location where the person may be found, if known. The request should also provide a brief statement of the facts of the case and be accompanied by the following documents: (a) Evidence that the person sought is the person charged or convicted; (b) The text and explanation of the law describing the related offenses and penalties; and (c) The text and an explanation of the law setting forth the statute of limitations applicable to the trial and punishment. If the request for extradition relates to a person who has not yet been convicted, it shall be accompanied by: (a) A copy of the charging document, or an equivalent document issued by a judge or judicial authority; and (b) Such evidence as in accordance with the laws of the Requested State, would be necessary to justify the apprehension and commitment for trial of the person sought if the offense had been committed there. The Extradition Treaty with the United States also provides for the provisional detention of any charged or convicted person. The application for detention of an individual may be made through diplomatic channels or directly between the Department of Justice of the United States of America and the Ministry of Justice of Costa Rica. The Provisional detention terminates within sixty days after the apprehension of the person sought if the Requested State has not received the request for extradition and the supporting documents required by law. Likewise, if the person sought agrees to a voluntary extradition the person is then surrendered to the Requesting State without further proceedings.

According to the Ministry of Foreign Relations during the 2002 to 2004 period there were 68 extradition requests filed. Of those requests 49 were from the United States, 2 from Canada, 2 from Germany, 3 from Italy and the rest from Spain, Belgium, Panama, Nicaragua, Argentina, France, Poland, Guatemala, Rumania, and Guatemala.

CHAPTER 4

COMMERCIAL AND FINANCIAL TRANSACTIONS

This chapter will cover the laws that govern and regulate commercial and financial transactions carried out within Costa Rica. For commercial transactions, the main source of legislation is the Commercial Code which was passed by the legislature in 1964 and since then has undergone several additions and amendments. The Commercial Code specifically governs corporate formation, contracts, sales, negotiable instruments, and bankruptcy. Article 2 of the Commercial Code states that commercial disputes will be resolved in order of priority by looking at (1) the Commercial Code (2) the Civil Code (3) commercial custom and usage and (4) general principles of law.

Book Three of the Commercial Code sets forth the laws which regulate negotiable instruments such as promissory notes, checks and bills of exchange, all of which will be discussed in more detail in this chapter. Although there is no specific compilation of laws in the form of a code to govern financial transactions, there are specific laws governing the purchase and sale of securities and monetary exchange policies which provide the background for understanding the financial system of Costa Rica.

1. CORPORATE FORMATION

Under Costa Rican law, there are three types of legal entities which offer limited liability to its shareholders. These are the Limited Partnership *(Sociedad en Comandita)*, Limited Liability Company (Sociedad de Responsabilidad Limitada), and the most commonly used, the corporation *(Sociedad Anonima)*.

1.1 LIMITED PARTNERSHIPS

The Limited Partnership *(Sociedad en Comandita)* is made up of at least one general partner with unlimited liability for all the debts and obligations of the partnership and one or more limited partners whose liability is limited to the value of their capital contribution. The limited partners are prohibited from actively participating in the administration of the partnership. If they actively participate their limited liability status is eliminated. The limited partner's contributions to the partnership must be in the form of cash, property or commercial patents. Contributions in the form of services or credit are not allowed.

1.2 THE LIMITED LIABILITY COMPANY

The Limited Liability Company (Sociedad de Responsabilidad Limitada) was created as an alternative to the corporation. It is simpler to operate since it does not require many formal acts to function. Ease of operation makes it easily adaptable for use by small business enterprises. The main characteristics of the limited liability company are that (i) the liability of the shareholders is limited to the amount of their capital contribution; (ii) the capital is divided into individual registered shares which cannot be sold to the public; thus, there is no public market for the shares; (iii) the company is made up of a minimum of two shareholders and there is no limit as to the maximum number of shareholders allowed. A company formed under these regulations is generally characterized by the ending S.R.L. or LTD.

The company is managed by one or several managers who may or may not be shareholders. While the simplicity of operation is a benefit of this form of incorporation the drawback is the limitation on the ability to transfer ownership of the Limited Liability Company to third parties.

1.3 THE CORPORATION

The Costa Rican Corporation (*Sociedad Anonima*) is the most widely used corporate form of business organization in Costa Rica. The main feature of the corporation is that the liability of the shareholders is limited to their capital contributions and stock ownership in the corporation is easily transferable to third parties.

A. Formation

A Costa Rican corporation may be formed in two ways. The most common method is referred to as simultaneous subscription. This method requires at least two corporate incorporators to personally appear before a Costa Rican Notary Public to execute the articles of incorporation. The second method, known as subsequent subscription, is rarely used since it involves formation by a promoter as opposed to incorporators. In the discussion that follows all references pertain to the formation of a corporation by simultaneous subscription.

To form a Costa Rican corporation, the Commercial Code requires that at least two individuals execute before a Notary Public the articles of incorporation and subscribe at least one share of stock each. There is no requirement that the incorporators be either residents or citizens of Costa Rica. A citizen of any country can incorporate in Costa Rica.

The articles of incorporation by law must contain the following information:

(1) Incorporation Date: The articles must specify the date and the place where the corporation is formed; (2) Identification of the Incorporators: Include the name, nationality, identification number for each incorporator. In the case of Costa Ricans it is their national identity card (cedula) and for non Costa Ricans their passport number or residency card number. The incorporator must also set forth their occupation, marital status, and domicile; (3) Corporate Name: Prior to the year two thousand, the Mercantile Registry would only allow the use of corporate names that were in Spanish. Since then, it is possible to register corporate names in English by providing the Spanish translation to the name. Generic names or names that have similarity with already recorded companies will not be allowed. The initial step in setting up a corporation is to ensure that the name you want is available for registration; (4) Corporate Purpose: In Costa Rica the corporate purposes are generally stated in very broad and encompassing terms unless the incorporator wishes to limit the purpose; (5) Duration: The articles of incorporation must list the duration and its possible extensions. The law prohibits an indefinite term and the most common practice is to list a duration of ninety-nine years to avoid doing extensions on the term; (6) The Capital Stock: The amount of authorized capital and the manner in which it shall be subscribed must be set forth in the articles of incorporation; (7) The Capital Contribution: Indicate the manner in which the capital is paid, whether by cash, property, or other capital contribution of the shareholders; (8) The Legal Domicile: The Costa Rican corporation must have a legal physical location in Costa Rica. In addition the articles of incorporation can specify that the corporation may have offices or branches in countries outside of Costa Rica; (9) The Board of Directors: The corporation by law must have a President, Secretary and Treasurer. There are no nationality requirements for these positions. The articles of incorporation must name the per-

sons that will occupy those positions at the time of incorporation. The same person may not occupy two or more positions. You need to have a different person for each of the required positions. Those named to the Board must either be present in order to sign the articles of incor poration or, if they are not incorporators then they can accept their positions by letters of acceptance; (10) The Enumeration of Powers: Within the articles of incorporation you must specify the type of power that each of the directors or officers will have to bind the corporation. Alternatives are having only the President with unlimited power of attorney or having the President and Secretary acting jointly to have unlimited power of attorney. How this is set up depends solely on your requirements. (11) Profit and Loss: The law requires that the articles of incorporation indicate how the allocation of profit and losses will be handled; (12) Dissolution: The articles of incorporation must indicate how the corporation will be dissolved or liquidated; (13) Resident Agent: A Costa Rican corporation must also name a Resident Agent if the President of the corporation is not residing in Costa Rica. The Resident Agent must be a Costa Rican Attorney who maintains an office in Costa Rica and is capable of receiving judicial and administrative notices on behalf of the corporation.

Once the articles of incorporation are drafted by the Notary Public and executed by the incorporators and the initial Board of Directors of the corporation, the Notary will prepare an extract of the incorporation and this document along with the applicable registration fees must be filed in the Costa Rican National Registry. Upon filing, the National Registry will assign the document to a Registrar within the Mercantile Section who is in charge of reviewing the documents' content and recording the registration.

At the same time, legal notice of the incorporation must be published in the official newspaper, La Gaceta to put third parties on notice of the registration in case there are oppositions to the corporate name that is being recorded. The corporate registration process generally takes about thirty five days and once complete the National Registry will return the original incorporation document to the Notary Public that drafted it who in turn will deliver it to the incorporators. Once the document is approved it is formally recorded and the document is stamped with the volume (*Tomo*) and entry number (*Asiento*) where it has been recorded.

The recording system is computerized and the registration information for the corporation will be the document presentation number for the document which is identified with a volume number (*Tomo*) and entry number (*Asiento*). In the past the corporation was also issued a corporate identity card number (*cédula júridica*) which would serve as the identification document for the corporation. The National Registry no longer issues the identification card. (Refer to Appendix 4 for sample Articles of Incorporation)

The corporate registration information is relevant since you will require it when you purchase an asset in the name of your corporations, install utilities, open a bank account and any carry out any other transaction where you must demonstrate that you are authorized to act on behalf of the corporation. To do these transactions you may be asked to provide a Personeria Juridica. This document is a prepared by a Costa Rican Notary Public and is an extract of the corporate information that is filed in the National Registry on a corporation. It is the equivalent of a Certificate of Corporate Standing since the Notary is certifying that the corporation is filed in the National Registry and the legal capacity of the Board of Directors to bind the corporation.

Once the incorporators have the original incorporation documents back from the National Registry they can file their request with the Costa Rican Revenue Department (*Tributación Directa)* to legalize the corporate books of the corporation. Some Attorneys include this service in the cost of the incorporation and will do this for you as part of the incorporation process while others will charge extra for the service.

By law, the Costa Rican corporation must have six corporate books; three of these are minute's books to record: Board of Director's meetings, Shareholders' meetings, and a Shareholder Log Book. The other three books are for accounting purposes and include: Inventory and Balances, General Ledger and Account Ledger. (See Appendix 5 for corporate book legalization request form) Depending on the activity or inactivity of the corporation it may be required to file a tax return at the end of the Costa Rican fiscal year which is September 30. The corporate tax returns are due by December 15th of each year. (See chapter 11, The Tax System, for more details on corporate taxation).

B. Capital Structure

Costa Rican law requires that the articles of incorporation also set forth: (1) The amount of paid in capital; (2) The number, par value, and classes of shares; and (3) The terms and method of payment for the shares.

Costa Rican corporations use the par value method, which is an artificial value set forth in the articles of incorporation and appearing on the face of the certificates for shares. As such, a corporation can issue common shares which must have a par value which can be denominated in Costa Rican currency or in United States dollars. The law prohibits issuing common shares without any value or issuing bearer shares. (See Appendix 6 for sample share certificate.)

In addition to common shares, the corporation may issue preferred shares as long as the class, preferences, rights, and limitations are set forth in the articles of incorporation. All shares are indivisible; this means that one share confers only one right. If there are several persons who own one share they will have to elect one representative to act on behalf of that share.

The corporation may issue stock certificates which must set forth the following: (1) the name, domicile, and duration of the corporation; (2) the date of subscription of the articles of incorporation; the Notary Public who drafted the articles of incorporation; and the registration numbers for the corporation from the National Registry; (3) the name of the shareholder at the time of incorporation; (4) The capital stock of the corporation and the total number of and value of each share; (5) The series, number and class of stock which the certificate represents. Each certificate must be signed by the corporate officers who are authorized in the articles of incorporation to sign the certificates. This is generally the President and Secretary of the corporation.

Stock in a Costa Rican corporation is freely transferable by endorsing the stock certificate to the name of the recipient and having the transferor sign and date the endorsement of the certificate. The transfer of stock can then be logged in the Shareholder Log Book of the corporation to formally document the transfer.

C. The Shareholders Meetings and Voting

The corporation will consider a shareholder of record that individual or entity which has been registered as such in the shareholders' log book. Each common share has the right of one vote. Thus, the Costa Rican corporation uses the concept of "straight voting" whereby each shareholder may cast the number of votes equal to the number of shares they hold.

The Commercial Code only requires that the names of nominative shareholders be entered in the shareholders' log book. The book can in turn be kept at the legal domicile of the corporation. There is no requirement that information contained in the shareholders log book be recorded publicly. As such, the shareholders log book is a confidential document and information contained therein may not be revealed without a court order from a Costa Rican judge.

Shareholder meetings are divided in two categories, general and special. The general meetings can be made up of all the shareholders while the special meetings are limited to those shareholders who have specific rights18. Furthermore, the general meetings are divided into ordinary and extraordinary. Extraordinary meetings are those which modify the corporate existence or which authorize the issuance of a class of shares or bonds which have not been set forth in the articles of incorporation. All other corporate matters are dealt with in the ordinary meetings. The law requires that an ordinary meeting be held once a year. In order to make up a quorum, it is required that at least fifty percent (50%) of the voting shares be represented at the meeting. In order to adopt a corporate resolution it must be passed by a majority of the votes.

D. Managing the Corporation

Costa Rican law requires that as a minimum, a corporation have three members in its Board of Directors: President, Secretary and Treasurer to manage and control its affairs. There are no nationality or residence requirements for board members. The Board of Directors selects the corporate officers and has the power to remove them. Generally, the directors, officers and managers in a closely held corporation are the same individuals unless the shareholders elect to appoint different officers. The Board of Directors also may hire employees or agents and create new offices. Although the Board has the option of delegating its functions, it remains ultimately responsible for fulfilling its obligations.

E. Powers of Attorney

The Shareholders and members of the Board of Directors, if so permitted, may grant Powers of Attorney to third parties. The Powers of Attorney may be Special (*Poder Especial*) or General (*Poder Generalisimo*). The Special Power of Attorney is generally executed to accomplish a specific purpose such as purchasing a specific parcel of property, opening a bank account, or signing specific documents. The Special Power of Attorney is not registered in the National Registry. The General Power of Attorney on the other hand, must be recorded in the National Registry and it provides broad powers including the power for the attorney-in-fact to substitute their powers, all or in part, to another person.

1.4 THE FOREIGN CORPORATION IN COSTA RICA

The Costa Rican Commercial Code allows a foreign corporation to establish a branch or subsidiary in Costa Rican or transfer its domicile to Costa Rica, so long as it complies with specified requirements. In many respects, the requirements are similar to those for incorporating a Costa Rican corporation since the purpose is to ensure that the information about the foreign corporation is duly recorded in the National Registry (Corporate Section) to give third parties notice of that existence. In the case of a branch office, the law requires that the corporation appoint a legal representative in Costa Rica who will have full power of attorney to act on behalf of the corporation. The request must also set forth the corporate purpose for the branch and the parent company as well as the capital stock, names of the officers and managers and the duration of the parent company. Once recorded and approved, the branch office will be issued a Costa Rican corporate identity card which it can use to conduct business in Costa Rica.

To transfer the domicile of a foreign corporation to Costa Rica requires that the articles of incorporation of the foreign company authorize such a transfer. If so, the foreign corporation may file its articles of incorporation which must be translated and certified by a Costa Rican consulate along with a corporate resolution authorizing the transfer of domicile with the Costa Rican National Registry. The request must also set forth the names of the officers and managers of the corporation.

2. CONTRACTUAL OBLIGATIONS

2.1 REQUIREMENTS OF CONTRACT FORMATION

A contractual obligation is a contract which the law will enforce in some manner. In Costa Rica, a contract must contain the following essential elements in order to be enforceable:

(1) Capacity- In order to be a party to the contract one must have the competency and ability to understand the nature and effect of one's acts. Generally, this means that the contracting party must be of legal age, which in Costa Rica is attained at the age of eighteen. (2) Subject Matter- In order to establish the validity of an obligation, the essential terms of the contract must pertain to a certain subject matter. The subject matter can be a tangible item or matter that will come into existence sometime in the ascertainable future. In order to be valid the subject matter must have an ascertained value; otherwise it is invalid. Likewise, if the subject matter of the contract is physically impossible to accomplish or illegal, the contract is invalid. (3) Consideration- This is the inducement to a contract. It is the motive or cause which induces a contracting party to enter into a contract. Generally, a contract is supported by consideration if the promisee gives up something of value, or refrains from doing something he was legally free to pursue in exchange for the act or promise of the promisor. (4) Consent-This refers to the intention of the parties to enter into a contract. For a contract to be formed, the parties must reach an agreement to which they mutually assent. This mutual assent is generally reached by way of an offer and acceptance. (5) Legal Formalities- Generally, unless specifically provided for by law, (some laws may specifically require written contracts) there is no legal formality which must occur in order to have a valid contract. As such, whatever the form or language in which the agreement is executed will bind the parties to the terms and performance which they have agreed to.

With that said I highly recommend that any transaction that you enter into in Costa Rica be put in writing and have your Attorney advise you on any possible pitfalls of the transaction or business that you are entering into. The enforcement and litigation of contractual disputes in Costa Rica is very tedious and time consuming and certainly something you want to avoid whenever possible.

2.2   OFFER AND ACCEPTANCE

As previously discussed, the mutual assent required for the formation of a contract generally takes place through what is called an offer and acceptance. In other words, one person proposes a bargain, the offer, and the other person who agrees to this proposed bargain gives his acceptance. The legal effect of an offer is that it creates a power in the other party to enter into a contract by making his acceptance. Once the offer is accepted the contract is perfected unless the law requires further formalities.

The party who makes the offer (offeror) is free to revoke his offer at any time before it is accepted. It must be noted that the revocation by the offeror will not become effective until the other party (offeree) has received notice that it is being revoked. Likewise, if the acceptance varies, modifies, or adds conditions to the terms of the offer it will not be considered an acceptance but a counter offer. Since the offeror is in effect, the master of his offer he may set the time limit for acceptance. At the end of this time period the power of acceptance by the offeree lapses and thus automatically terminates. If no time period for acceptance is specified the law provides that the offer is terminated if not accepted within three (3) days. This time period is extended to ten (10) days if the contracting parties reside in Costa Rica but is not located in the same province and sixty (60) days if they reside outside of Costa Rica.

2.3 THE EFFECT OF FORMATION

Once formed, the contract and its terms become legally enforceable between the contracting parties. Pursuant to Costa Rican law, the rights and duties which may arise from a contract may be freely assigned or delegated. The only exceptions are for contracts which involve rights and duties of a personal character. If the contracting party delegates his duties under the contract to a third party he may still be held liable unless the third party delegator ratifies the contract.

Costa Rican law also recognizes the validity of a contract which is to benefit a third person. Thus X and Y may make a contract in which

Y makes a promise which will benefit X; in return for X's promise to give performance which will benefit Z rather than Y. In this situation Z is said to be a third party beneficiary. The rights which inure to a third party beneficiary to enforce the contractual obligations depend on whether the third party beneficiary is either a donee beneficiary or a creditor beneficiary. If the promisee entered into the contract for the purpose of conferring a gift on a third party, the third party is referred to as a donee beneficiary. However, once the third party beneficiary accepts the benefits of the contract the promisor is legally obligated to perform directly to the third party.

2.4 DEFENSES TO FORMATION

The Civil Code sets forth certain defects in the formation of a contract which may be grounds for nullification of the contract. The most common defenses include:

(1) Mistake: A contract is voidable on grounds of mistake if there is a mistaken belief about an existing fact which has a material effect on the agreed exchange of performances or if there is a mistake as to the subject matter of the contract. Note that a simple clerical error or mathematical miscalculation will not make the contract voidable but may allow the party to rectify the error.

(2) Duress: The defense of duress arises if the party can demonstrate that he was unfairly coerced into entering into the contract by violence or threats. Generally, a subjective standard is applied to determine whether the party's free will has been overcome. That is their age, sex, and condition is taken into consideration.

(3) Illegality: A contract is void if its subject matter is illegal, or the participation of one or both of the parties is illegal, contrary to public morals, and/or public policy.

(4) Impossibility: A contractual obligation may be discharged if it becomes physically impossible to perform. The impossibility which arises must be absolute and permanent in nature. Typical types of impossibility may include the destruction or unavailability of the subject matter of the contract; death or incapacity of the party; and or supervening illegality.

2.5 BREACH OF CONTRACT AND DAMAGES

Contractual obligations must be performed according to the terms stipulated in the contract. If details as to performance were not stipulated to in the contract, then performance must be carried out pursuant to the established business custom. Likewise, if the contract omitted details as to the location where payment is to be made then it shall be presumed that payment will be made at the debtor's place of business.

Failure to perform or a defective performance gives rise to a breach of contract unless the breach is attributable to an act of God or fortuitous act. If a breach of contract is established, the damaged party may be entitled to compensatory and consequential damages. Compensatory damages compensate the injured party for the injury it has sustained. Consequential damages are those that flow directly from the breach of contract i.e. a proximate cause of the breach.

On some occasions, parties negotiating a contract may make an explicit agreement as to what each party's remedy for breach of the contract will be. Such an agreement, as to the consequences of breach and placed in the contract itself is called a liquidated damages clause. Costa Rican law specifically recognizes liquidated damage clauses. The Civil Code provides that if a contract contains a liquidated damages clause then both parties must abide by the agreed upon amount.

3. COMMERCIAL TRANSACTIONS

In general, the law applicable to contractual obligations discussed above is also applicable and interrelated to commercial transactions. However, the Commercial Code has sought to distinguish commercial transactions to provide uniform commercial practices through custom, usage, and agreement by the parties. Since the Commercial Code provides a separate chapter which specifically governs merchants and commercial transactions it is necessary to discuss its application.

3.1 SCOPE AND DEFINITIONS

The Commercial Code defines a merchant as (i) persons with legal standing who carry out a trade or business; (ii) all corporate entities incorporated pursuant to the provisions of the Commercial Code; (iii) foreign corporations and their subsidiaries who engage in commercial transactions within the country. A commercial transaction is defined by the Commercial Code as: (i) commercial transactions carried out by business enterprises or individuals in the normal course of business; (ii) the purchase, sale or lease of real property; (iii) the purchase/sale of aircraft and ships, bonds, securities, and corporate stock.

3.2 OFFER AND ACCEPTANCE

When the parties to a commercial transaction negotiate a contract face-to face or by telephone, to buy or sell goods, the contract will be considered formed once they mutually agree on the terms, object and price. When negotiating via mail, if a written offer provides that the power of acceptance will continue for a specified time period then that period is applicable. If both parties are located in the same city and no time for acceptance is specified, then the offer must remain open for five (5) days. This increases to ten (10) days if the parties are located in different cities and to thirty (30) days if one of the parties resides in a foreign country. This time period begins to run when the offeror deposits the offer in the mail. A contract is formed when the offeree notifies the offeror of his acceptance. If his acceptance contains additional terms or conditions, the contract is not considered formed unless the offeree accepts the modifications and so notifies the offeror.

3.3 SELLER'S OBLIGATIONS

A. Delivery of the Goods

Unless otherwise agreed, the place for delivery of goods is the seller's place of business. The following evidence will constitute proof that delivery has been made and accepted: (i) A delivery acknowledgment signed by the buyer; (ii) tendering a bill of lading to the buyer; (iii) if the buyer affixes his trademark or brand to the goods with the acquiescence of the seller; (iv) by tendering the keys to the item or good that was sold; (v) a certified document issued by a government official; (vi) any other method which is a customary business practice.

B.   Risk of Loss

Once the contract has been formed and the buyer takes possession either actual or by title, any loss or damage to the goods are the sole responsibility of the buyer. On the other hand, if the seller has sold the goods but has not delivered them to the buyer, the risk of loss will remain with the seller in the following cases: (i) if the goods sold are of such a nature that they are not easily identifiable or distinguished; (ii) If the buyer had a right to inspect the goods but was unable to do so prior to their destruction so as to voice his acceptance; (iii) when the goods sold were to be delivered according to a specific number, weight or measurement; (iv) if the sale of goods was made conditional on an agreed delivery date; (v) if the buyer was willing to accept the goods but the seller was in breach as to the delivery of the goods.

C. Warranty of Goods

A warranty, in general, is the seller's agreement or representation about the goods that they have sold. The Commercial Code recognizes an express warranty. However, it only arises if the seller specifically guarantees the quality of a good. The length of time of the warranty is that which is established by the seller. If no time period is established, the law will assume a one year warranty.

3.4 BUYER'S OBLIGATIONS

The general obligation of the buyer to a commercial transaction is to accept and pay for the goods in accordance with the terms of the contract.

A. Right to Inspect the Goods

Before the buyer accepts and pays for the goods, he has the right to inspect the goods to insure that they conform. Once the buyer receives and inspects the goods and subsequently accepts them, he may not later allege a defect as to quality or quantity. The buyer has five (5) days from the date he receives the goods to provide the seller with written notice that the goods are non-conforming unless otherwise agreed upon by contract.

A buyer may also accept the non-conforming goods and request indemnification for the breach of the contract. A right to file an action in court for delivery of non-conforming goods expires three (3) months from the date of delivery.

B. Acceptance

The form of acceptance depends on the conduct of the buyer. If the buyer has had a reasonable opportunity to inspect the goods and he notifies the seller that he accepts the conforming goods, he has accepted them. Likewise, if the buyer notifies the seller that he is willing to retain the goods despite their nonconformity, he also has accepted the goods.

3.5 REMEDIES FOR BREACH OF CONTRACT

Once a contract for the sale of goods is perfected, each of the contracting parties has a right to demand performance. The party who breaches the contract by failing to perform will be held liable for damages.

If the buyer wrongfully rejects the goods, the seller may consider the contract canceled. This action discharges the seller's duties under the contact towards the buyer and allows him to retain any remedy for breach of contract. The seller may then maintain an action to recover the price of the goods; this, in effect, allows the seller to sue to recover the price of the contracted goods. The seller can also request the resale of the goods. In order to do so, the seller requests that the goods be deposited with the court who in turn may resell the goods.

4. BANKRUPTCY

The Commercial Code, Articles 851 to 967, empowers the courts to entertain bankruptcy proceedings. A merchant or a corporate entity may declare itself bankrupt and initiate a judicial proceeding for bankruptcy if it complies with certain requirements. In Costa Rica, bankruptcy proceedings are quite restrictive and its application is limited to the "re-organization" of the business enterprise as opposed to a discharge of all obligations. Likewise, there is no personal bankruptcy and these provisions are only applicable to a merchant or a corporation engaged in business.

4.1 WHO MAY FILE FOR BANKRUPTCY

A. Voluntary Request by Debtor

A debtor or corporate administrator may voluntarily file for bankruptcy ten (10) days after it has stopped making payments to its creditors. The petition for bankruptcy must include the following documentation: (i) A balance sheet indicating all assets and liabilities including a breakdown of the names and addresses of each creditor and the outstanding balance; (ii) an indication of any accounts receivable due; (iii) a detailed description of the reasons why the debtor has ceased payment of his obligations; (iv) a cash flow statement of the debtor's business and personal expenses; (v) the exact date on which the debtor ceased payment of his obligations; (vi) all the debtors' accounting and financial statements including books, invoices, and receipts.

B. Involuntary Request by Creditor

A creditor who holds a claim against the debtor may request the involuntary bankruptcy of a debtor if he can show that the debtor is past due on one or several accounts or that he has failed to pay his obligations to third persons. The situation varies if the creditor is a mortgage or lien holder. In this case, they must prove that the property which is the basis of the lien or mortgage is insufficient collateral to cover their debt before they are allowed to request bankruptcy of the debtor.

The other grounds which may justify the filing of a bankruptcy proceeding include: (i) if the debtor conceals his whereabouts; (ii) if the debtor, without cause, closes his business; (iii) if the debtor conveys his assets to some of his creditors; (iv) if the debtor engages in fraudulent activities; (v) pursuant to the discretion of a judge.

C. The Court's Ruling on the Bankruptcy Petition

If the bankruptcy petition complies with all the legal requirements referred to above, the court must declare the debtor bankrupt within twenty four (24) hours after filing. In addition to declaring the debtor bankrupt, the court also issues an order that is published in the Judicial Bulletin (Boletin Judicial) and which: (i) prohibits the payment and delivery of tangible property to the debtor; (ii) prohibits the National Registry from accepting documents for recordation which could result in a lien on the property of the debtor; (iii) provides notice to all banks, commercial institutions etc., not to deliver to the debtor any stocks, negotiable instruments or merchandise; (iv) provides notice to the post office that all mail addressed to the debtor be delivered to the bankruptcy trustee; (v) it notifies the Immigration Service not to issue a travel visa which would allow the debtor to leave the country; (vi) gives the criminal courts notice of the bankruptcy so that they may investigate the reasons for the bankruptcy and thus rule out fraud. The code requires that the court rule on a bankruptcy petition within twenty-four (24) hours under the assumption that the longer it takes to rule the more time the debtor may have to dissipate the assets of the estate and thus result in less distribution to potential creditors. The effect of the code is that it places the debtors' estate on hold until a trustee is appointed and the composition of the estate is determined.

4.2   THE BANKRUPTCY TRUSTEE

The trustee is the official representative and administrator of the bankrupt estate. The trustee's duties are established in articles 873-884 of the Commercial Code. To be eligible as a trustee, the individual must be an Attorney who is not a government official. The trustee must be of legal age and reside within the jurisdiction where the bankruptcy proceeding was filed.

The duties of the trustee are to ensure the efficient and prompt liquidation of the estate. The trustee is subject to removal if he neglects to properly carry out his tasks. The Costa Rican Commercial Code specifically outlines the duties of the trustee as follows:

(1) to receive all the accounting books and inventories any assets;

(2) to monitor all communications and orders issued by the court;

(3) to locate and take possession of property of the estate and collect any accounts receivable;

(4) to file a financial report, including a statement of receipts and disbursements;

(5) to convert the property of the estate into cash;

(6) to file a distribution plan which must be approved by the creditor's committee.

The trustee is under a fiduciary duty to the creditors and may not engage in any actions contrary to their interest.

4.3 THE CREDITOR

A. Creditor's Claims

Generally, for the creditor's claim or interest to be recognized in the bankruptcy proceeding, a proof of claim should be filed (*legalización de creditos*). Claims are paid in order of priority: first, secured claims (those that are secured by collateral) are paid, then, claims for wages and salaries and finally unsecured claims (those not secured by collateral).

B. Creditor's Committee

The creditor committee (*Junta de Acreedores*) is made up of all the creditors which have properly filed a proof of claim as of the required deadline for filing the proof of claim. These creditors are then given legal notice by publication in the Judicial Bulletin (*Boletin Judicial*) that a creditors' meeting will be held. The creditors' meeting is held in court chambers unless otherwise agreed and is presided over by a Bankruptcy Judge.

At this meeting, the creditors and the trustee among other things, classify the claims which have been filed against the estate, discuss and approve any measures which are necessary to accomplish the preservation and subsequent liquidation of the estate. This task is accomplished by majority vote of the creditors. Each creditor, who has an approved claim, has one vote and each resolution or plan presented to the creditor committee must be approved by a majority in order for it to take effect.

4.4 THE ADJUDICATION OF BANKRUPTCY

Once the creditor committee has approved a distribution plan, the trustee prepares a summary of its actions along with the proposed distribution plan which he presents to the court. The judge reviews the report and makes his final findings which in effect become the final judgment. It is important to note that at any time after the proof of claims as been filed but before the distribution of the estate is accomplished, the debtor may enter into an agreement with his creditors' and thus dismiss the bankruptcy proceeding. Once either of these procedures is completed and the court has determined that the bankruptcy was justifiable, the debtor is discharged. The effect of the discharge is to free the debtor from all debts that arose prior to the filing of the bankruptcy petition.

4.5 CULPABLE OR FRAUDULENT BANKRUPTCY

Article 863 of The Commercial Code makes it mandatory for a Civil Court to transfer a copy of the bankruptcy file to a criminal judge for investigation. The criminal judge is in charge of conducting the investigation to determine if the debtor has committed a criminal offense by engaging in culpable or fraudulent bankruptcy. The Penal Code defines these offenses as follows:

(1) Culpable bankruptcy may occur if there is an excessively disproportionate disparity between the expenses incurred by the debtor and his capital; or as a result of gross negligence on the part of the debtor in operating his business including gambling, speculation or abandonment. (2) Fraudulent bankruptcy is established if the debtor engages in conduct such as (i) creating fictitious debts and expenses, (ii) fraudulently conveying or concealing assets of the estate, (iii) benefits one creditor at the expense of others, (iv) destroying or falsifying financial documents and books. A debtor convicted of a fraudulent bankruptcy may not be discharged from bankruptcy until he serves his criminal sentence and repays all the creditors in full.

5. NEGOTIABLE INSTRUMENTS

In Costa Rica, the laws which govern negotiable instruments and commercial paper are also regulated within the Commercial Code. Since stocks and bonds are governed by additional laws their discussion will be undertaken in the subsequent section on securities' regulation. Here I will address three of the most common forms of commercial paper used in Costa Rica and those are: the promissory note (*pagaré*), the bill of exchange (*Letra de Cambio*) and the check (*cheque*).

5.1 THE PROMISSORY NOTE

The promissory note is a documentary instrument by which a person or entity that subscribes it promises unconditionally to pay another a determined sum of money within a determined time frame. Costa Rican law is very formal in establishing the requirements necessary to create a promissory note. The promissory note must contain the following:

(1) Words in the document to the effect that it is a promissory note;

(2) The promise pure and simple to pay an established amount of money;

(3) Set forth the expiration date of the promissory note;

(4) The name of the individual or entity to which payment must be made;

(5) The place and the date on which the promissory note is signed;

(6) The name and the signature of the person who has issued the promissory note along with the name and signature of any co-signers to the note.

At the time of drafting special attention must be paid to ensure that all the requirements established by law are contained within the document otherwise you may have difficulty at the time of enforcement based upon a defectively executed document. (See Appendix 7 for sample Promissory Note)

Costa Rican law allows the creditor of a promissory note to sue for collection pursuant to the summary executory process. In these cases, if the debtor defaults on the payment schedule set forth in the document, the law allows the filing of a lien against any and all property of the debtor for the amount of the promissory note plus an additional 50% to cover interest and legal expenses. Generally, the lien is ordered by the court and placed on the assets before the debtor is even served with the lawsuit, to prevent the dissipation of assets. If the debtor has no assets which can be attached then it may be difficult to collect upon the promissory note.

5.2 THE BILL OF EXCHANGE

The bill of exchange which is referred to as a *Letra de Cambio* is more commonly used in Costa Rica than the promissory note because it is more flexible as a negotiable instrument and thus easier to negotiate and transfer. The instrument is used to secure an obligation to pay a specified sum of money at an agreed upon interest on an agreed upon date or payable on "demand". The instrument is an unconditional promise to pay and this means that the parties cannot alter, modify or make the *Letra de Cambio* subject to other conditions or obligations. If the terms of payment are conditioned on other obligations or performance, it is diverting the intent of the *Letra de Cambio* and this could affect its enforceability. The person or entity that signs the document is responsible for repayment of the loan obligation. As is the case with the promissory note, failure to pay allows the holder of the instrument to file a lawsuit pursuant to summary executory procedure for its collection. However, special care must be taken to ensure that the document contains all the legally required variables or else enforcement may be barred. To be legally recognized as a *Letra de Cambio* de document must contain the following:

(1) The words *Letra de Cambio* within the text of the document;

(2) The mandate pure and simple to pay a specified sum of money;

(3) The name of the person that is agreeing to pay;

(4) The expiration date of the document;

(5) Set forth the place where payment must be made;

(6) The name of the person to whom payment must be made;

(7) Set forth the date and the place where the document is issued;

(8) The name of the person issuing the note; With very limited exceptions, if the *Letra de Cambio* omits any of the legal requirements set forth above it will not be enforceable as an executory instrument.

(See Appendix 8 for sample Bill of Exchange)

5.3 THE CHECK

The Commercial Code defines a check as an unconditional order of payment by which one person orders a bank, the payee, to pay a sum of money to a third party know as the beneficiary. If the beneficiary of the check is an individual, the law allows that person to endorse that check once to a third party; after that, no subsequent endorsements are allowed. If the beneficiary is a corporate entity, the law does not allow endorsement of that check to a third party. Instead, the corporate entity may only deposit the check into an account in the name of that corporate entity; or cash it at the issuing bank.

If you have been issued a "bad check" because of insufficient funds or the check was from a closed account there are two avenues to pursue the payee of the check, civil or criminal. If the case is filed in civil court then it proceeds under the summary process. Bear in mind that if the person that wrote you the check has no assets which you could collect upon or wages that could be levied upon then pursuing the civil remedies will likely be a waste of time. On the criminal side, the Penal Code stipulates that issuers of "bad checks" may face a fine or prison sentences which can range from 6 months to 3 years. The law requires that the defendant be notified of the criminal complaint and allows them five days from the date they are served to pay the amount of the check to the beneficiary of the check. If they pay, the criminal complaint is dismissed; if not, the case against the defendant proceeds.

In general, you will find that most businesses in Costa Rica will not accept checks as a form of payment because they are well aware that collecting on bad checks is a lengthy and tedious proposition so many prefer to avoid it altogether. With the increase in the numbers of credit card and debit card providers within the country, this is becoming the preferred method of payment.

6. THE FINANCIAL SYSTEM

The entity charged with keeping the pulse on the Costa Rican financial system is the Central Bank of Costa Rica (*Banco Central de Costa Rica*).

Pursuant to law, the Central Bank is charged with establishing monetary policy, issuing currency, establishing reserve requirements and regulating financial institutions within the country. The banking system in Costa Rica is divided between government owned banks and private banks. Only those banks that are authorized by the *Superintendencia General de Entidades Financieras (SUGEF)* may operate in Costa Rica. The SUGEF is responsible for auditing the Costa Rican financial institutions to ensure the stability and operation of the financial system. At the present time there are three government owned banks, thirteen private banks and ten finance companies. The banks authorized to operate in Costa Rica pursuant to the SUGEF are:

Government Owned Banks:

Banco de Costa Rica, Banco Nacional de Costa Rica, Banco Credito Agricola de Cartago Banco Popular y de Desarrollo Comunal.

Private Banks:
Banco BAC San Jose, S.A., Banco BCT, S.A., Banco Catahy de Costa Rica, S.A., Banco Internacional de Costa Rica, S.A., Banco Improsa, S.A., Banco Lafise, S.A., Banco Promerica, S.A., Citibank, (Costa Rica), S.A., Scotiabank de Costa Rica, S.A., HSBC Costa Rica, S.A.

Banks are required to have a financial reserve that must be deposited with the Central Bank of Costa Rica. There is no deposit insurance in Costa Rica. The government does have a blanket guarantee for deposits held in the three government owned banks. Private banks are not covered by the government guarantee.

Many of the private banks in Costa Rica also operate their own "offshore" banks generally located in the Caribbean. In most instances the activities of their offshore branch is unregulated by the Costa Rican bank regulatory agency. As such, if you purchase a Certificate of Deposit from the local Costa Rican branch office the deposit is governed by Costa Rican law. If the bank issues the Certificate of Deposit from its offshore branch then regulation of that deposit falls outside of the scope of the Costa Rican regulatory agency.

You can view detailed and up to date financial information on each of the financial institutions regulated by SUGEF at their web site www. sugef.fi.cr

7. SECURITIES REGULATION

The Costa Rican financial markets are made up of Public (government) and Private Sector instruments which are traded in the Costa Rican Stock Exchange (*Bolsa Nacional de Valores*). The issuance and sale of these securities is governed by the Securities Regulation Law of 1998 *(Ley Reguladora del Mercado de Valores)*. The law created the Securities Regulation Office (*Superintendencia General de Valores-SUGEVAL)* which is in charge of regulating the sales of securities as well as securities brokers and the protection of investors and dissemination of information relevant to the securities market. The web site for SUGEVAL is www.sugeval.fi.cr and contains the list of authorized brokerage houses and securities regulations. The Securities Regulation Office is in turn overseen by the National Financial System Supervisory Council (*Consejo Nacional de Supervisión del Sistema Financiero*) which is made up of five members from the private sector, the Minister of the Treasury and the President of the Central Bank.

7.1 THE STOCK EXCHANGE

In Costa Rica there is only one stock exchange and that is the *Bolsa Nacional de Valores (BNV)*. The stock exchange was officially established in September of 1976 as the "commercial exchange" and was originally regulated by provisions in the Costa Rica Commercial Code. It later evolved into its current structure which is a private corporation *(Bolsa Nacional de Valores, Sociedad Anonima)* run by a Board of Directors and managed by a General Manager. By law, the stock exchange must be owned by the brokerage houses. The objective of the stock exchange as set forth in its internal regulations adopted in 1999 is defined as creating, developing and strengthening the securities market in an efficient manner.

As of this edition, there were twenty-eight (28) brokerage houses authorized to operate in Costa Rica. A brokerage house is generally a private company that is authorized by the stock exchange to trade securities and financial instruments within the stock exchange on behalf of their clients or for their own account and provide investment advice and account administration services for their clients. Each brokerage house in turn employs individual stock brokers (agents) which must be licensed by the stock exchange and are the individuals responsible for carrying out the transactions on behalf of their brokerage houses.

There are more than two hundred licensed brokers who work for the various brokerage houses.

In order to establish a central depository and custodian of financial instruments which were being traded within the stock exchange, a central depository known as CEVAL *(Central de Valores)* was created in 1994. Among others, the function of CEVAL is to hold on deposit the financial instruments from the financial intermediaries and mutual funds; administer the financial instruments held on deposit by collecting amortization and interest and; execute the liquidation and payment of the financial instruments it holds; issue new or replacement certificates. The Stock Exchange is located in Santa Ana, a western suburb of the city of San José. Statistics on trading volume is available on their web site at www.bnv.co.cr

7.2 THE OFFER AND SALE OF SECURITIES.

The Securities Law considers any of the following to be a "security" *(valor)* and for which the securities regulations are applicable: (1) The shares issued by a corporation *(Sociedad Anonima)* as well as any instrument which gives the rights to subscription to shares. (2) The obligations or instrument provided that represents a loan or credit in favor of the issuer. (3) Those documents which by their legal nature or commercial practices are negotiable instruments such as promissory notes or bills of exchange. (4) The certificate of participation issued by a closed investment fund. A "public offering" *(oferta pública)* of a security is defined by the Securities Law as any offer whether express or implied which purports to issue, place, negotiate, or transact in securities by transmitting it to any member of the public or specified groups.

A public offering will be presumed if any of the following criteria are applicable: (1) The offering is made within the national territory (Costa Rica) by publicity in the communication media such as television, radio, press and the Internet. (2) The offering within the national territory (Costa Rica) of securities which have the same characteristics and similarity to other securities which are regulated and authorized by the Security Regulatory Agency (SUGEVAL). According to the regulations, it shall not be considered a public offering if (1) the offer is made by foreign (non-Costa Rican) issuers through the Internet so long as the issuer or intermediary has clearly established that the offer is not directed to the Costa Rican market and takes reasonable measures to prevent the purchase of those securities from Costa Rican citizens. (2) the offer is made by a national issuer (Costa Rican) pursuant to foreign law which is made through the Internet and which establishes passwords to their site in order to prevent persons residing in Costa Rica or Costa Rican citizens from accessing the site.

The offer of securities without authorization can result in injunctions and sanctions. The type of sanction will depend on the gravity of the infraction; the harm caused, the intentional nature of the act, the financial capacity of the offender, the duration of the un-authorized conduct and the recidivism of the infringer.

7.3 INVESTMENT FUNDS

The passage of the Costa Rican Securities Law (*Ley Reguladora de Mercado Valores No. 7732)* in 1998 allowed the formation of investment fund management companies to administer investor funds. In order to form an investment fund company the law requires that it be under the supervision of the Securities Regulatory Agency (Superintendencia General de Valores- SUGEVAL) and that it comply with the following requirements: (1) Be a corporate entity whose sole purpose is the administration of funds, (2) have a minimum capitalization of thirty million Colones, (3) that none of the directors, managers, officers of the proposed company have a criminal conviction and that they be of recognized moral and ethical standards and experienced in the field. (4) Any modifications in the control of the investment management company must be authorized by SUGEVAL. As of this edition the following were registered and authorized with SUGEVAL as investment fund management companies:

Aldesa, SFI, BAC San Jose, SFI, BCT, SFI, Banco de Costa Rica, SFI, Banco Nacional, SFI, Cathay, SFI , CPG, SFI , Fondos Cuscatlan, SFI (now owned by CITIBANK), Gen Net, SFI, HSBC, SFI, Interbolsa, SFI, Improsa, SFI, INS-Bancredito, SFI, Lafise, SFI, Multifondos de Costa Rica, SFI, Mutual, SFI, Sama, SFI, Scotia, SFI, Popular, SFI, Valores Serfin, SFI, Vista, SFI (Source SUGEVAL)

In order to offer an investment fund to the public in Costa Rica it must be approved by the Securities Regulatory Agency (SUGEVAL). The regulatory agency categorizes funds as either closed or open-end funds. In an open-end fund, the investor can buy and redeem units in the fund when they add or withdraw their money from the fund since the Fund has the obligation to purchase back the investment unit. A closed-end fund issues a set number or shares which are traded on the Costa Rican exchange. The price is determined by the investor demand for the fund and the fund does not have the obligation to purchase the investment from the investor.

The funds can further be categorized by the composition or mix of the instruments in which it invests. In Costa Rica the most common funds are those which invest in government (public) debt, private debt (stocks and bonds) a combination of the two or real estate investment funds. Furthermore funds are also categorized by the investment strategy of the fund management company for a particular fund. Those can be: (1) Short Term Funds *(Fondos de Corto Plazo)*, (2) Growth Funds *(Fondos de Crecimiento)*, (3) Income Funds *(Fondos de Ingreso)*, (4) Money Market Funds *(Fondos de Mercado de Dinero)*, (5) Stock Funds *(Fondos Accionarios)*, (6) Real Estate Investment Funds *(Fondos Inmobiliarios)*.

In the past the vast majority, 96% of the funds were invested in Costa Rican government debt. Many of them were invested in long term government bonds because of the higher rate of return. During the rush to real estate in mid 2000 many new funds aimed at real estate investments were created in the form of Real Estate Investment Trusts known locally as *Fondos Inmobiliarios*.

7.3 PENSION FUNDS

Under Costa Rican law 3% of the employee's wages are set aside to fund an Employee Capitalization Fund *(Fondo de Capitalización Laboral)*. Half of that is earmarked for the Mandatory Pension Plan. At the present time the following entities are authorized by the Costa Rican government as Pension Fund Managers

BAC San Jose Pensiones, Banco de Costa Rica, OPC, Banco Nacional Vital OPC, CCSS, OPC, INS Pensiones OPC, IBP Pensiones, OPC, Banco Popular OPC, Vida Plena OPC.

The employee can select which Pension Fund Manager it elects to manage its pension fund. If the employee does not make the selection then the manager by default is the government owned, Banco Popular.

8. CONSUMER PROTECTION

Costa Rica adopted its consumer protection law in 1995. The law, titled Law for the Promotion of Competition and Consumer Protection *(Ley de la Promocion de la Competencia y Defensa Efectiva del Consumidor No. 7472)* establishes certain fundamental rights to which a consumer is entitled. These rights range from a right to true and accurate information as to goods and services sold as well as a protection from deceptive advertising practices and abusive trade practices. The law imposes certain obligations on producers and merchants and prohibits any actions which are aimed at restricting the supply of goods and services.

Violations of the consumer protection law may be pursued by the consumer on an administrative or judicial level. If a complaint is filed at the judicial level, the case will proceed pursuant to the summary court procedures established in Article 432 of the Code of Civil Procedure. Prior to filing a lawsuit, parties are required to attend a conciliation conference with the judge in an effort to settle their dispute.

9. INVESTMENT SCHEMES

Costa Rica has always been a haven for dubious investment schemes and there is a popular saying among expats that if you want to become a millionaire in Costa Rica you better come with two million since you are likely to lose one.

Many developers did take advantage of the real estate boom of 2004-2007 and those that were able to get in early and out before the US real estate market crashed did very well for themselves. During this boom period in Costa Rica it was common to see real estate agents and developers tooling around in their "Hummers" all over the coastal areas of Costa Rica.

During this period there were also their share of real estate schemes some more egregious than others. Costa Rica became flooded with boiler rooms where high pressure sales pitches and mass internet e-mail campaigns were unleashed on consumers worldwide taking advantage of Costa Rica's popularity. In many cases the project infrastructure that was promised was never delivered and in others proper legal title to the lots sold was never provided.

While New York had "Bernie Madoff" who admitted to a $50 billion ponzi scheme Costa Rica had "Enrique", the most popular of the investment schemes in Costa Rica. The "Villalobos Brothers" as they were known had according to government sources over 6,000 investors and raised $404 million dollars. The "brothers" paid it's depositors between 3% to 3.5% interest per month on funds invested. By many accounts they had been in business for more than a decade and never missed a payment. Until it all came tumbling down and many expats living in Costa Rica lost their life savings in the scheme. There are all kinds of theories and speculations regarding their demise. A copy cat enterprise called "Savings Unlimited" also collapsed soon after when its founder fled the country with funds taken from more than 2,000 investors. Both are currently wanted by Interpol.

As the financial markets became less attractive and real estate more appealing the schemes changed from financial investments to real estate schemes of all sizes and colors. They promised huge rental returns, massive appreciations and so on and so on.

CHAPTER 5

EMPLOYER-EMPLOYEE RELATIONS - THE LABOR CODE

When employing others in Costa Rica you must abide by the labor regulations of Costa Rica to avoid problems with employees and with the Costa Rican Labor Department.

1. THE LABOR CODE

All employer-employee relations are governed by the Labor Code *(Codigo de Trabajo)*. When the Costa Rican Labor Code became law in 1943 Costa Rica was struggling with social unrest and this law was passed as an attempt to harmonize the employer-employee relationship and coordinate labor and capital in an equitable manner. In general terms the employer should be aware that Costa Rican labor regulations and court interpretations are weighed in favor of the employee.

1.1 THE WORK CONTRACT

The Labor Code presumes an employer-employee relationship exists if there is an exchange of services for money and the employer exerts direction and control over the work of the employee. The law recognizes both written and oral labor contracts. Depending on the type of business or employment that is involved you may want to document the employment relationship in writing to avoid misunderstandings in the future.

1.2 EMPLOYER REGULATIONS AND POLICY

The Labor Code requires that every employer draft and implement written employment policies and regulations that inform the employees of their rights and obligations. Generally, these regulations discuss working hours, work breaks, holidays and pay days. The Code requires an employer to incorporate into their employment policy manual all applicable rights and duties of the employee. Specifically, the Code requires that the written policy manual contain the following provisions: (i) Name of the employer; (ii) description of the type of work carried out by the employer; (iii) specify the location (s) where the employee must render services; (iv) working hours and wages; (v) work breaks; (vi) a description of the base salary by category of worker and incentive pay, if any; (vii) the day and place where wages are to be paid; (viii) guidelines on safety and hygiene; (ix) any special guidelines regarding women and minors; (x) names of management personnel including the management person who will be responsible for employee relations; (xi) a description of the disciplinary procedures to be followed.

1.3 WAGES, HOURS AND VACATIONS

A. Minimum Wage

The parties are free to negotiate the amount of wages paid so long as it does not fall below the established minimum wage. The right to a minimum wage is provided for in the Costa Rican Constitution. The minimum wage scale is established by the National Council on Wages and is revised every six months. Once the wage scale is approved it is sent to the Ministry of Labor and approved by way of Executive Decree. The wage scale that is published contains the established minimum wage for more than two hundred positions, including skilled, unskilled and professional personnel. The wages may be paid by the hour, day, biweekly or monthly as agreed upon between the parties. See Figure E below for a sample of the minimum wage scale for selected occupations. Keep in mind that these wages are adjusted every six months and you can obtain a copy of the wage scale known locally as Decreto de Salarios Minimo at most book stores in Costa Rica. If you are paying your employee above the minimum wage scale and the National Council on Wages publishes a legal wage increase you are not obligated to provide your employee with that wage increase. The employee is bound by the legal wage increase dispositions only as to those employees that are paid according to the minimum wage scale.

Figure E Minimum Wage for Selected Occupations

Occupation	Min. Wage	Period	$1 =546¢
Agricultural Laborers	¢ 6,024.00	day	$11.03
Construction Laborer	¢ 6,024.00	day	$11.03
Carpenter	¢ 6,559.00	day	$12.01
Gardener	¢ 6,559.00	day	$12.01
Machine Operator	¢ 6,559.00	day	$12.01
Domestic Maid	¢ 107,830.00	month	$197.49
Guard	¢ 193,677.00	month	$354.71
Vocational school graduate	¢ 219,498.00	month	$402.01
Receptionist	¢ 193,677.00	month	$354.71
Secretary	¢ 203,772.00	month	$373.20
Messenger	¢ 193,677.00	month	$354.71
Cashier	¢ 203,772.00	month	$373.20
General Office	¢ 193,677.00	month	$345.71
Medical Technician	¢ 235,220.00	month	$430.80
Bachelors Degree	¢ 331,376.00	month	$606.91
Licenciate Degree	¢ 397,665.00	month	$728.32

Source: Decreto de Salarios Mínimos, No. 34612 - MTSS

Bear in mind that the minimum wage scales are generally below the actual market salary. As such for certain job positions where it is difficult to recruit employees you will have to pay higher salaries. For example bilingual employees in call center operations can make anywhere between $650 to $1,500 dollars per month.

A. The Work Week

Pursuant to the Labor Code the normal ordinary work week is forty-eight (48) hours per week maximum. The work period for an ordinary day shift is from 5:00 A.M. to 7:00 P.M. An employee who works a regular day shift (jornada diurna) may not work more than ten (10) hours per day, eight (8) hours per day if the type of work is dangerous or hazardous. If the employees are at the executive and managerial level, the limitations are a maximum of twelve (12) hours of work per day.

The Labor Code makes further distinctions between day and night shifts. A night shift (*jornada nocturna*) position is work that is carried out between 7:00 P.M. and 5:00 A.M. The night shift by law may not exceed six (6) hours per day and thirty six (36) hours per week. The Labor Code also provides for a mixed work shift which can be seven (7) hours per day and forty-two (42) hours per week maximum. The mixed shift is made up of work carried out both during the day and extending into the night shift. For example a worker could begin work at 3:00 P.M. and leave at 11:00 P.M. It is important to establish with the employee what is the "ordinary" shift that will be worked since any hours which exceed these established maximums will be considered overtime and must be paid at time and a half. When this occurs the hours worked in excess of the legally established maximum are considered extra (jornada extraordinaria) and will be compensated accordingly. However, the ordinary and the extraordinary work periods together may not exceed twelve (12) hours per day.

B. Time Off and Vacations

(1) Legal Holidays: The Labor Code considers the following as paid legal holidays: January 1 (New Years Day), April 11 (Juan Santamaria day), Easter (Holy Thursday and Good Friday), May 1 (Labor day), July 25 Nicoya Annexation day), August 15 (Mothers day), September 15 (Independence day), and December 25 (Christmas). Unpaid legal holidays include August 2 and October 12. An employee which is required to work on a legal holiday must be paid double wages.

(2) Vacations: Workers are entitled to two weeks paid vacation for each fifty (50) weeks of continuous employment with the same employer. The vacation pay is calculated by taking the wages earned during the last week which is worked prior to the vacation. If the employee is terminated prior to accumulating fifty (50) week's worth of employment they are entitled to one (1) vacation day for each month of employment. The later amount is paid to the employer upon termination. Subject to specific exceptions, the Labor Code does not allow employees to accumulate vacation time Likewise, the two-week vacation period may not be broken up; the maximum allowed by the Code is to divide it into two parts. It is the employer who establishes the date on which the employee may take their vacation.

1.4 THE CHRISTMAS BONUS

By law, every worker who has worked for an employer for at least one year is entitled to an additional month's wages as a Christmas bonus. This payment is commonly referred to as the *Aguinaldo* and must be paid regardless of job performance. The bonus must be paid by the employer between December 1st and the 20th. If an employer terminates an employee prior to December, the Christmas bonus must be pro-rated and paid to the employee when he or she is terminated. To calculate the amount of the bonus, add the total wages paid to the employer from December 1 through November 30 and divide that amount by twelve (12).

For domestic servants the law requires that you add an additional 50% to the wages paid as in kind payments (food and housing) in calculating their Christmas bonus.

• *Quick Reference:* Example: If an employee earned 200,000 Colones during the first two months of their employment and then 300,000 Colones during the next ten months the calculation of the Christmas Bonus would be as follows:

Wages at 200,000 X 2 = 400,000
Wages at 300,000 X 10 = 3,000,000

Total Wages earned over 12 months is 3,400,000 divided by 12 months is equal to 283,333 Colones which would be the amount of the Christmas Bonus.

1.5 TERMINATION OF EMPLOYMENT

The major surprise for foreigners in Costa Rica is the difficulty involved in firing a worker. The Labor Code has strong protection of the worker's right to job security and employees cannot be fired without cause. As such, under certain circumstances, terminating the employment of an employee triggers legal obligations which require payment to the employee. This depends on whether the employment is terminated for cause or not as set forth in the Labor Code.

A. Termination for Cause

Article 81 of the Labor Code itemizes the grounds which justify an employer's reasons for terminating an employee. If an employee's dismissal is justified by cause as set forth in the Labor Code, the employer will only be liable for payment of wages and unused vacation time and will not incur further financial obligations to the employee. The dismissal must be well substantiated since the employer carries the burden of proving that the termination was for cause should the employee file a complaint against the employer with the Labor Court. Bear in mind that labor court's in Costa Rica will resolve disputed issues of fact in the light most favorable to the employee and it is upon the employer to defend against these presumptions.

B. Terminations without Cause

If the termination of an employee is not for cause as set forth above, the employer might be financially liable to the employee. In order to fully understand the way in which the financial obligations known as Prestaciones Laborales are due it is essential to define these obligations and explain how they are triggered.

(1) Pre-Termination Notice (Pre-Aviso)

Before an employer can fire an employee without cause they must provide the employee with the required notice that the employment will be terminated. This is referred to locally as the Pre-Aviso. It is extremely important to follow the legal requirements established in the Labor Code regarding pre termination notice since failure to do so will trigger additional obligations. The amount of notice required depends on the length of time which the employee has worked for that particular employer. If the employee has worked with the employer more than three (3) months but less than six (6) months he is entitled to one (1) week notice of termination; two weeks if between six (6) months and one (1) year and one month prior notice if they have been employed more than one (1) year. The notice should be delivered in writing unless the employment agreement was verbal then the notice can be given verbally in the presence of two witnesses.

The employee can continue to work during this notice period and will be entitled to one paid day off a week in order to look for new employment. On the other hand the employer may decide that he does not want the employee to remain on the job and in lieu of written notice, the employer may pay the employee a sum of money equivalent to the salary which would have been earned during the notice period.

If payment is made in lieu of notice then the amount to be paid is based upon the total average wage earned during the six months prior to the termination or fraction thereof if they have not worked for six months.

• *Quick Reference:* Pre Termination Notice

If your employee has worked for you:
More than 3 months but less than 6 months then notice =1 week
More than 6 months but less than 1 year then notice = 2 weeks
More than 1 year then notice = 1 month.

(2) Severance Pay *(Cesantia)*

If an employee is terminated without cause by the employer or if the employee quits for cause, they are entitled to severance pay. In Costa Rica the severance payment works as a built in unemployment compensation system since the burden falls on the employer to subsidize the employee while they search for other employment. The Labor Code provides that severance pay shall be based on the length of time which the employee has worked with the employer. The manner in which severance pay is calculated and distributed is set out in the Law for the Protection of the Worker *(Ley de Protección al Trabajador)* which provides as follows:

If the employee has worked with the employer for more than three (3) months but less than six (6) months then they are entitled to the equivalent of seven (7) days wages.

If the employee has worked from six (6) months to one (1) year they are entitled to fourteen (14) days of wages

If the employee has worked for more than one year then the following schedule applies for each year worked up to a maximum of eight years:

No. of Years Worked	Days of Severance
1	19.5
2	20
3	20.5
4	21
5	21.24
6	21.5
7	22
8	22
9	22
10	21.5
11	21
12	20.5
13	or more 20

• *Quick Reference:* Severance.

If your employee has worked for:

More than 3 months but less than 6 months then severance = 7 days wages
More than 6 months but less than 1 year then severance = 14 days wages
More than 1 year then severance = days listed in the table above.

The Law for the Protection of the Worker also requires the employer to pay 3% of the amount of the severance on a monthly basis to a compulsory employee pension fund which will be discussed in more detail in the following section.

The severance payment is based upon the average wages earned by the employee in the six months preceding the termination or fraction thereof if they have not worked for six months prior to the termination.

There is a cap on the number of years that are to be paid to an employee as severance and this has been set at eight (8) years. This means that if an employee has worked for fifteen years and fired without cause the severance payment is capped at eight years.

(3) Accumulated Vacation Pay *(Vacaciones)*

When an employee is terminated, any unused vacation time must be paid. As discussed above, an employee is entitled to two (2) weeks' vacation for every fifty (50) weeks of work. The vacation pay is determined by multiplying the employee's daily (gross) wage by the unused vacation days.

• *Quick Reference:* If the employee has worked less than 50 weeks prior to termination:

Payment = 1 week for each month worked.
If the employee has worked more than 50 weeks:
Sum of total wages earned by the employee for 50 weeks is added and then divided by 50 to obtain the Average Weekly Wage (AWW).

Vacation payment due = AWW multiplied by 2.

(4) Pro-rated Christmas Bonus *(Aguinaldo)*

To calculate the amount of the Christmas bonus add the total wages paid to the employer from December 1 through November 30 and divide that amount by 12.

C. A Sample Termination

In order to illustrate the manner in which the termination provisions of the Labor Code operate, we will create a fictional employee who works as an assembly line worker earning a gross wage of 400,000 Colones per month.

Juan has been employed by Industrias Tech, S.A. for three years and has not used any of his allotted vacation time for the present year.

Industrias Tech, S.A. needs to terminate Juan because of a decline in sales. Pursuant to the Labor Code, this is considered a termination without cause which triggers the severance payment. Since Juan has worked for Industrias Tech, S.A. more than a year he must be given a one month written notice (preaviso) that his employment will be terminated. In lieu of such notice, Industrias Tech, S.A. may pay Juan the preaviso by tendering 400,000 Colones which is the equivalent wage of one month. Since Juan has worked for more than a year and the termination is not for cause he is also entitled to severance pay (Cesantia) equal to twenty and one half (20.5) days wages for each year worked up to a maximum of eight years. Since Juan worked for three years the amount would be 273,333 Colones for each year worked. Since Juan did not use his allocated vacation time during the year he is entitled to payment for this unused portion. Since he is being terminated during his third year of employment he is entitled to two weeks' vacation payment.

Juan is also entitled to a pro-rated Christmas Bonus. Since he is being terminated in month two, the wages earned to date would be two months for a total of 800,000 Colones which are divided by 12 and this gives us the prorated Christmas bonus of 66,666 Colones. The final wage statement for Juan would look as follows:

Pre-termination notice (*Preaviso* 30 days): ¢400,000
Severance pay (*Cesantia* 20,5 days X 3 Years) ¢820,000
Unused Vacation (*Vacaciones* 15 days) ¢ 200,000
Pro-rated Christmas bonus (*Aguinaldo*) ¢66,000
Total: ¢ 1,486,000

1.6 DOMESTIC SERVANT EMPLOYEES

The Labor Code has a separate chapter which regulates the employment of domestic servants. The Code defines a domestic servant as an individual that labors in private residential homes. According to the Labor Code, the first thirty (30) days of service for a domestic employee constitute a trial period during which either party may terminate the employment agreement without prior notice and without being obligated to pay severance pay. The maximum work day for a domestic employee is twelve (12) hours and must include a one hour rest period. The guidelines discussed above regarding the termination of employees also apply to domestic employees. However, the Labor Code provides that the food and lodging provided to the domestic employee shall constitute "in kind" payments for purpose of calculating termination and the Christmas bonus. The "in kind" payment is set at 50% of the wages received by the domestic employee.

The employer must also be aware that when terminating a domestic servant without cause they are liable for the pre notice payment and severance payment as well which are calculated taking into account and additional fifty per-cent (50%) of the wage that was earned as "in kind" payment.

For example: If you hire a maid for the sum of ¢200,000 per month; the law will assume an additional 100,000 Colones as "in kind" payment. As such when you terminate the employee without cause the basis for the calculation must include the "in kind" payment.

1.7 PREGNANT EMPLOYEES

The Labor Code expressly protects employees that are pregnant and/or in the nursing phase. Article 94 of the Labor Code states that an employee that is pregnant or in the nursing phase may not be terminated without cause. To terminate these employees for cause requires authorization from the Ministry of Labor. To guarantee these benefits the employee that is pregnant must notify here employer as soon as possible and provide a medical certificate from the Costa Rican Social Security Administration (CCSS) verify the condition.
In these special cases the employer is liable to the pregnant employee for one (1) months wages prior to the birth of the child and for three (3) months wages while she is nursing the child.

2. THE EMPLOYEE CAPITALIZATION FUND

The Worker Protection Law (*Ley de Protección al Trabajador*) created the Employee Capitalization Fund (*Fondo de Capitalización Laboral)* which is funded by the employer and is equal to 3% of the gross wages of the employee. The capitalization fund is in turn divided into two parts. The first is the creation of a Mandatory Complimentary Pension Plan (*Regimen Obligatorio de Pensiones Complementarias)*. Prior to this law an employee that retired relied solely on the contributions made to the Costa Rican Social Security Administration (*Caja Costarricense de Seguro Social)* for their retirement. Although the social security retirement system remains in effect it is now complimented by the Mandatory Complimentary Pension Plan *(Regimen Obligatorio de Pensiones Complementarias)*. Of the 3% contributed to the capitalization fund 50% of it is destined for the Mandatory Complimentary Pension Plan. The remaining 50% is destined for an employee savings plan referred to locally as the *Ahorro Laboral*. The employee may withdraw the funds in the savings plan (1) if the employment relationship is terminated for any reason, (2) to the beneficiaries of the employee in case of death, (3) every five years during the employment relationship.

The funds allocated to the Employee Capitalization Fund are administered by private pension operators who must be authorized and regulated by the government. The agency responsible for oversight is the Pension Fund Regulation Agency *(Superintendencia de Pensiones-SUPEN)*.

3. LITIGATION OF EMPLOYMENT DISPUTES

In Costa Rica employees generally are very well informed about their rights provided for in the Labor Code. The Ministry of Labor has specialized offices which cater to employees that have questions or complaints about employment conditions and disputes. The office will assist employees in calculating their severance payments based upon the facts provided by the employee to the labor advisor. Based on that information the labor advisor prepares a written estimate of rights known locally as an *Estimación de Derechos* which is then given to the employee to deliver to the employer. *(See Appendix 9 for sample of Estimación de Derechos form)* This document is not legally binding upon the employer since it is an estimate which is based solely upon information provided by the employee to the Labor Department official who prepared it. However, it can be used as a negotiating tool to arrive at a settlement between the employee and employer.

If no agreement is reached in disputed issues between an employee and employer then a lawsuit may be filed before the Labor Court with jurisdiction over the parties. As part of the proceeding the Labor Court judge will schedule a conciliation meeting so that the parties can meet together with the Judge to reach a settlement of the dispute. However, the conciliation meeting is not mandatory but it can be a good option to resolving the dispute if there is willingness between the parties. If not, then the case proceeds and the Judge begins gathering evidence and subsequently sets the trial date. At trial, each of the parties presents their evidence and witnesses to the Judge who in turn will issue a written resolution setting forth the facts and legal conclusions which are the basis for the judgment. As indicated before, the labor courts will generally resolve all elements of proof in the light most favorable to the employee.

Depending on the labor court and the type of case involved the average time it takes for a labor case to get to trial in Costa Rica is two years.

4. INDEPENDENT CONTRACTORS

Simply labeling an agreement as an "Independent Contractor Agreement" is not enough to refute the presumption of the Labor Code that an employer-employee relationship exists. In addition, any doubts in this regard will be resolved in the light most favorable to the employee. In ruling on these issues the Court will generally look at the reality of the entire relationship between the parties regardless of what the contract stated.

The determining factor is the amount of direction and control that was exerted over the worker.

In recent years the growth of companies that offer temporary or seasonal workers has increased. This outsourcing must also be carefully planned and structured to avoid having those employees come back directly to you alleging rights under the provisions of the Labor Code which could make you liable for their claims.

Local businessmen always try and be creative to structure employee relationships in a way that it doesn't overburden their business. However, many of these structures don't hold up when challenged in court by a disgruntled employee. The Costa Rican labor system is very rigid and biased in favor of the employee.

5. LABOR UNIONS AND SOLIDARITY ASSOCIATIONS

5.1 LABOR UNIONS

The amount of labor unions that are active in the private sector in Costa Rica has decreased over the years. Labor unions were strong in the banana growing sectors of Costa Rica but as the participation of multinational corporations in that activity decreased so did the influence of the labor unions. This combined with new legislation that allowed for the creation of labor solidarity associations with the authorization to negotiate directly with employers on behalf of their association diminished the role that the labor unions played in the past. The Labor Unions do remain strong in the public sector and they have tremendous influence on political decisions affecting government run enterprises such as the telephone, electric and the insurance business which is a government monopoly.

5.2 SOLIDARITY ASSOCIATIONS

Labor solidarity movements are employee labor associations which are set up to benefit the employees and to act as a balance between the employer and employee relationship. The right of employees to form a solidarity association is set forth in the Law of Solidarity Associations *(Ley de Asociaciones Solidaristas)* which was passed in 1984. Although the law did not come into effect until 1984, the solidarity movement began in Costa Rica in 1947. The labor association is formed by the workers of a particular company. For example, if company Y had fifty employees they could all get together and form the employee association of company Y. The law requires that in order to form an association there must be at least twelve (12) workers. The association also acts as a credit union providing its members with savings plans and loans. There are currently more than 2,100 solidarity associations in Costa Rica. In turn, all the labor associations are members of the Costa Rican Solidarity Movement Association *(Movimiento Solidarista Costarricense)* which provides training, seminars and information on the solidarity movement in general. Their web site which contains the list of all labor associations in Costa Rica is www.solidarismo.com.

6. INJURIES ON THE JOB / WORKERS COMPENSATION

The Labor Code establishes guidelines to provide for worker's occupational health and safety. Legislation covering worker's compensation was expanded in 1982 and incorporated into the Labor Code.

6.1 WORKERS COMPENSATION INSURANCE

Every employer must carry workers' compensation insurance to insure their workers against work related accidents. The workers' compensation policy is sold and underwritten by the National Insurance Institute *(Instituto Nacional de Seguros)* (See Appendix 10 for a worker's compensation policy application form.) The employer may also be responsible for independent contractors if they are under his ultimate direction and control. If a worker is injured and the employer did not procure insurance as required, the employer will be personally liable for all expenses incurred by the worker as a result of the injury. Municipal inspectors and inspectors from the Ministry of Labor and from the National Insurance Institute are responsible for ensuring that all employers carry worker's compensation insurance. Any business that is in violation of these provisions may be shut down.

The cost of the policy is determined by the National Insurance Institute after reviewing the application and assessing the risk involved in the business or occupation of the employer. The range is generally 2 to 3% of the amount of the payroll reported on the application form.

6.2 WORKER'S COMPENSATION FOR DOMESTIC EMPLOYEES

The National Insurance Institute (INS) has a worker's compensation policy that is designed for homeowners or renters that employ domestic help such as a maid and a gardener. The policy will not cover a guard or chauffeur. This policy is known as *Riesgos de Trabajo Domestico* and is available if you have a maximum of two full time domestic employees. If more employees are hired then the INS will require that you obtain the regular worker's compensation policy. The idea behind this policy was to facilitate the procedures whereby employers could insure domestic employees without the hassle involved in applying for and maintaining the regular worker's compensation policy.

6.3 WORKER'S COMPENSATION CLAIM PROCESS

A work accident occurs when the worker, in the course and scope of his employment, incurs an injury that results in a temporary or permanent incapacity to work or death. A worker is considered to be under a temporary disability if his injury impedes his ability to work but is only of a temporary nature. This status ends when a doctor determines that the worker is at maximum medical improvement and is returned to work full duty or at the end of two years.

The Code subdivides the permanent disability as follows; (1) Permanent minor disability occurs when the worker's impairment to the body as a whole is from 0.5% to 50%; (2) Permanent partial disability from 50% to 67%; and (3) Permanent total disability if the impairment is greater than 67%. The percentage of impairment is determined from the impairment guidelines in Article 224 of the Labor Code as interpreted by a medical disability panel which is made up of five members. Panel members represent the Ministry of Labor, Social Security Administration, Ministry of Health, the Medical Association, National Insurance Institute, and a labor representative.

Once an injury occurs on the job, the employer is responsible for filing a Notice of Injury form with the National Insurance Institute (Instituto Nacional de Seguros) within eight (8) days of the date of injury. The injured worker has a right to claim a benefit for all medical services and rehabilitation incurred as a result of the injury. In addition, the worker is entitled to claim wage loss for the period of time which he is out of work as a result of the injury. Depending on the nature of the disability, the wage loss which the worker may claim can range from 60% to 100% of his wages and may continue for two years for temporary disability and up to ten (10) years for permanent total disability.

7. THE SOCIAL SECURITY SYSTEM

Costa Rica has a compulsory social security system which provides each and every citizen with medical care, disability payments, and retirement benefits. The system is administered by the Social Security Administration *(Caja Costarricense de Seguro Social CCSS)*. The system operates by way of compulsory contributions from employers, employees and the government all of which are pooled together. Employers are required to fill out a monthly payroll report with the Social Security Administration and this report is used as the basis for calculating the social security contributions. (See Appendix 11 for sample payroll reporting form.)

In Costa Rica, the law stipulates that all workers must be reported and covered by the Social Security Administration. It has been customary practice in Costa Rica to report employees for social security purposes at a lower salary then is actually being paid to the employee as wages. This way the employee obtains the medical coverage that is needed but less is taken out of their pay check. On the other hand, the employer has to contribute less towards the social security account of the employee. In other cases, the employer does not even report the employee on social security and instead lets the employee obtain their own social security account as an independent worker. The problem with both of these scenarios arises when the employment relationship terminates and a disgruntled employee reports the employer to the social security administration for not having included them in the social security contribution or for under reporting their wages. This could in turn result in a claim by the Social Security Administration against the employer for back payment of social security contributions which could also include fines and penalties as well.

7.1 MEDICAL BENEFITS

The medical benefits coverage provided by the Social Security Administration (CCSS) includes coverage for: medical assistance and surgery, hospitalization, prescriptions, dental care, maternity-related expenses, and burial expenses. Coverage is financed by mandatory contributions based upon the gross wage of the employee. The employer contributes 9.25% and the employee 5.5%. Those that are self-employed must contribute 13.25%.

7.2 DISABILITY AND DEATH BENEFITS

The disability and death benefits coverage provides the worker with protection in the event of a disability which would render the employee incapable of working. The death benefits portion provides survivors benefits to the worker's family. As is the case with the medical benefits coverage these benefits are financed by the employer contributions of 4.75% and employee contributions of 2.5%

7.3 RETIREMENT BENEFITS

An employee in Costa Rica may apply for retirement benefits at the age of sixty-five if that person has contributed at least 240 monthly quotas to the Social Security Administration. The amount of the pension is established by taking the highest 48 salaries earned in the five years preceding the date of retirement up to the maximum which is periodically reviewed by the Board of Directors of the Social Security Administration. As a compliment to this retirement pension the Mandatory Complimentary Pension Fund created by the Law for the Protection of the Worker which was discussed in section two above also provides the worker an additional source of retirement income.

7.4 GOVERNMENT CONTRIBUTION

In addition to employer/employee contributions indicated above, the medical, disability, retirement, death, and survivors benefits discussed are also funded by the government. The Social Security law specifically legislates several items which are to be earmarked for funding Social Security, those include: (1) value added tax on the importation of all liquor, wines, perfumes, beer, soft drinks, mineral waters, (2) a 15% tax on all products produced and sold by the National Distillery; (3) 15% consumption tax on locally manufactured beer; (4) 2% of any and all payments made by the three branches of government and the Municipalities (subject to exemptions.)

The following table summarizes all of the compulsory contributions required under Costa Rican law:

Deduction	Employee	Employer
Funds Administered by Social Security		
Health and Maternity	9.25%	5.5%
Disability/Retirement/Death	4.75%	2.5%
Subtotal 1	14 %	8%
Funds Earmarked for Other Institution		
Popular Bank Compulsory Savings	0.50%	1%
Vocational School Funding (INA)	1.5%	0%
Family Social Assistance	5.0%	0%
Social Assistance (IMAS)	0.50%	0%
Capitalization Fund	1.0%	0%
Mandatory Complimentary Pension	0.50%	0%
Employee Savings Fund	3.0%	0%
Total	**26%**	**9%**

CHAPTER 6

REAL ESTATE TRANSACTIONS AND FINANCING

Purchasing property in Costa Rica requires the buyer to do ample research and get competent legal advice to ensure that you will not have
any problems down the line. This Chapter is designed to introduce the
reader to all the legal principles which are related to the purchase and
ownership of real estate in Costa Rica.

1. PROPERTY RIGHTS

Costa Rican law recognizes the absolute right to ownership of real
property. By real property we mean land, and generally whatever is
erected or growing upon or affixed to land. This means that the owner
of the property has the exclusive right of possessing, enjoying and dis-
posing of their property as they see fit, unless prohibited by law.

1.1 THE PROPERTY RECORDING SYSTEM

The Costa Rican government operates a national property recording
system which assists the public in determining ownership of title to
land and any liens, annotations or mortgages which may be recorded
against the property. The recording system is centralized in the National Registry *(Registro Nacional)* which is under the supervision of
the Ministry of Justice. The Property Section *(Registro de la Propiedad)* of the registry acts as a depository of documents which have been
executed and filed in the system.

The Civil Code specifically requires that all documents related to title
to real property and or which pertain to interests in property be recorded in the property section of the National Registry. The documents filed in the property registrar must as a minimum set forth: (i) a
legal description of the property; (ii) the type, value, and conditions of
the instrument which is being recorded; (iii) a description of the right
on which the recorded instrument is based; and (iv) the full name of
the grantor and grantee of the recorded instrument.

The Costa Rican recording system operates on the doctrine of "first in time, first in right" or what is known as a "race" filing system. Under this system the first one to file an interest against the property has established a priority right. For example, assume a property owner gives a mortgage to X but X fails to record it in the National Registry. Subsequently property owner sells the property to Y who has not notice of the mortgage. Under this scenario Y would take title to the property free from the mortgage because it was not recorded and as such could not have had any notice of it.

The Property Section of the National Registry is fully computerized and indexed. The property records database can be searched by property owner name index or by a title registration number assigned to each and every property known as the Folio Real. The Folio Real number is generally a six digit number followed by a dash and three additional digits which designate the ownership interest. For example a property located in the Province of San José with title number 240918-000 means that the first six numbers are the title registration number for the property and the –000 means there is only one undivided interest to the property. If the property is held jointly by husband and wife then the extension would read –001 and –002 to reflect two interests in one title. Properties which are part of a condominium development will have the letter "F" after the title number which stands for filial to reflect that it is recorded as part of a condominium development. For example, a condominium development with the name of Valle Azul Condominium may have ten titled parcels within the development and each of them would have their own title number which may look as follows 098141-F-000. The National Registry can issue certificates of title or provide a registry report on a particular property. The registry report provides detailed information on a particular property including the name of the title holder, the boundary lines of the property, liens, annotations and other recorded documents which affect title. (See Appendix 12 for sample property title report known as Informe Registral)

2.   TYPES OF PROPERTIES

As the demand for Costa Rican real estate grew over the past few years so did the different type of property offerings to cater to that demand. As such you can find in Costa Rica a vast amount of different types and styles of properties.

2.1 CONDOMINIUM PROPERTY *(Propiedad en Condominio)*

A condominium type property in Costa Rica may be built around a certain theme. You can have a colonial style single family home condominium or you can have a high rise building and anything in between. The common theme behind the condominium is that it generally has a private gated entrance and common areas which are shared by the owners of the property within the condominium. All condominium property will have a condominium regulation and a home owner's association to govern the affairs of the condominium.

2.2 URBANIZATIONS *(Urbanizaciones)*

Urbanizations are the opposite of the condominium property since they are generally comprised of individually titled parcels of property accessed via public roads as opposed to the private internal roads established in a condominium. In urbanizations there are generally no home owners association and no common areas. If you purchase land in urbanization you can build whatever the local zoning law allows such as apartments, townhomes or a single family home.

2.3 ESTATE LOTS *(Parcelas)*

Estate lots exist in Costa Rica due to an anomaly in the Costa Rican Agrarian Law designed to protect the small farmers when Costa Rica was mostly and agriculturally based country. An estate lot is a lot that has more than 5,000 m2 (53,819.55 Sq.Ft. / 1.23 acres) because that is the minimum allowed by the agrarian law in order to subdivide a property. Developers have used this form of property title because it is faster to subdivide a property and title the individual estate lots than it is to do so as a Condominium or Urbanization type development. Since it is not a condominium you cannot legally place the type of restrictions or limitations that you could on a property registered as a Condominium. Some Municipal governments impose construction limitations on estate lots restricting construction to a certain percentage of the lot size.

2.4 RAW LAND *(Lotes or Fincas)*

Depending on its size raw land will either be referred to as a lote or a finca and is generally un-improved land which may or may not have utilities or services located upon it depending on the location. You can find raw land available in many areas of Costa Rica with prices varying in great degree by their location.

3. PURCHASING PROPERTY

Regardless of the type of property that you wish to purchase in Costa Rica you will have to interact with the Costa Rican real estate transfer process.

3.1 FINDING THE PROPERTY

A. Real Estate Agents

In many cases your first contact when you decide to buy property in Costa Rica will likely be through a real estate agent. In many developed countries the real estate agent is a licensed and bonded professional who can be held legally and financially liable for misrepresentations or negligence.

In Costa Rica there are no laws that regulate real estate agents. As such many foreigners have set up real estate offices in Costa Rica because of the lack of licensing requirements to adhere to. Many don't even have Costa Rican legal residency status which would authorize them to work in Costa Rica and they simply do so illegally. There are however, many well qualified and reputable real estate agents in Costa Rica and you need to ask for references and ask other expats for recommendations to make sure you are dealing with somebody that is well qualified.

The Costa Rican Chamber of Realtors [CCBR] is a voluntary association of realtors and they require future members to take real estate courses before they will allow them to join the association. The CCBR has been around since 1974 and has tried for many years to have a real estate licensing law passed in the legislature but their efforts have not been effective.

As a purchaser of real estate you should also keep in mind that the legal duty of the realtor is with the Seller who is paying their commission unless you as the Buyer have retained the realtor as a Buyer's agent. The realtors in Costa Rica generally charge commissions which range from 5% to 10% of the sales price of the property. You will find that in the coastal and rural areas many of the realtors will request a 10% commission. You will also learn that in Costa Rica there is no Multiple Listing Service (MLS) that shares property listings among all realtors. As such, some realtors may have listings that others don't and vice versa.

Many sellers are reluctant to sign exclusive listing agreements with one broker when they can have several brokers offering the property for sale. As a result you may have several agents showing the Buyer the same property.

As the Buyer you should check all facts related to the property you intend to purchase through your own legal representative and not rely solely on what an agent or real estate developer tells you. Most reputable real estate agents are happy to cooperate with your Attorney to verify all property and title information.

3.2 TITLE TO THE PROPERTY

A. The Title Search

Once a buyer has identified a particular piece of property they are interested in purchasing, the buyer through their Attorney should conduct an initial property title search in the National Registry. To initiate the search, the buyer should request that the seller provide them with the full name of the registered owner and the property title number *(folio real)*. The title search will reveal the legally registered owner of the property as well as alert you as to any liens or encumbrances that may affect title to the property.

A preliminary title search can be conducted online at the website of the National Registry which is www.registronacional.go.cr. It is also possible to obtain at the National Registry a certified certificate of title *(Certificado de Propiedad)* which will certify the legal condition of the property on the date the certificate is issued.

Costa Rica follows the doctrine of first in time, first in right. This means that recorded instruments are given priority according to the date and time in which they are recorded. Since the certificate of title issued by the National Registry is prima facie evidence of the condition of title on the date issued, any instrument not recorded at the time the certificate is issued may be deemed invalid. Obviously, every situation and property differs and in some cases a review of the National Registry records alone may not be sufficient to uncover liabilities or encumbrances. That is why it is highly recommended that you retain the services of a Costa Rican Attorney to conduct the title review for the property.

B. The Survey Map *(Plano Catastrado)*

The seller should also provide the buyer with a copy of the legally registered survey map for the property. This survey map is known locally as the Plano Catastrado. All official survey maps must bear the stamp of the Catastro Nacional and include their registration number which in turn means that it has complied with the applicable standards of format and accuracy as certified by the surveyor that prepared it. The National Registry will not allow the transfer of a property unless a reference to a recorded survey map is indicated within the deed and its existence sworn to by the Notary Public that is preparing the deed. The survey map will provide the buyer with the necessary tool to inspect the boundaries of the property that is to be purchased. Depending on the property, it may be wise to retain your own surveyor to walk the property with you and review the survey map that you have been provided. *(See Appendix 13 for Property Survey Map known as Plano Catastrado).*

In certain areas of the country I would recommend a re-survey of the property that you will purchase done by a surveyor that is hired by you as the Buyer. It is not uncommon to have survey maps that contain errors and or outright misrepresentations. After all, the survey maps are done by local topographers and the quality and integrity of the professional doing the work varies. In a bustling coastal town we have run across survey maps that "disappear" areas set out as public access roads in a residential development. The property owner that purchases based upon those survey maps could have trouble in the future if they build on the areas which are designated as public areas since the right of the government to enforce a public access does not have a statute of limitations. In other areas we have seen survey maps that are outright falsifications. As such, it is always best to have your Attorney and surveyor verify the authenticity of the survey map that is the basis of the property purchase.

If you are purchasing a parcel of land which is being segregated from a larger tract of land, then it will also be necessary for the Municipal authority where the land is located to approve the segregation of the parcel. This approval is generally stamped on the Survey Map (plano catastrado) and is known as a visado municipal. In the case of segregation it is a pre-requisite for registration to have the municipal approval. Without it the National Registry may refuse to record the transfer of the property into the name of the buyer.

Do not pay the full purchase price on any property based upon a promise by the Seller that the Municipal approval will be forthcoming. In those cases put the funds in escrow and make the sale contingent on the Municipal approval.

3.3 THE PROPERTY CLOSING PROCESS

A. The Property Purchase Agreement

Once the buyer is satisfied with the initial title search on the property the buyer or their real estate agent will provide the seller with a purchase offer that will set forth the terms of the offer to the seller. If the purchase offer is accepted then a formal Property Purchase Agreement known locally as either an Opcion de Compra or a Promesa Reciproca de Compra-Venta can be drafted and signed by the parties to the transaction. In this type of agreement, the seller agrees to sell and the buyer agrees to buy at a specified price and within a stipulated time frame. The buyer tenders an agreed upon deposit to either the seller or to an independent party approved by both buyer and seller who can serve as the escrow agent of the deposit pursuant to the terms of the contract

Due to the proliferation of foreign real estate agents in Costa Rica many have brought with them boiler plate purchase agreement forms used in their country of origin. As a Buyer you need to be extremely cautious about relying on forms that have not been vetted by a Costa Rican Attorney since their enforcement in a Costa Rican court of law may be compromised if it was not drafted taking into account Costa Rican law.

I once had a real estate agent object to my Purchase Agreement because it was longer than the one page boiler plate form he was using which made it "easier to make the sale". The boiler plate form left so many issues up for interpretation that in the event of a dispute resulting in litigation it would become a nightmare. As such, in drafting the purchase agreement it should be as thorough as possible and take into account any possible conflicts or problems that may arise. After all this is the document that governs the relationship between the Buyer and the Seller all the way to the property closing.   (See Appendix 14 for Sample Reciprocal Promise to Buy and Sell)

B. Property Due Diligence and Pre-Closing Checklist.

When researching a property that you want to purchase and prior to closing on the property you need to ensure that the following items are addressed to your satisfaction:

1. Utilities. Make sure the Seller is current with the payment of the basic utilities which are: Electric, Water, & Telephone,

2. Property Taxes. Make sure the Seller has paid the property taxes and ask them to produce a certificate of payment issued by the Municipal government where the property is located.

3. Condominium Sales. If you purchase in a Condominium then request from the Seller (i) a copy of the regulations for the condominium *(CCR's known locally as Regalmento del Condominio)*. (ii) Request a letter from the Condo Association indicating that the condo unit that is being sold is current with all fees and assessments. (iii) I also like to request a copy of the Condominium Balance Sheet. After all when you purchase a condo you are inheriting its financial condition as well.

4. Review the property inventory. If the property you are purchasing includes a home and an inventory list of items it is very important for insure that the items described in the inventory list are as warranted before closing.   You would be surprised how many misunderstanding arise at closing because of a poorly drafted and detailed inventory list.

5. Understand the Property Survey Map *(Plano Catastrado)* . Be sure that you have walked the boundaries of the property you are purchasing with your official property survey map *(plano catastra-*

do) in hand. If you have doubts about the proper location of the boundaries or the measurement of the property then hire your own surveyor to conduct an overview of the officially registered survey plan. This process is known locally as a replanteo.

6. Check Zoning. If you are purchasing undeveloped land it is very important to obtain a Zoning Use *(Uso de Suelo)* from the local Municipal Government where the property is located. This will ensure that you are able to use the property for what you want to use it for. Some properties have restrictions and construction coverage limitations and you need to be aware of this before you purchase.

7. Occupants or Tenants. Make sure there are no occupants or tenants in the property before you purchase. If there are, you must ensure that a mechanism is in place to guarantee to you that they will be out of the property before you pay the full purchase price. In Costa Rica tenants have rights that might make it difficult to remove them.

8. Verify that Development or Building Permits are in Order. If you are purchasing new construction ask for copies of the construction permit and development plans to ensure the project development is in compliance with local laws. This information is provided by the local Municipal government where the property is located.

C. Earnest Money Deposits.

As in most real estate transactions worldwide it is customary in Costa Rica to tender a deposit. In Costa Rica a deposit is known locally in several different names such as *deposito de garantia, arras confirmatorias or reserva.* The amount of the deposit is whatever is negotiated between the buyer and the seller. The seller will generally try and get as large of a deposit that they can get away with. The more customary deposits are in the 5% to 10% range. The deposit is refundable depending on the contingency or conditions indicated in the Purchase Agreement but generally non-refundable for failure to complete the transaction within the time period specified in the Purchase Agreement. Be sure you fully understand the conditions of your earnest money deposit.

In real estate transactions that we handle we prefer to designate our separate escrow company as the escrow agent for the earnest money deposit. Some Sellers will accept this while others will insist on holding the earnest money deposit themselves or with their Attorney. You will have to treat this on a case by case basis. Regardless, the conditions of escrow and disbursement of the earnest money deposit to either the Seller or the Buyer needs to be fully addressed and understood by all parties to the transaction. On many occasions we find contracts that are vague regarding the disbursement of the earnest money deposit and vague as to what constitutes a breach of the closing terms and conditions of the agreement

D. How is Title to the Property Transferred ?

In Costa Rica, property is transferred from seller to buyer by executing a property transfer deed known as an Escritura de Traspaso, before a Notary Public. *(See Appendix 15 for an example of a property transfer deed.)*

Unlike common law countries such as the United States and Canada, where the role of the Notary is limited to authenticating signatures, in Costa Rica the Notary Public *(Notario)* have extensive powers to act on behalf of the State. The Notary Public, who must also be an Attorney, may draft and interpret legal documents as well as authenticate and certify the authenticity of documents.

In selecting the Notary to draft and record the property transfer deed the local custom is that the buyer may select their Notary/Attorney to draft the transfer deed if the buyer he is paying all cash for the property. On the other hand, if the purchase price is financed there are generally three alternatives to selecting the Notary/Attorney: (1) If a large percentage of the purchase price is being financed by the seller or a banking institution and a mortgage needs to be drafted to guarantee payment then the seller or banking institution may require that their Notary/Attorney draft the transfer deed. (2) If a property is purchased 50% cash and 50% financed it is common that both Attorneys for the buyer and seller jointly draft the transfer deed and mortgage in one single document, known as co-notariado. (3) Or, the buyer may insist that his Notary/Attorney draft the transfer deed and let the sellers Notary/Attorney draft a separate mortgage instrument. In this case, since the mortgage is being drafted separately it carries a higher registration fee.

Whichever way you proceed it is important to establish early on in the process who will handling the transaction and the fees involved so that information can be incorporated into the Purchase Agreement. After all you don't want to show up at the closing table and be surprised.

With the large increase of real estate development projects in Costa Rica many developers eager to have the sale done as quickly as possible and using high pressure sales tactics use their own contracts and may even claim that legal advice is not necessary. If you proceed in any transaction in Costa Rica without your own independent legal advice and have problems down the line your recourse may be very limited and when available is an extremely lengthy process.

E. Forms of Property Ownership

At the buyer's option, the property can be purchased individually, jointly with other persons or in the name of a corporation. In Costa Rica it has become common to use Corporations for several reasons. First, if properly structured, transferring ownership to the corporation can protect the property from the personal liabilities which may be incurred by you as an individual. Costa Rican courts in general tend to respect the corporate entity, as separate from the individual and with limited exceptions will not pierce through the corporation to get at the individual. Second, as an inheritance tool. If properly structured the corporation can pass to your heirs thus avoiding probate of the underlying real estate asset.

Another reason corporations are common in real estate transactions is because real estate developers began titling properties in their subdivisions or condominium development in the name of Costa Rican corporations. The developer would then turn around and sell to the property buyer the corporation which already owned the asset instead of transferring the real estate. Why ? because the transfer of the corporate stock did not trigger the 1.5% real estate transfer tax and other property related closing costs. The Costa Rican Department of Revenue has been taking a closer look at this practice by reviewing some real estate developments and their property transfer methods. As in any real estate transaction in Costa Rica you are best to consult with your own Attorney to ensure that you clearly understand the transactions that you are entering into.

Another viable alternative available to married couples is to declare your property to be homestead. The Costa Rican Family Code allows married couples to homestead their property at the time of purchase if the home will be the family dwelling. A property so designated *(Afectación Familiar)* cannot be mortgaged or encumbered by one of the spouses since it requires consent by both spouses. Likewise, the designation shields the property from the creditors of either spouse. Only the joint debts of the spouses can be filed against the property.

The decision as to ownership should be based upon your particular situation and after consultation with your Attorney.

F. Closing Costs

Unless agreed otherwise, it is customary for the buyer and seller to share equally in the closing costs. The typical real estate closing will involve the following costs:

(1) Real Estate Transfer Tax. - The government collects a property transfer tax (Impuesto de Traspaso) which is equal to 1.5% of the registered value of the property. The National Registry will not record a transfer deed unless the transfer taxes and documentary stamps have been paid.

(2) Documentary Stamps -The government also requires that documentary stamps be affixed to the deed. These stamps amount to approximately 1.1% of the registered value of the property as follows: Legal Bar Association Stamp ¢25.00 for every ¢100,000.00 *(Timbre del Colegio de Abogados)*; Municipal Stamp: ¢2.00 for every ¢1,000.00 *(Timbre Municipal); * Fiscal Stamp: ¢2.00 for every ¢1,000.00 *(Timbre Hospitalario)*; Agricultural Stamp ¢1.00 for every ¢1,000.00 *(Timbre Agrario); * National Archives Stamp ¢20.00 *(Timbre del Archivo Nacional)* The National Registry also imposes its own tax of .05% on documents presented for recordation to the National Registry. *(Derechos de Registro)*

(3) Notary Fees - The Notary that drafts and records the contract for sale and carries out the closing is entitled by law to a Notary Transaction Fee. The Notary Fee is established by law and compliance with the minimum fee schedule is mandatory for all Costa Rican Attorney's / Notaries. For real estate transactions the current minimum fee schedule is:

First 10 Million Colones 2%
Excess of 10 to 15 Million Colones 1.5%
Excess of 15-30 Million Colones 1.3%
Excess of 30 Million Colones 1.0%

Bear in mind that this fee is for drafting and filing the property transfer deed. Any additional services including the drafting of purchase agreements, escrow and the like may carry additional fees

G. The Two Tiered Property Value System

At this point in time it is appropriate to clarify the difference between the registered value of a property and the actual sales price paid for the property. For many years it has been entrenched in the local culture to have two purchase prices for a property. The actual sales price which is the real price paid for the property and the other which is a lower price that is declared by the parties in the property transfer deed (escritura). By doing so the parties are basing all transfer taxes, registry fees and documentary stamps upon the lower registered value of the property as opposed to the actual sales price. Doing so is a form of tax evasion and the Costa Rican tax authorities are aware of this practice but up to date have had little resources to pursue all offenders. Instead they have been focusing on larger real estate developments that are selling multiple units.

If you decide to engage in this practice you certainly do so at your own risk. In the past couple of years the local Municipal governments have been carrying out property appraisals and some Municipal governments are very efficient at updating their property records and valuations.

H. The Registration of the Transfer Deed

Now that you have finalized the closing, exchanged the money and taken possession of the property that is everything you have to do, right? Unfortunately, that's not the case. The original transfer deed *(Escritura)* must be filed in the National Registry. It is the obligation of the Notary that drafted the transfer deed to ensure that the deed is presented *(Anotado)* and subsequently registered *(Inscrito)* in the Property Section of the National Registry. I have underlined the words presented and registered to highlight the importance of following up with the

Notary to ensure registration. To file the deed, the Notary that drafted the document must print out the deed on their special bar coded legal paper and attach their security tag *(Boleta de Seguridad)* to the document. The National Registry issues these security tags to each Notary in Costa Rica as a security measure to control the admission of documents within the National Registry. Documents without the Notary security tag will not be admitted for registration in the National Registry. Although filing the document guarantees your priority (i.e. first in time first in right) it does not automatically guarantee registration. If the document complies with the formal requirements of submission then the National Registry will accept it for processing by date stamping the document and assigning it a document entry number (citas del Diario) which is also stamped on the face of the document. *(See Figure F for sample document entry stamp)*

With this number one will be able to track the document throughout the registration process. The document is then scanned into the Registry computer system and each document is randomly assigned to one of several registrars within the property section department that are responsible for reviewing the document and conducting the relevant title search for the property prior to authorizing the registration of the document.

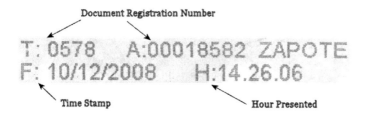

Document Registration Number

T: 0578   A:00018582 ZAPOTE
F: 10/12/2008   H:14.26.06

Time Stamp   Hour Presented

Figure F National Registry Document Entry Time Stamp

The National Registry will not register a transfer deed unless all the transfer taxes and registration fees are paid. Also, any prior instruments which encumber the property, such as mortgage, liens, judgments, and or judicial annotations must be lifted before your transfer deed will be registered. The Registrar will also make sure that the information in the document which was submitted for registration correctly matches the property against which the document is being recorded. If the document contains errors which can be corrected then

the Registrar will note the errors, log it into the co[r]
return the document to the Notary that presented i[t]
can be corrected and the document resubmitted. I[n]
ment could remain un-recorded because of errors
not corrected. The Notary Code Law provides that [c]
remain defective for one year will be cancelled and ᵖ[r]ᵉsen-
tation priority lost. If the error is a material error which cannot be
corrected then the Registrar will cancel the original annotation of the
document.

Once a transfer deed is accepted for registration without errors, the
Registrar approves the document by signing their name to the document and logging the authorization with their security code in the
computer records of the National Registry. The completed document
is then attached to the original deed and returned to the Notary that
filed it who should deliver it to the user. Assuming the transfer deed
contains no defects which could delay registration, the transfer deed
should be registered by the National Registry within 45 to 60 days after presentation. In any event, follow up with the Notary to ensure
registration, otherwise you will run into problems in the future when
you decide to resell the property and find out that your sale was not
registered.

• *Quick Reference:* Property Purchase Check List

• Request the title number (folio real)
• Request the survey map (plano catastrado)
• Have a title search done (Estudio Registral)
• Carefully walk the property boundaries with the survey map
• Certify that all Municipal property taxes and assessments are paid
• If desired, arrange for property inspection to be done of the house
• Be sure the property is not affected by future highway development
• If your purchase to build consult Municipal government for restrictions
• If you purchase with a house then request copy of house plans and
  building permit
• Make sure any domestic employees you keep have been paid off by
  the seller
• Make sure any tenants or occupants to the property leave before
  you close.

PROPERTY AND MUNICIPAL TAX LIABILITIES.

In Costa Rica all properties are subject to a property tax known locally as Impuesto de Bienes Inmuebles and which is administered by the local Municipal government where the property is located. The current property tax rate is .025% of the recorded value of the property. The property tax is due on a quarterly basis.

In order to determine the tax basis for a property the Municipal government relies on three factors: (1) Voluntary Declaration by the Property Owner *(Declaracion de Bienes Inmuebles)*.In this case the Municipal government has specialized forms and requests the property owner to complete the form with all the information on the property. When the property owner turns in the form the Municipal government will calculate the value based upon its database on property values for the area and construction costs. If you complete the form and it is accepted by the Municipal government then you will not have to file the form again for five years. (2) Municipal Appraisal *(Avaluo Municipal)*: If you do not fill out the declaration form then the Municipal government may send out its property appraiser who will then set the value of your property. Some Municipal governments have an appraisal department established and functioning while others do not. As such, some Municipal governments may be more efficient than others in initiating the appraisal process. (3) Transfer of Property Title or Recording a Mortgage: If you transfer title to your property then the value that is established in the transfer deed, if higher than the current tax basis, will be established as the new valuation for your property. For example, if your tax basis is $50,000 on the property but you sell it for $150,000 and that is the value reported on the property transfer deed *(Escritura de Traspaso)* then this will be the new tax basis for the property for calculation of property taxes. The same case applies if you take out a mortgage on the property and the amount of the mortgage is higher than the current tax basis of the property, then the value of the mortgage would be become the value of the property for property tax purpose

The Municipal government also collects a general services tax which includes garbage pickup, water, sewage, etc. *(Servicios Urbanos)* The amount charged depends on the municipality where the property is located.

5. BEACH PROPERTY

Beach property is given separate consideration because it is an area which has generated much confusion among would be buyers. The confusion arises when a buyer desires to purchase a piece of property on the coastline which in many cases is not legally titled property.

5.1 The Maritime Zoning Law

In Costa Rica the ownership of shoreline property is regulated by the Maritime Zoning Law *(Ley Sobre La Zona Maritimo Terrestre)*. The Maritime Zone encompasses two hundred (200) meters of beach frontage which is owned by the Costa Rican Government. Of the two hundred meters regulated by the maritime law, the first fifty (50) meters of tideland are zoned as the "public zone" *(Zona Publica)*. These zones are open to the general public, and private possession or occupation of this area is prohibited by law. The remaining one hundred and fifty (150) meters farther inland are zoned as a "restricted zone" *(Zona Restringida)*. The law allows the local Municipal government to grant leases called Concesiones for the occupation and use of this area for terms that range from five to twenty years. *(See Figure G below for an illustration of the Maritime Zone and Appendix 16 for Maritime Concession Application Form)*

There are coastline properties that were titled before the 1977 Maritime Law came into effect and as such those properties do have legally registered title. These properties are rare and extensive title research such be conducted before you purchase this type of property. There have been numerous frauds and fake titles created as the value of these properties increased in the past couple of years.

The first determination that must be made is if there is an existing legally valid concession already granted for the property or if it will be necessary to apply for a concession for the first time. If a valid concession exists then the holder of the concession may assign his rights to that concession to a purchaser. The assignment of rights must be ratified by the Municipal government with jurisdiction over the property. If a prior concession exists there should be a file open in the Municipal government and it would be wise to obtain and review a copy of the entire file before you purchase any assignment of rights. This is another area where fraud and corruption have been prevalent. In some cases the local Municipal officials approved concessions which they were legally not authorized to do.

In order to apply for a concession for possession of land in the maritime zone for the first time, the applicant must prove that they have had actual and open possession of the particular property. The property must also have a duly recorded property survey map *(plano catastrado)* which has been approved by the Municipal government where the beach property is located. This generally requires an inspection by the Municipal government to verify the information on the survey map.

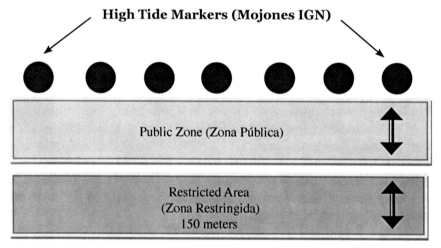

The concession request is filed with the Municipal government where the coastline property is located. The concession department of the Municipality will review the application and if it is in agreement will submit the application to the Municipal Council who must vote on the application and then issue a written resolution in response to the application. The Municipal resolution is the document that confers the concession and will state the terms and conditions of the concession. Once approved the concession is submitted to the Concession Department of the Costa Rican Tourism Institute *(I.C.T.)* who will ratify the Municipal resolution and enter the Concession in their database and which will subsequently be recorded in the Registry of Concessions in the National Registry of San Jose *(Concesiones Maritimo Terrestre)*.

By law, before a concession can be granted, the particular beach area where the property is located must have an approved Coastal Zoning Plan *(Plan Regulador Costero)* in place. Prior to this the National

Geographic Institute *(Instituto Geografico Nacional)* must place the high tide markers called mojones on the shoreline property that is to be zoned. The zoning plans are approved by the Costa Rican Institute of Tourism *(Instituto Costarricense de Turismo).* Only the actual concession will clearly define the rights and terms of occupation and use which the occupant has to the property.

If you have a concession and the beach area where you located did not have a Coastal Zoning Plan in place when your concession was approved it is an illegal concession.

In the past since the local Municipal governments did not have the funds to implement all the coastal surveys and tide markers it became common practice for the Municipal government to allow private parties to hire their own surveyors and then submit the documents to the Municipal government for approval. Due to abuse and corruption this practice is no longer allowed. All documents required for the approval of a zoning plan must be done by the Municipal government with jurisdiction over the particular beach area.

• *Quick Reference:*   If there is no Zoning Plan approved for your coastal area you DO NOT have a legal concession.

Although local governments will collect a land use tax known as a canon from occupants of land located in the maritime zone it does not mean that a concession has been granted. As such, the payment of a canon is simply recognition of the right to possession. On many occasions people purchase a right of possession believing that they automatically have a concession from the government. This is not the case. The granting of a government concession is a separate procedure and a zoning plan for the area must be approved by the Costa Rican Tourism Institute before a concession will be authorized.

Also, in the past Municipal governments have granted concessions to individuals without complying with the legal pre-requisites established in the law. Although this practice has been common for many years it is risky to rely on a concession that has not complied with each and every aspect of the law. As the value of beach properties increase so does the scrutiny by administrative agencies to ensure compliance with applicable laws.

The Office of the Comptroller General *(Contraloria General de la Republica)* has audited the actions of the Municipal governments to enforce the Maritime Zoning Law and issued a strong reprimand to those governments for their failure to properly regulate development on the maritime zone and lack of enforcement of existing laws. (Informe No. DFOW-AM-11/2004).

Interestingly the last time an evaluation of the maritime zone was done was in 1993 when the Tourism Institute (I.C.T.) commissioned a study to determine the amount of illegal constructions on the public area of the maritime zone. At that time in the Municipality of Santa Cruz alone it was determined that there were sixty-four illegal constructions. The new report by the Office of the Comptroller General determined that those illegal constructions were still there. Since the time of that report 2004, the Maritime Zone Departments of the local governments have begun an aggressive campaign to remove all illegal structures from the Public Zones specified in the Maritime Law. This has resulted in the demolition of several hundreds of structures that were in violation of the law.

The Maritime Zoning Law also restricts foreign ownership of land under concession. Pursuant to the law, the following may not acquire a concession: (1) Foreigners, unless they have been residents of Costa Rica for at least five years; (2) Corporations with bearer shares; (3) Corporations domiciled outside of Costa Rica; (4) Costa Rican corporations incorporated by foreigners; (5) Corporations with 50% or more ownership by foreigners. Any transfer which is carried out in violation of the law shall be deemed void.

All kinds of schemes have been developed by local Attorneys to by-pass these regulations including providing nominee corporate officers or nominee shareholders of local corporations to own the concession or setting up private trust agreements with the beneficial owners of the concession. There is a growing local resentment of the complete foreign ownership of the Costa Rican coastlines and as such it is difficult to predict how heavy handed the government will become in enforcing the law.

Those of you that decide to purchase property subject to the Maritime Zoning Law should consult with an Attorney before you proceed. This area of the law is very complex and dotted by potential pitfalls if not thoroughly researched.

6. EASEMENTS

An easement (servidumbre) is the right of one person to go onto the land in possession of another and make limited use of it. Typically, easements are created in order to give their holder the right of access across a tract of land. Generally easements involve two pieces of land: (1) the dominant tenement, which is the land whose owner is benefited by the easement and (2) the servant tenement, which is the land whose owner is burdened by the easement.

6.1 CLASSIFICATION OF EASEMENTS

An easement is classified as either affirmative or negative. The affirmative easement entitles the holder to enter upon the servant tenement and make affirmative use of it for such purposes as laying and maintaining utility lines, draining lines, water lines etc. An affirmative easement confers to the holder a benefit to use the servant estate, which when absent, would be an unlawful interference with the right of ownership.

The negative easement prevents or prohibits the servant tenement owner from doing some act or making a particular use of their land. An example of a negative easement is one that prohibits the owner from building a structure in excess of a certain number of floors.

6.2 HOW EASEMENTS ARE CREATED

The Civil Code provides that easements which are continuous and apparent may be created by express grant, last will and testament, and by prescription.

(1) By Express Agreement

Since an easement is an interest in land it can be created by express agreement between the parties.

(2) By Prescription

To acquire a prescriptive easement, the person must have used it in an open and notorious manner for a continuous period to the adverse interest of the owner.

6.3 TERMINATION OF EASEMENTS

Since an easement may be created by agreement of the parties it can also be terminated when the stated conditions to which the parties agreed expire. If the expiration term is not specified, the Civil Code provides for different ways in which an easement can be terminated.12

A. Release

The person that enjoys the benefit of the easement (dominant tenement) may execute a release and thus terminate the easement.

B. Merger

If the title to both the servant and dominant tenement come into the hands of a single person, the easement is extinguished.

C. Non-Use of the Easement

A showing that the owner of the easement has not used it for an extended period of time will result in its cancellation.

D. Destruction of Property

If the property is involuntarily destroyed or altered so that the easement cannot be used, it may be extinguished. If the condition which affects the easement ends, it may be automatically revived.

• *Quick Reference:* Easements. If you are purchasing a property and have any question regarding the existence or location of an easement it highly recommended that you retain the services of your own property surveyor so that they can clearly and unequivocally render a report to you regarding the existence of any easements. In some cases a title search will reveal the existence of recorded easements but it will not reveal any non-recorded easements or implied easements. Do not purchase any property unless you walk the boundaries and clearly understand what you are getting.   In most cases, the Attorney or Notary Public that carries out the property transfer does not conduct a physical inspection of the property and as such has no way of knowing if there are un-recorded easements.

7. ADVERSE POSSESSION

Adverse possession is the occupation of property by an individual in such a manner that the occupation is adverse to the interests of the title holder of the property.

7.1 ESTABLISHING THE CLAIM FOR POSSESSION

In Costa Rica, the law will recognize the claims of an adverse possessor in real estate if certain requirements are established. Specifically, Articles 853-864 of the Civil Code requires that the possessor or squatter *(precarista)* as they are commonly called exert possession of real property in a continuous, open, and peaceful manner for a period of no less than ten years.

Once the ten years have transpired, the possessor may file in the Court that has jurisdiction over the property an action to quiet title known as Información Posesoria. Once the action is filed, the court will publish in the legal journal, Boletin Judicial, notice of the case requesting third parties that have an interest in the case make an appearance to preserve their rights. If accepted without opposition, the judge will issue a judgment in favor of the possessor and order the National Registry, Property Section to record title in their name.

7.2 LEGAL ACTION AGAINST AN ADVERSE POSSESSOR

The key factor in taking action against an adverse possessor or squatter is time. Once it is discovered that an adverse possession of your property has occurred it is important to take legal action quickly. If the discovery is made within three months of the adverse possession, the law allows the property owner to proceed by way of a Summary Court Procedure to request a restitution of possession to the legitimate owner *(Interdicto de Amparo de Posesion)*. At this stage, since the case proceeds pursuant to a summary process, the procedure to reestablish possession is relatively quick, by Costa Rican standards. If more than three months have passed since the possession was discovered, the property owner may not proceed pursuant to the Summary Court Procedure and instead must file an action against the possessor by way of an Ordinary Court Procedure *(Juicio Ordinario)*. This procedure is more intricate and can drag on for years and years.

7.3 AVOIDING AN ADVERSE POSSESSOR
AND SQUATTERS

Absentee owners of neglected or untended property are the primary targets of squatters and property theft gangs. Most problems occur with undeveloped land located in rural areas. The following are suggestions to avoid potential problems.

1. Make sure you have a legally registered property survey map *(plano catastrado)* of your property; 2. Fence your property and keep the fences properly maintained; 3. Post a private property sign with your phone number within your boundary lines; 4. Let your neighbors know that you are the owner and provide them with a telephone number where they can contact you should a problem arise; 5. Walk your property boundary lines at least every two months. This way if you detect a squatter you can file a summary procedure action against them (remember that the statute of limitations for summary process is three months); 6. If you reside outside of Costa Rica you will need to hire a caretaker to look after your property. The caretaker that you hire should sign a contract with the property owner which clearly defines the responsibilities and duties of the caretaker. After all, you don't want your caretaker to wind up being your adverse possessor, which has happened. 7. If you reside outside of Costa Rica, conduct a title search on your property every six months or so to ensure that no movements have been recorded against the property. From time to time there is property theft gangs that with the help of unscrupulous Attorneys or Notaries forge the property owner's signature or fabricate powers of attorney alleged to have been granted by the property owner.

The gang would then "sell" the property generally to a foreign corporation which would in turn resell or mortgage the property to an innocent buyer or lender. Keep in mind that these precautions are for raw undeveloped land that is left untended by absentee owners.

8. RIGHTS INCIDENT TO POSSESSION

8.1 WATER RIGHTS

The right of individuals over water depends on how the water is classified. Water is generally classified as waterways, surface waters, and underground waters.

(A) Waterways: The waters of the ocean and the sea are considered navigable waterways and one may not interfere with their free use. All coastal waterways, rivers and lakes are part of the public domain and the use of this water is determined by administrative regulation.

(B) Surface waters: the water which naturally flows onto the property may be used at the convenience of the owner.

(C) Underground waters: Generally, water under the surface is subject to the control and ownership of the surface owner with restrictions imposed by the regulating authority.

Access to water is becoming a large issue in the coastal areas of Costa Rica where water scarcity can be an issue.   If you purchase in those areas be sure to clearly understand where the source of your water is coming from and that you have legal documents to ensure your access to those water sources.

8.2 THE FRUITS OF THE LAND (FRUCTUS)

Property ownership also includes the surface rights which may include natural vegetation or growing crops. The Civil Code divides these surface rights into two categories, natural fructus and industrial fructus.

(1) Natural Fructus: Natural fructus is natural vegetation which grows on the land (i.e. plants, trees, shrubs). These are considered part of the land and fructus naturales will pass with the conveyance of the land.

They are and remain real property until they are actually severed from the land.

(2) Industrial Fructus: Industrial fructus are annual growing crops which occur as a result of the cultivation and labor of man. These are generally considered personal property. This becomes important when you purchase land that it is being cultivated by a third party. At the time of purchase you must ensure that the third party that is cultivating the land is compensated for the value of the crops. Otherwise, they may file suit against the property owner to recover their investment in the crops and any improvements in the land.

9. SECURITY INTERESTS IN REAL ESTATE

In general terms, a security interest on real estate operates to secure some obligation to pay a loan. If the loan is not paid when due the holder of the security interest has a right to take title to the real estate.

9.1 THE MORTGAGE

The most widely used financing vehicle is the mortgage. A mortgage is an interest in land created by a written instrument providing security for the performance of a duty or the repayment of a debt. The creation of a mortgage occurs between two parties. The mortgagor *(debtor)* who is the owner of the land and the mortgagee *(creditor)* who is the holder of the mortgage *(i.e. an individual, bank or finance company)*.

In Costa Rica, a mortgage can only be created by way of a written instrument which is prepared and witnessed by a Costa Rican Notary Public and recorded in the property section of the National Registry. Unless the mortgage instrument is executed in this prescribed manner it will not be accepted for registration by the National Registry. *(See Appendix 17 for sample mortgage deed.)*

A. Mortgage Closing Costs

In addition to any points which the lender may charge, it is customary for the borrower to pay for all the costs of drafting and recording the mortgage instrument in the National Registry. A mortgage can be created simultaneously at the time of sale by adding a mortgage clause in the transfer deed, or a separate mortgage instrument can be drafted. The reason for choosing one method over the other will depend on the particular type of transaction involved. The typical mortgage closing costs involve the following costs:

(1) National Registry Fee. (2) Documentary stamps which in the case of a mortgage involves the Municipal stamp *(Timbre Municipal)*, Agrarian stamp *(Timbre Agrario)* and the Legal Bar Association Stamp *(Timbre Colegio de Abogados)*. These registration fees and stamps total about 0.43% of the amount of the mortgage. (3) Notary Fees. The Notary that drafts the mortgage document charges according to the Notary Fee schedule which is:

First 10 Million Colones 2%
Excess of 10 to 15 Million Colones 1.5%
Excess of 15-30 Million Colones 1.3%
Excess of 30 Million Colones 1.0%

The typical costs for a $100,000 mortgage would be as follows:
Mortgage amount: $100,000.00

National Registry Fee:	$ 100
Bar Association Stamp	$ 25
Municipal Stamp	$ 200
Agrarian Stamp	$ 100
Subtotal 1 - Fees	$ 425
Notary Fee	$ 1,300
Total	**$ 1,725**

9.2 MORTGAGE FORECLOSURE

Foreclosure is the method by which the mortgage property or proceeds from the sale are applied to the satisfaction of the debt or obligation. The most common method of foreclosure is by judicial sale of the mortgaged property. In Costa Rica, such a procedure is authorized by the Civil Code and the process to initiate the lawsuit is governed by the Collections Law *(Ley de Cobro Judicial)* which came into effect in 2008.

Under this law the only defense in a mortgage foreclosure action is payment of the outstanding obligation. This means that a mortgage foreclosure will proceed according to summary process and the action is simply one of execution. If the proceeding is accepted by the court it will set a date for auctioning the property. Although there are exceptions, the legal procedure to foreclose on property ranges under the new collection law can range from three to six months depending on the complexity of the case.

9.3 MORTGAGE BONDS *(CÉDULAS HIPOTECARIAS)*

The Costa Rican Civil Code provides an alternative financing tool in the form of negotiable mortgage bonds which are guaranteed by real property. In order to issue these mortgage bonds the property must not be encumbered by other mortgages.

The manner in which this works is that an owner of real property decides to issue mortgage bonds with a given value. The owner appears before a Notary Public and drafts a written instrument requesting that the Property Section of the National Registry issue mortgage bonds upon a particular piece of property. Once the request for mortgage bonds is filed in the National Registry it takes approximately two months for the Registry to record the document and prints the mortgage bond certificates. For example, if the owner wants fifty thousand dollars worth of mortgage bonds they may request that five certificates of ten thousand dollars each be issued. The National Registry delivers the bonds to the owner of the property and reflects the issuance by placing an annotation on the title number of the property. This annotation puts third parties on notice of the mortgage bonds issued against a particular piece of property. The owner does not become personally liable for the mortgage bonds. Instead, the bonds are backed by the property that is pledged. As needed, the issuer of the bonds can pledge them for cash or exchange them or offer them as collateral for other loans. (See Appendix 18 for Mortgage Bond.)

10. THE LANDLORD-TENANT RELATIONSHIP

A Leasehold is an estate in land. This means that the tenant who occupies a property acquires a present possessory interest in that property and certain rights and liabilities flow from this property relationship between the landlord and the tenant. In Costa Rica these rights and duties are governed by the Civil Code *(Codigo Civil)* and the Tenancy Law *(Ley General de Arrendamientos Urbanos y Suburbanos)*

10.1 THE TENANCY LAW

The law which governs Landlord-Tenant relations, Ley General de Arrendamientos Urbanos y Suburbanos, in Costa Rica has been in effect since 1995. The law it replaced had been in effect from 1939-1995 and it created a housing shortage because under that law it was not profitable to build housing for rental due to the strong limitations on rental increases and acquired rights passed on to the tenant.

The current law is much more balanced in the Landlord-Tenant relationship. The Costa Rica law borrows extensively from Landlord-Tenant legislation in Chile, Mexico and Uruguay. The law applies to written and verbal contracts which relate to real property used for residential or commercial purposes. Those contracts that are not encompassed by the Tenancy Law must be resolved pursuant to the Civil Code provisions. The Tenancy Law is divided into twelve chapters as follows:

1. Objectives and the Rental Contract- Chapters I -IV

According to the Legislature, the purpose of the law is to harmonize the right of each individual to decent and adequate housing with the right of freedom of contract and economic development. With that in mind, it should be pointed out that any agreement which contravenes the clauses of the Tenancy Law is deemed invalid. As to the content of the rental contract, the law specifies that the written agreement must contain as a minimum the following information (a) Name and personal data of the contracting parties; (b) Legal description of the property; (c) Detailed description of the property and its condition; (d) Furniture or items which are to be included in the rental contract; (e) The specific use for the property (i.e. residential, commercial) (f) Price, method and place of payment; (g) The rental term; (h) Legal domicile for service of process; (i) date of the contract. (See Appendix 19 for sample residential lease.)

2. Landlord Duties -Chapter V

The landlord has a duty to deliver to the Tenant the premises in habitable condition for their peaceful and quiet enjoyment. Failure to comply with these duties may result in a constructive eviction entitling the Tenant to damages. In the case of emergency repairs, the law gives the Landlord ten days from the date of notice, to effectuate emergency repairs. The manner in which notice is given must comply with the law. If the Landlord after having received proper notice of the need of conducting emergency repairs fails to comply then the Tenant may carry out the emergency repairs and withhold a portion of the rent to cover their cost.

3. Tenant Duties - Chapter VI

(1) Duty to pay rent: The Tenant has a duty to pay rent on the date specified in the contract. (2) Use of the Property: The Tenant may not alter the intended use of the property without the written consent of the Landlord. Failure to comply with these provisions gives rise to a cause for eviction. (3) Duty to preserve the condition of the premises:

A Tenant has a duty to maintain the premises in good condition and return it in the condition it was received. The Tenant will be liable to the Landlord for any deterioration or damage caused to the property that is the result of the Tenants negligent or intentional act. To ensure that the tenant is keeping up the condition of the leased property, the law gives the Landlord the right to inspect the premises during reasonable hours once a month.

4. The Price and Term of the Rental Contract- Chapters VII-VIII.

(1) Duty to Pay Rent: The landlord and the tenant may freely establish the price of the rent. It is the tenant's responsibility to pay the rent on the agreed upon date and at the agreed upon place. If no place is specified for the payment of the rent then the law will presume that it is at the leased premises. (2) Rental Increase: In residential leases, the law establishes a formula for rental increases in Colones that may not exceed 15% per year. If the inflation rate for a particular year exceeds 15% then the government will set the maximum rate allowed for that year. If the residential lease contract is in U.S. dollars, the law does not allow an annual increase for the lease term. For non-residential leases, such as commercial leases, the parties are free to set the period, form and amount of the rental increase. (3) The Duration of the Lease: The duration of the rental contract may not be for a period of less than three years. This means that if a landlord signs a one year lease and the tenant refuses to vacate at the end of the year he has the right to automatically renew, whether the Landlord approves of it or not, until completing the three years authorized by the Tenancy Law. In order to terminate the Lease contract the Landlord must give the Tenant a three month written notice. Failure to do so will result in automatic renewal of the three year lease term.

5. Transfer, Assignments and Subleases. - Chapter IX

(1) Transfer: If the leased premises are sold or transferred, the rental contract goes along with the sale and the tenant cannot be removed.

(2) Assignments and Subleases: The Tenant is not authorized to assign or sublease the leased premises unless there is an express authorization from the Landlord to do so. If the Tenant does not comply with these provisions the law will presume that the tenant has abandoned the premises which may result in a rescission of the contract.

6. Rules Governing Low Income Housing - Chapter X

The law contains several provisions which are only applicable to residential properties that have been approved by the Mortgage Housing Bank (Banco Hipotecario de la Vivienda) as low income housing.

7. Termination of the Rental Contract - Chapter XI

(1) Causes for Termination: Pursuant to the Tenancy Law a rental contract may be terminated if (a) The contract is deemed null and void pursuant to Articles 9,10,14, 23, and 24 of the law; (b) Rescission of the contract pursuant to Article 30 and 38 of the law; (c) Eviction pursuant to Article 27 and 28 of the law; (d) Loss or destruction of the leased premises; (e) Expiration of the lease term; (f) Expropriation of the property.

(2) Termination for Cause Attributable to the Tenant: The landlord may request the termination of the contract if the tenant: (a) Does not pay the rent as agreed; (b) Fails to preserve the condition of the leased premises; (c) Does not abide by condominium by-laws; (d) Changes the intended use of the leased premises; (e) Fails to comply with the landlords request for an inspection of the premises; (f) Damages the leased premises; (g) Abuses the scope of the lease pursuant to Article 78, 79 , 81, and 85 of the law.

(3) Termination for Causes Attributable to the Tenant: The Tenant may request that the contract be terminated if the landlord: (a) Does not deliver the premises in a habitable condition; (b) Fails to maintain the property or complete agreed upon repairs, (c) Alters the premises or engages in construction without the authorization of the Tenant; (d) Interferes with the peaceful and quiet enjoyment of the leased premises; (e) Fails to pay for agreed upon utility services.

8. Eviction and Rental Increase Procedures - Chapter XII

Legal actions for eviction of a tenant or for a rental increase must be filed in the court where the property is located *(Juzgado de Menor Cuantia)*. The action proceeds pursuant to the Summary Procedure (Proceso Sumario) set forth in Article 432 of the Costa Rican Code of Civil Procedure *(Código Procesal Civil)*.

10.2 PROCEDURES TO REMOVE A TENANT

A. The Complaint in Summary Procedure

The Costa Rican Code of Civil Procedure specifies that tenant eviction cases may proceed pursuant to the summary procedure as set forth in the Code. The purpose of summary procedure is to expedite the judicial process. Summary procedure is available if the grounds for removal of the tenant is based upon: (1) A breach of the terms of the contract as set forth in Article 114 of the Tenancy Law (*i.e. lack of payment, failure to preserve condition of the premises, non-payment of condominium fees)*; (2) termination of the rental contract and or other grounds which are established by law.

The eviction process for non-payment of rent pursuant to the summary procedure is initiated by filing a complaint with the court and serving the tenant with a summons. The complaint must indicate the names of the parties, the factual and legal basis for the complaint, and the legal description of the property. Along with the complaint the landlord must include (a) a copy of the lease contract, if any; (b) a certificate of property ownership setting forth the legal description of the property. This can be issued by the National Registry or a Notary Public; (c) an appraisal of the property prepared by a licensed Engineer or by the Property Tax Revenue Department. This condition is cumbersome since it may require hiring an appraiser to prepare a report just when you are in a hurry to get rid of a tenant who may not be paying rent. Failure to comply however may result in the case being dismissed.

Once served with the complaint, the tenant has five (5) days in which to respond to the complaint for eviction by filing an answer setting forth any of their defenses. If the tenant files an answer and formally opposes the complaint for eviction the court will allow three (3) days for the taking of evidence. At the close of this evidentiary period the court will analyze the evidence presented before it and issue its final judgment. If the tenant fails to respond and/or oppose the complaint for eviction the court will enter a default judgment which orders the tenant to vacate the property. If the tenant fails to comply with the order then the police with proper jurisdiction can be commissioned to carry out the order of eviction.

It is difficult to estimate the time frame involved in an eviction proceeding. They can range anywhere from two (2) months to one year depending on the court where the action is being litigated and the defense tactics which are being used to oppose it.

B. The Writ Of Possession and Damages

Once the court issues a Final Judgment it issues a Writ of Possession which commands the police to restore possession of the premises to the owner. If need be, the police is authorized to place the personal property of the tenant in storage at his expense. Once the tenant is removed and the eviction complete, the landlord is entitled to file with the court a separate motion, known as an *Incidente de Cobro de Alquileres,* requesting back rent, interest, and damages, if any, incurred as a result of the eviction action. If the landlord has prevailed in the lawsuit they can also file a motion requesting that the tenant pay for their Attorney fees and costs *(Incidente de Cobro de Honorarios).*

11. CIVIL LAW TENANCY

The Tenancy Law discussed above is applicable to all real property which is destined for residential use. The same Tenancy Law also applies to real property that is used for any commercial, industrial, artistic, professional, technical, cultural, educational, and recreational or activities that provide public services. The law specifically sets forth what kind of establishments are not covered under the Tenancy Law, those are: (1) Hotels, pensions, hostels, boarding places or similar establishments. (2) Houses and locals destined for tourism and which are located in areas appropriate for tourism activities. So long as the rental is seasonal in nature. (3) The stands provided in markets or fairs. (4) Parking lots and vehicle storage places, (5) The leases on advertising banners, (6) The occupation by tolerance of a person in a constructed facility. (7) The housing provided to the administrator, guard, peon, caretaker, or employee related to their employment. (8) The farm house which is occupied when the main purpose of the lease is the use of the agricultural land. All of the proceeding cases which are specifically excluded by the Tenancy Law are regulated by the applicable provisions of the Civil Code. Those that are destined exclusively for agricultural use are regulated by the Agrarian Code.

The court procedure for enforcing civil law tenancies are the same ones followed by the Tenancy Law except the foundation for the action must be allowed by the Civil Code. For example, an action filed for nonpayment of rent of a property that is not within the parameters of the Tenancy Law would have to be based on Article 1147 of the Civil Code which allows the landlord to request the resolution of a lease when one of the parties breaches their obligation, in this case the obligation to pay rent.

11.1 ADMINISTRATIVE EVICTION

An administrative eviction is an eviction which is carried out by an administrative office of the government, generally the police, as opposed to a judicial branch such as the Court. In Costa Rica a request for an administrative eviction is filed with the Ministry of Public Security. The legal department of the Ministry of Public Security reviews the petition and based upon the evidence and facts presented will either grant or deny the request. If granted, the Minister of Public Security will sign and issue an order to the police to carry out the eviction. The administrative eviction is more commonly used to remove squatters, employees or guests from property that they were either illegally occupying or were occupying by the mere tolerance of the owner and the tolerance was rescinded. The administrative eviction can also be used in the case of guests for hotels, pensions, and hostels where the stay is intended to be temporary as opposed to permanent.

12. CONDOMINIUM LAW

The word condominium means control over certain property owned jointly with one or more other persons. The main characteristic of the condominium is that the condominium purchaser acquires ownership title in the unit together with an undivided tenancy in the common interest with other unit owners in the common areas.

In Costa Rica, the law that regulates Condominium properties has been in effect since 1999 and is called the Law Regulating Condominium Property *(Ley Reguladora de La Propiedad en Condominium)*. In the past couple of years the boom in condominium development properties has given rise to an entire industry catering to condominium administration and management.

12.1 CREATING THE CONDOMINIUM

Under the law the real estate developments that can be recorded as a condominium development include: (1) Buildings or structures designated as residential, commercial locals, offices, parking lots either built or to be built. (2) The structures which are built on one piece of property to be titled by different owners. (3) Constructions which are already built and are either residential, commercial, tourism or industrial may be recorded under the condominium law if they meet the necessary technical specifications. (4) The owner of a concession right destined for commercial or tourism development. (5) Projects in urbanization's which are to be developed in phases.

The condominium is created by drafting and recording a declaration in the National Registry. The declaration will contain, among other things, a legal description of the underlying land, a description of the building structures that will comprise the project, a legal description for each unit, and a description of the common areas. The declaration will also assign to each unit a percentage which is determined by dividing the initial value of the unit by the value of the whole project. This percentage is then used to determine the unit owner's percentage interest in the common areas.

The condominium law also requires that the declaration which is filed in the National Registry set forth the By-Laws which will govern the administration of the condominium.

Before a condominium can be legally recorded in the National Registry to create individualized property title numbers it must fulfill all the permitting requirements established by law. At the very least most condominium projects will require environmental impact review and compliance with both local and national construction regulations.

12.2 THE UNIT AND COMMON AREAS

The common areas are made up of those areas so designated in the plans of the condominium property. Common areas include the ground on which the condominium buildings are located, entry ways, parking areas, gardens and all other parts of the property that are necessary for the existence, maintenance and safety of the structure. The common areas may not be transferred, pledged or liened in any manner since they are an intrinsic part of the property as a whole.

A. Rights and Duties of Unit Owners

The condominium law allows a unit owner to freely transfer, mortgage, encumber, and/or contract out their ownership interest in the condominium.

Unit owners are required to use their property in accordance with the restrictions included in the condominium declaration document. In addition, the condominium law expressly prohibits any acts by unit owners which would interfere with the quiet use and enjoyment of the property by other unit owners or which threatens the health, safety and welfare of the building. The exterior decoration and facade of the units must be uniform and cannot be varied.

The unit owners are required to proportionately contribute to the expenses incurred by the condominium to administer, maintain and operate the common areas. The condominium law specifically states that the unit owners are responsible for following common expenses: (i) Any tax liability that affects the property, (ii) insurance premiums, (iii) expenses relative to the administration, maintenance and cleaning of the building and the common areas, (iv) costs of utilities incurred in operating common areas, (v) authorized repairs and improvements made to the building or the common areas, (vi) expenses incurred by the administrator, (vii) other expenses which have been authorized by the owner's association, (viii) the cost of acquiring common goods.

12.3 MANAGING THE CONDOMINIUM AND THE OWNERS ASSOCIATION

A. Administration and Management of the Condominium

The condominium law requires that the condominium be managed by an administrator. This administrator is appointed pursuant to the by-laws for the condominium which was filed with the declaration. The law requires that the by-laws provide for (i) the method for appointment and termination of a condominium administrator; (ii) specify the method of assessment of unit owners to cover common expenses; (iii) The frequency in which the property owners will meet and who will preside at the meeting; (iv) use and limitations of the common areas; and (v) the sanctions which can be imposed and the mechanisms to resolve disputes; (vi) the method to approve any modifications to the exterior façade of the condominium.

The condominium administrator has a duty to care for the administration and maintenance of the property. This includes collecting all assessment fees and maintaining financial statements relative to the income and expenditures of the association.

B. The Owners' Association

The purpose of an owners association is to promote and enforce uniformity within the condominium and to allow the unit owners to pool their resources for the benefit of the association.

Each owner is a member of the owners' association and has the right to votes equal to their percentage of ownership in the condominium. A quorum of the owners' association requires that 2/3 of the value of the building be present. If quorum is not present a second call will be made and quorum will be reached with whatever representatives are present.

Any resolutions adopted by the owners' association must pass by majority vote present at the meeting. The resolutions passed by the owner's association are legally binding on all the owners. The resolutions must be recorded in the minute's book which must be maintained by the owners association. A unit owner who disagrees with any resolutions of the association may pursue legal action to challenge the resolution within three months after the resolution is adopted.

In most new condominium development projects the developer is the one that names and controls the Association until such time as the project is sold out and the new owner's take over the association. As such when you purchase in a condominium project read the by-laws before you purchase since it will be very difficult later to get the property quorum of members to change the existing by-laws.

13. CONSTRUCTION AND DEVELOPMENT

All construction in Costa Rica is regulated by the Costa Rican Building

Code. Also applicable are the regulations from the Institute of Housing and Urban Development (Instituto Nacional de Vivienda y Urbanismo), the Association of Architects and Engineers *(Colegio Federado de Ingenieros y Arquitectos de Costa Rica)*, and the Municipal regulations from the Municipal government where the property is located. Enforcement of the building regulations rests with the Municipality which has jurisdiction over the property. The Municipal Building Department and will generally be able to provide you with the requirements for building. *(See Appendix 20 for sample request for a municipal building permit.)*

13.1 CONSTRUCTION PERMITS

The law requires that any application for a construction permit be presented by a licensed Architect or Engineer. As such, once the decision has been made to build a home, condominium, or initiate a real estate development project a local Architect or Engineer should be sought out to guide you through the process which can be troublesome and lengthy without expert assistance.

The best way to avoid surprises when you get ready to build or develop is to make sure that the property you purchase is suitable for your intended purpose. To ensure this you should conduct some preliminary studies on the property to ensure that obtaining a building permit won't be a problem. First, request a zoning opinion *(Certificado de Uso de Suelo)* from the Municipal government where your property is located. (See Appendix 21 Zoning Request)

If the Municipal government where the property is located has adopted a master zoning plan then they will issue you a written certification in response to your request and setting forth the permitted use for your particular property. If there is no master zoning plan for the area then they will respond based upon their internal guidelines and directives for the particular area. With the same survey map you can also ask the Municipal government to indicate the required setbacks to the property on which you intend to build. (See Appendix 22 for Zoning Information for Selected Municipal Governments) Second, determine if the property you intend to build on has basic services such as water, electricity, telephone, and drainage. Third, make sure there are no restrictions placed on the lot which could result in the denial of a construction permit. It will not be enough to check the National Registry, you should also check at the Ministry of Public Works (M.O.P.T.) for future road construction projects; Ministry of Health (Ministerio de Salud); Housing and Urban Development (I.N.V.U) and the Municipality where the property is located (Municipalidad). Also, be aware of any environmental regulations which may affect your construction project by consulting with the Ministry of the Environment at their environmental impact office (SETENA) Also ensure the project does not violate national wildlife refuge and areas or areas deemed protected by the Forestry Law *(Ley Forestal)*

The procedures for requesting the construction permit will vary depending on the type of project that is involved. In the past, the government centralized all the government agencies that needed to sign off on construction plans in one office. That office housed representatives from the Ministry of Transportation, M.O.P.T (roads), I.N.V.U. (housing), I.C.E. (telephone), AYA (Water), S.N.E. (Electricity) C.F.I.A.. (Association of Architects and Engineers), and the Ministry of Health. However, as of this edition that office has been separated and the responsibility for permit approval is being delegated back to the Municipal government where the property is located as opposed to the national government.

The permit requirements will vary depending on the scope and size of the construction project. However, for a typical single family detached dwelling to be built on a residential lot that has all utility services, the permit process will be as follows: (1) Have the architectural blueprints signed by the Architect or Engineer that drafted them and the electrical plan by the Electrical Engineer that drafted it. (2) The blueprints must be filed with the Costa Rican Association of Engineers and Architects *(Colegio Federado de Ingenieros y Arquitectos)* along with the standardized consulting agreement *(Contrato de Consultoria)* between the Architect/Engineer and property owner. (See Appendix 23 for CFIA standard consulting contract) This contract is a requisite to obtaining a building permit. At this office they review the contract and establish the per meter cost for the type of construction that you intend to build. The amount fixed then works as the basis for the fees paid to the Architect/Engineer and for the construction permit fees.

Once approved by the Costa Rican Association of Engineers and Architects, they will stamp the blueprints and return them to the Architect/Engineer who can then proceed to the next phase. (3) The blueprints are now ready for filing before the Municipal government where the property is located and who is responsible for issuing the building permit. The process varies depending on the Municipal government but they will generally require that you: (1) Fill out a construction permit application (Solicitud de Permiso de Construcción). (2) Obtain a worker's compensation policy from the National Insurance Institute (I.N.S). Since the purpose of the permit is to build, the law requires that the applicant provide proof that the property owner or their contractor has a valid workers compensation policy in effect before a construction permit is issued. The cost of the workers compensation policy will be based on the value of the construction which was established by the Costa Rican Association of Engineers and Architect in the consulting contract previously discussed. (3) Provide a certified copy of the property survey map (Plano Catastrado) for the property where the construction will take place. (4) Provide a certificate o title (Certificado de Propiedad) issued by either the National Registry or a Notary Public which sets forth details as to the owner and boundaries for the property. (5) Provide three copies of the construction blueprints. (6) Provide a municipal certification that the property is up to date on the payment of property taxes and municipal assessments. This can be requested at the Municipal government. (7) Provide the approval from the water company (AYA) regarding availability of water where the home will be built.

By law it is the Municipality which is delegated the responsibility to ensure that all constructions comply with building regulations. As such, you can expect periodic visits to your construction site by the Municipal building inspector who must certify that the construction is proceeding according to code.

The requirements are more extensive for condominium projects, commercial construction, and urbanization projects which also require approval by the Costa Rican Institute of Housing and Urban Development (INVU) and environmental impact evaluation by the Costa Rican Environmental Compliance Department (SETENA)

Whether you choose a turnkey type builder who will agree to a fixed cost, or decide to act as your own General Contractor and subcontract the labor and materials of your construction be sure you have a well specified construction contract that defines the obligations of each of the parties involved and leaves nothing up to interpretation.

• *Quick Reference:* Construction Permits for a Residential Home.

• Hire an Architect or Engineer
• Prepare contract between property owner and Architect/Engineer
• Draft construction blueprints
• Draft house electrical plan
• Review and approve final blueprints
• Prepare C.F.I.A. standard consulting contract
• File blueprints and standard consulting contract with C.F.I.A.
• Prepare Municipal request for building permit
• Obtain workers compensation policy at INS
• File the permit request and supporting documents with the Munici
  pality
-Application
-Blueprints
-CFIA Consulting Contract
-Copy of property survey map
-Certificate of Title
-INS workers compensation policy
-Property tax and municipal services payment receipts
• Retrieve the building permit from the Municipal government.

13.2 FEE SCHEDULES FOR ARCHITECTS
AND ENGINEERS

All Architects and Engineers in Costa Rica must be licensed by the Costa Rican Association of Engineers and Architects. *(Colegio Federado de Ingenieros y Arquitectos).* This governing body establishes the fee schedule that can be charged by its members. Most fees are based upon a percentage of the value of the construction project. According to the regulations of the Association of Architects and Engineers the level of participation of a licensed Architect or Engineer in a construction project is separated into two phases. Phase I is drafting the construction plans and obtaining the permits and Phase II is supervision and execution of the actual construction.

A. Phase I: Construction Plans and Permits

This first phase is further subdivided into several distinct professional services which can be provided to the client by the Architect or Engineer.

The percentages cited are those that the Association of Architects and Engineers has established as the minimum fee which may be charged.

Furthermore it is the Association which establishes the per meter cost of the construction which in turn determines the total value of the construction. As previously discussed the Association of Architects and Engineers reviews all construction plans to ensure that the values established meet the parameters they establish. In essence, the Association of Architects and Engineers has the right to establish the minimum per meter cost of construction which ultimately benefits their members who charge a percentage of the cost of construction.

The current fee structure is broken down as follows: Preliminary Studies *(Estudios Preliminarios)* 0.5%, which may or may not be required depending on the scope of the project. Preliminary Project Design (Anteproyecto) 1% to 1.5%, Generally, during this stage the Architect or Engineer will meet with the client to discuss construction requirements.

With this information the Architect/Engineer will prepare drafts of the proposed construction project for review by the client. These drafts should include site planning and preliminary work drawings. When you contract for this service be sure you agree with your Architect or Engineer beforehand what he is going to provide for you. Construction Plans and Technical Specifications *(Planos de Construcción y Especificaciones Técnicas)* is 4%. This is one of the most important steps in the overall construction project since execution of the project will depend upon the quality and accuracy of your construction plans.

Once you and your Architect/Engineer have agreed on the layout and design of the project they will begin drafting the plans. In Costa Rica, a complete set of plans should include: a site plan, distribution plan, elevation and transversal and longitude perspectives, roof design and drainage, design of footings and support beams, structural plans, electrical design, mechanical and sanitary system design, as well as a plan which details all the interior finishing's of the construction. The more detailed the plan the easier it will be for you to send out the plans for bids. Budgeting *(Presupuesto)* For an additional 0.5% your Architect or Engineer will provide a global construction budget for your project. The cost goes up to 1% for an itemized construction budget. Here the Architect/Engineer prepares a material lists based upon your construction plans and prepares a construction budget for you.

B. Phase II. Control and Execution.

This stage involves the actual construction and project supervision. The regulations authorize three kind of supervisory tasks each of which requires a larger amount of time and responsibility by the Architect or Engineer. Inspection *(Inspección)* is 3% of the total value of the construction project. Here you're Architect /Engineer will visit the construction site at least once a week and will inspect it to ensure that the construction plan specifications are being followed by the general contractor. They will also verify the quality of the materials being used and review invoices being presented by the General Contractor. Supervision *(Dirección Tecnica)* is 5% of the total. This requires more direct involvement by the Engineer or Architect in the day-to-day operation of the project. Administration *(Administración)* is 12% of the total value of the project, here the Architect or Engineer takes complete responsibility for the day-to-day management and overall execution and completion of the project. *(See Appendix 23 for CFIA standard consulting contract and Figure I for Fee Schedule).*

The option you choose will depend upon the type of project involved, the reliability of your builder / general contractor and the amount of time you are willing to dedicate to the construction project. All told, phase I and II can range from 9% to 18% of the estimated value of the construction project.

As such, it is common practice to negotiate fees with the Architect or Engineer. Most builders will be eager for your business and, depending on the scope of the project will be willing to work out an agreement which is tailored to your particular needs. Before you sign any contracts be sure that you understand the fee structure and know exactly what is and is not included in the fee. Likewise, clearly define the responsibilities that your Architect/Engineer is going to assume. Do the same thing with your general contractor and any sub contractors. A well drafted construction contract can avoid misunderstandings between yourself and those that you have hired to build your project or development.

Figure H.   Summary of Fee Schedule for Architects and Engineers

ITEM	FEE
Preliminary Studies	0.5%
Pre-Project Design	1.0% to 1.5%
Construction Plans / Technical Specs.	4%
Budgeting	0.5% to 1.0%
Inspection	3.0%
Technical Direction	5.0%
Complete Administration	12.0%

Source: Contrato de Servicios Profesionales Para Consultoria Colegio Federado de Ingenieros y de Arquitectos de Costa Rica (C.F.I.A.)

14. PROPERTY INSURANCE

In Costa Rica, the sale of insurance has been for many years a government monopoly where the law prohibited private insurance companies from underwriting insurance policies in Costa Rica.

As such, the only authorized insurer in the past was the National Insurance Institute *(Instituto Nacional de Seguros)*. The Institute sells insurance through its network of brokers and authorized agents. More information is available on the insurance provided by the Institute at their web site which is www.ins.go.cr

On August 7th of 2008 the Costa Rican legislature approved the Law Regulating the Insurance Market *(Ley Reguladora del Mercado de Seguros No. 8653)* This new law will open the insurance market to private companies to participate in the insurance business. As of this edition the government was in the process of establishing the Insurance Regulatory Office which would be a precursor to issuing insurance licenses to private companies. In the interim the information set forth below on coverage's are those provided by the Costa Rican Insurance Institute (INS).

14.1 PROPERTY DAMAGE

The most common policy sold by the Institute to insure real property is an umbrella policy known as "Hogar Seguro 2000" which insures homes and their contents. The coverage's, and applicable deductibles are as follows:

Item	Coverage	Deductibles
A	fire and lighting	none
B	mutiny, strike, work stoppage, vandalism, hurricane, cyclone, explosion, smoke, falling objects.	$100 per claim $100 per claim
C	floods, landslides, earthquakes and tremors	20%

If one chooses coverage's A, B and C, the annual premium payment will be about 0.34% of the amount of insurance provided.

14.2 PROPERTY CONTENTS INSURANCE COVERAGE

You can extend coverage to include the contents of your home. The Institute (I.N.S.) estimates the contents of your home at a standard rate of 35% of the insured value of the property. If the homeowner feels that this amount will be insufficient to cover the contents they can request coverage based upon actual cash value of the items in the home.

The Institute also sells a Home Theft Policy that will insure the contents of your home which have been itemized. A detailed list and description of each item is required. Premium payments will depend upon several factors that are analyzed by the Institute on a case by case basis.

14.3 TITLE INSURANCE COVERAGE

Title Insurance is a product developed in the United States and mostly sold in the United States to insure against financial loss from defects in title. Title Insurance in the United States was created in 1876 since land title searches were done by conveyancers, who personally searched titles or obtained an abstract (summary) to determine ownership of the land and encumbrances to that title.

Title Insurance arrived in Costa Rica following United States purchasers of property in Costa Rica. Since the Costa Rican insurance monopoly at the time prohibited the sale of insurance by private companies they labeled the local product a Title Guaranty. The concept of title insurance is relatively new for Costa Rica and something that is not commonly used by locals and aimed mostly at United States buyers.

To determine whether or not you need title insurance on your property purchase in Costa Rica you must ask yourself: -What am I specifically looking to be covered against - then carefully read the insurance exclusions in the policy to make sure that the coverage you will be relying on are not those excluded from insurance coverage. Another consideration to take into account is where any disputes for coverage will be litigated. Some policies provide that any coverage dispute must be settled in Costa Rica before Costa Rican courts while others indicate that a United States court will have jurisdiction of the dispute.

There are at least five title insurance companies operating in Costa Rica and your local Real Estate Attorney can arrange for title insurance coverage with any one of them if you wish to purchase the coverage. The rates of coverage will vary among the different companies but you can expect to pay around 1% of the amount you are insuring the property for.

CHAPTER 7

FAMILY LAW

1. MATRIMONY

1.1 TYPE OF MARRIAGES RECOGNIZED UNDER COSTA RICAN LAW

Costa Rican law legally recognizes two procedures for marriage; the civil ceremony or church matrimony.

A. The Civil Matrimony

A civil marriage ceremony can be performed by a Judge, Mayor, Provincial Governor or Notary Public. Once the ceremony is carried out a declaration of marriage must be completed and filed in the Civil Registry. This declaration must include the following information: the name of the parties, nationality, status, age, occupation, identification number, residence, parents' name and nationality, and the date, place and time of the wedding ceremony. The legal rights and obligations which arise from matrimony occur when the declaration is registered in the Civil Registry. *(See Appendix 24 for civil marriage document)*

B. The Church Matrimony

The great majority of Costa Ricans (85%) consider themselves Roman Catholics. Many Costa Ricans have strong ties with the Catholic church. Under Costa Rican law a marriage ceremony carried out by a Catholic priest has the same legal effect and validity as a civil ceremony. The marriage ceremony performed before a Catholic priest must be registered in the Civil Registry just like the civil ceremony. Since the law specifically refers to the Catholic church, couples from other religious denominations must resort to a civil matrimony procedure for their marriage to be legal.

1.2 MARRIAGES NOT RECOGNIZED BY LAW

The Family Code sets forth specific categories of marriages which by law are determined to be illegal, void, or prohibited.

A.   A Marriage Is Legally Impossible:

(1) If one of the parties is not either single, widowed or divorced;

(2) If the marriage is between blood relatives;

(3) If the marriage is between siblings related by blood;

(4) If an individual is charged with the murder of his or her spouse; then that individual may not marry the surviving spouse of the murdered victim;

(5) If it is between persons of the same sex.

B. A Marriage may be Declared Void:

(1) If consent to the marriage was procured by way of threats, duress or misrepresentation as to the identity of one of the parties to the marriage;

(2) If it is determined that one of the parties lacked the capacity to form voluntary intent;

(3) If one of the parties is a minor under the age of 15;

(4) On the grounds of impotence which is incurable and which occurred before the marriage;

(5) If the marriage ceremony is performed by an unauthorized government official.

C. A Marriage Is Prohibited:

(1) If one of the parties is under the age of 18 and has not been legally emancipated;

(2) For a previously divorced female if the marriage will take place within 300 days of her divorce, unless she provides official medical certification that she is not pregnant;

(3) Between a guardian or his descendants and the orphan under their care;

(4) If prior notice is not published in the official bulletin, unless the official carrying out the ceremony dispenses with the requirement.

1.3 PREMARITAL LEGAL FORMALITIES

In Costa Rica, the government takes an active role in promoting the importance of the family. Under Costa Rican law, the government has an affirmative duty to protect the family. Consequently, the government imposes certain legal requirements which prospective couples must satisfy before it will authorize a marriage. The parties must file with the Civil Registry office the following documentation:

(1) Birth certificate of each party;

(2) Certificate of marital status issued by the Civil Registry; *(This document certifies that the parties have not been married in the past or that they are legally divorced or widowed.)*

(3) List of two persons who will serve as witnesses to the matrimony. *(name, marital status, occupation, identification number and residence of the witnesses must be provided.)*

(4) If one of the parties is a minor (less than 18), then they must provide proof of emancipation with parental consent;

(5) If the female was divorced within one year, then she must provide an official medical certification indicating that she is not pregnant;

(6) The parties must give public notice by publishing a statement in the official bulletin for eight consecutive days manifesting their intent to marry. The purpose of this is to provide notice of the marriage and allow those opposed to voice their objections. The notice requirement may be waived by the official that is carrying out the ceremony. The government will authorize the marriage once these legal requirements are complied with. It should be noted that in a church marriage the Catholic church may impose additional requirements.

1.4 PREMARITAL AGREEMENTS

The Family Code recognizes the validity of premarital agreements which allocate the distribution of present and future assets. The premarital agreement must be signed in the Notary Public protocol book and must be registered in the National Registry in order to be valid.

The requirement that the premarital agreement be executed before a Notary Public and then recorded in the National Registry of Costa Rica could affect the enforcement within Costa Rica of premarital agreements drafted outside of Costa Rica. A ruling from the Second Chamber of the Supreme Court supports this proposition. In their decision the Court ruled that a premarital agreement drafted in Mexico between a Canadian and United States couple would not be recognized in Costa Rica as it relates to their Costa Rican assets because the Mexican premarital agreement could not be recorded in Costa Rica as is required by Costa Rican law. As such be sure you following the formalities required by Costa Rican law or your premarital agreement many not have any validity in Costa Rica.

2. MARITAL DISSOLUTION

The Family Code provides two methods for dissolving a marriage. Dissolution of marriage by mutual consent or by judicial decree.

2.1 DISSOLUTION BY MUTUAL CONSENT

The dissolution of marriage by mutual consent involves an agreement between the parties to dissolve the marriage. Dissolution by mutual consent was not recognized in Costa Rican law until it was incorporated into the Family Code in 1970. Prior to that time, the only manner in which to obtain a divorce decree was pursuant to a judicial proceeding after a determination of fault had been established.

In order to request dissolution of marriage by mutual consent, the law requires the parties to have been married for at least two (2) years prior to their filing. If the parties have been married for less than two years they are not eligible for mutual consent dissolution and must proceed by way of a judicial determination. To initiate the process, the parties must appear before a Costa Rican Notary Public and draft a marital termination agreement in which they agree, among other things, to (i) child custody, (ii) child support, and (iii) spousal support, if any, (iv) an equitable distribution of the marital assets. Once the marital termination agreement is properly executed before the Notary Public it is filed with the Court along with a petition requesting the dissolution of the marriage. *(See Appendix 25 for marital dissolution agreement.)*

2.2 DISSOLUTION BY JUDICIAL DETERMINATION

If the parties to the marriage do not qualify or are unable to resolve their differences and cannot mutually agree on the conditions of their divorce they can file a petition for dissolution of marriage before a Family Court with proper jurisdiction. If the parties proceed by way of judicial proceeding, they must allege and prove the grounds for the dissolution.

A. The Grounds for Marital Dissolution

Article 48 of the Family Code lists the specific grounds which will support a petition for dissolution of marriage. These include:

(1) Adultery: Pursuant to the Code, adultery is a violation of the parties' duty to fidelity. Once alleged and proved, it is sufficient grounds for the judge to issue a decree of dissolution.

(2) An Attempt Against the Life of a Spouse or Child: Credible evidence which shows that one of the parties has made an attempt against the life of the other or of one of the children.

(3) An Attempt by One of the Spouses to Corrupt or Prostitute the Other or any of the Children: This generally refers to the acts of one spouse to force or coerce the other to have sex with third parties, and or if it is determined that the children are being sexually abused.

(4) Spousal or Child Abuse: This refers to the physical and or psychological abuse inflicted by one spouse against the other or against the children.

(5) Judicial Separation for at Least One Year: If the parties have been legally (court approved) separated for at least one year then they may raise this as grounds for the dissolution of marriage. However, before the dissolution is granted, the parties must appear before the court for two reconciliation sessions in three month intervals.

(6) If the Spouse is Legally Declared Missing: Before this is pleaded as

grounds for divorce, the party must request a judicial declaration that one of the parties to the marriage is missing. In order to obtain this declaration there must be a two year period wherein the party has not been seen or heard of.

(7) De facto Separation: If the parties have been separated for at least three (3) years.

In order to obtain a decree of marital dissolution in Costa Rica the petitioner must plead and prove one of the above referenced grounds as the basis for the petition. Furthermore, the Code establishes a one year statute of limitations for initiating an action for marital dissolution based upon items (1) through (7) listed above. This means that the petitioner must file a petition for dissolution within one year of the time that he or she becomes aware of the facts that give rise to the complaint otherwise the action is time barred.

2.3 RECOGNITION OF FOREIGN DIVORCE DECREES

If a couple was divorced outside of Costa Rica but requires that the dissolution of marriage be recorded in Costa Rica they will have to petition the Costa Rican Supreme Court to have the foreign judgment recognized. This judgment recognition proceeding is known locally as an Exequatur proceeding and is filed before the First Chamber of the Supreme Court.

The foreign judgment that is the basis of the recognition action must be certified, authenticated by the Costa Rican Embassy or consulate in the country of origin and translated in Spanish by an official translator. Of all the judgment recognition actions filed before the First Chamber of the Supreme Court the vast majority, 85%, were for recognition of foreign divorce decrees.

2.4 LEGAL (JUDICIAL) SEPARATION

The Family Code allows couples who have been married for at least two (2) years to obtain a decree of judicial separation. This document allows couples to legally separate but maintain the legal status of their marriage.

The decree of judicial separation is granted by the court only after establishing the grounds for separation. The Code specifically provides for the following grounds to support a petition for legal separation.

(1) Any of the grounds which the Family Code establishes for dissolution of marriage;

(2) Abandonment by one of the spouses;

(3) Neglect by one of the spouses to support their children and spouse;

(4) Serious offenses- If alleged, it is up to the judge to determine the gravity of the offense;

(5) Mental or physical impairment of one of the parties which continues for more than a year and threatens the life or health of the other spouse;

(6) A criminal conviction resulting in a prison sentence of three (3) years or more. This cause of action may only be filed when one of the spouses has been incarcerated for a continuous period of no less than two (2) years;

(7) Mutual consent of the parties;

(8) The de facto separation of the couple for one year after having been married for at least two years.

The effect of a judicial separation is the same as that of a decree of dissolution of marriage except that in the judicial separation the legal bonds of matrimony are not dissolved. The judicial separation does allow the parties to liquidate their marital assets and determine child custody and support.

3. IMPUTED MARRIAGE – THE FREE UNION

Under Costa Rican law the free union between a man and a woman which is open, public, known and stable for more than three (3) years shall have the same legal effect as a legally recognized marriage. In Costa Rica this relationship is referred to as *Union de Hecho*. Either party to the relationship may appear before a court with proper jurisdiction and request a judicial recognition of the status "free union".

The action must be filed no more than two years after the relationship has broken or the death of one of the parties. This recognition allows the party to participate in the property and assets of the other as well as request financial support.

4. CHILD SUPPORT

Costa Rican courts have jurisdiction to determine child support obligations. The Family Code defines support as food, housing, dress, medical attention, education, entertainment, transportation and others which may be within the financial possibilities of the person required to provide the support. The Court will take into account the needs and the lifestyle to which the beneficiary was accustomed in relation to the income capacity of the provider. The Petitioner must file suit in court with proper jurisdiction which is where either the petitioner or respondent resides. The complaint must indicate the name of the petitioner and the alleged provider, names of the beneficiaries, amount of child support requested, the financial status of both parties. The complaint filed must set forth the evidence relied upon.

Once filed, the court will open the proceedings and establish a temporary child support award which must be paid by the respondent while the case proceeds towards a final resolution. The respondent has eight (8) days in which to file a response to the complaint.

The amount of child support whether temporary or permanent must be paid within the time frame established by the court. Failure to pay child support can result in fines and a prison sentence which can range from one month to two years. Child support may not be waived and there is no time limit in which to file a child support enforcement action.

4.1 FINANCIAL SUPPORT OF OTHERS

The Costa Rican Family Code goes a step further regarding the financial support obligations of the family. Clearly, as discussed in the previous section, a parent is responsible for the financial support of their minor children. The Code however, also allows actions for the financial support of a spouse, ex-spouse, or a couple in a free union (living together unmarried). Also included is the parents right to receive financial support from their children as well as support for those family members with a disability. In Costa Rica the children have a legal obligation to support their elderly parents. The parents may file suit against their children to have a court award them financial support.

5. ADOPTION

Adoption is the process by which a parent who is not the natural parent of a child becomes legally recognized as that child's parent. In Costa Rica the placement of children for adoption requires the participation of the National Child Welfare Agency *(Patronato Nacional de la Infancia)*. This agency is a division of the government and it closely regulates adoptions in Costa Rica.

5.1. WHO MAY BE ADOPTED

The law authorizes the adoption of (1) minor children who have been legally declared abandoned. The declaration of abandonment may be made administratively by the National Child Welfare Agency when there is no opposition to the adoption, otherwise the declaration must be made by a Family Court Judge. (2) A minor child whose birth parents consent to the adoption. The consent must be proven to a Family Court Judge who has discretion in determining what is in the best interests of the child.

5.2 ADOPTION PROCEEDINGS

In Costa Rica, the Family Court has jurisdiction over adoption proceedings. To qualify for an adoption, the petitioner must be at least 25 years old (the law also requires that the adoptive parent be at least 15 years older than the adopted child) and show financial ability to support the adopted child.

If the adoptive parents are not Costa Rican citizens and reside outside of Costa Rica the law requires they demonstrate that (1) The couple has been married for at least five years, (2) That they comply with the established guidelines for adoption required in their country of origin, (3) That the relevant Child Welfare Agency in their country of origin have declared them eligible for adoption, (4) Demonstrate that a public or state agency in their country of origin will oversee the welfare of the child.

In essence, the adoption procedure consists of parental consent, notice of the adoption proceeding, background investigation of the adoptive parents, a judicial decree of adoption and secrecy of adoption records.

A. The Adoption Application and Home Study Evaluation

In order to initiate the adoption process, the interested party must file an application for adoption with the Family Court with proper jurisdiction.

The adoption request requires the applicant to provide a brief description of themselves and a description of the child they wish to adopt. The application must be accompanied by the following documentation:

(1) Marriage certificate of the applicants;

(2) Birth certificate of each applicant;

(3) Criminal background check from applicants' country;

(4) Financial statement indicating income and assets of applicants;

(5) Certification that both applicants are in good health;

(6) Certification that the child has been declared abandoned.

Once the application is filed, the court will appoint experts who will conduct a psychological and social home study of the child and the prospective adoptive parents. The study must be completed within fifteen days of the acceptance of the appointment by the experts. If the adoptive parents are domiciled outside of Costa Rica, the home study must be conducted by the public child welfare agency where the adoptive parents reside.

B. Notice and Hearing

The law requires that the request for adoption be published in the legal newspaper, Boletin Judicial. Once published, any opposition by third parties to the adoption must be filed within five days of the date of publication. The National Child Welfare Agency (PANI) is also made a party to the proceeding.

Once the home study reports have been filed with the court, the adoptive parents, the minor child and a representative from the National Child Welfare Agency will be required to appear before the Family Court Judge for a hearing. At the hearing the judge will explain to the adoptive parents the obligations which they must undertake and require their acceptance of those obligations in open court.

C. Final Decree and Registration of the Adoption

Once the court concludes its hearing on the adoption petition, it determines whether or not it is in the best interests of the child that the adoption petition be granted based upon the circumstances of the case. If the court grants the adoption petition, a decree of adoption is entered authorizing the adoption. The decree of adoption must be registered in the Civil Registry.

Once it is registered the adoption takes legal effect and the child becomes the legal child of the adopting parents, thus creating the same relationship as between legitimate children and their natural parents. The decree of adoption and all records which are registered are confidential and may only be disclosed by the Civil Registry with a court order.

5.3 INTERNATIONAL CONSIDERATIONS

An international adoption such as the procedure described above is a viable consideration. However, in addition to the procedural requirements set out by the Costa Rican government, the adoptive parents must also take into consideration the immigration and adoption laws of their own country.

CHAPTER 8

THE LAWS OF SUCCESSION (WILLS AND TRUSTS)

1. INTRODUCTION TO WILLS

This chapter discusses the law which applies to wills. In general, a will is an instrument which is executed in accordance with certain formalities that directs the disposition of a person's property at his death. Thus, a will operates as an instrument to transfer title to real and personal property at the death of the testator. However, when a person dies without a valid will, or when the will does not make a complete disposition of the estate of the deceased, then it is said that the person died intestate and the distribution of that property is governed by the intestacy laws.

1.1 INTESTATE SUCCESSION

As previously discussed, the distribution of the property of a person who dies without a will is governed by the laws of intestacy. In Costa Rica the laws of intestacy are contained in the Civil Code which provides that in the absence or invalidity of a will the estate of the deceased will pass to the legitimate heirs. The Code defines legitimate heirs as follows:

(1) First Degree -The spouse, children and parents of the deceased subject to the following conditions:

(a) If the spouse requested and was granted a legal (judicial) separation he/she may not inherit from the estate. On the other hand, if the spouse was separated (other than by legal decree) their right to inherit from the estate is only barred as to property acquired since the separation.

(b) If the spouse is deriving income from community property (i.e. property acquired during marriage that is not separate property) then the intestates 1/2 share passes to the surviving spouse. Since it is community property the other 1/2 does not pass to the spouse by inheritance since it already belongs to the surviving spouse by virtue of the fact that it is community property.

(c) A father may only inherit from a child that was born out of wedlock if the father recognized the child with his or her mother's consent or if the child was supported by his father for two consecutive years.

(d) If an unmarried couple lived together the surviving person may inherit if both had legal capacity to marry and co-habituated together in a singular and public manner for at least three years.

(2) Second Degree -The grandparents and other legitimate ascendants.

(3) Third Degree - The natural brothers and sisters on the mother's side.

(4) Fourth Degree -The nephews of the deceased. *(The Code refers to natural and legitimate children of the brothers and sisters on the mother's side.)*

(5) Fifth Degree -The uncles of the deceased. *(The Code refers to the deceased father's legitimate brothers and non-legitimate brothers of the mother or father.)*

(6) Sixth Degree- The State. If the estate does not pass to the preceding five degrees then the Code specifically directs that the property pass directly to the Board of Education for the district in which the property of the deceased was located.

1.2 TESTAMENTARY DISPOSITION

The manner in which a person can set forth their testamentary intent is by drafting a will. If executed in accordance with legal formalities, the will directs the disposition of the person's property at their death. Generally, a will has no operative effect during the testator's life and can be revoked or amended until the testator's death.

A. Types of Wills and Formalities

The Civil Code recognizes two types of wills, the noncupative will *(open will)* and the sealed will *(closed will).*

(1) The Open Will

The Civil Code recognizes two methods of executing an open will. Those are the notarized and attested wills. *(See Appendix 26 for instrument creating an open will.)*

(a) Notarized Will- If the testator does not hand write his will then it must be executed in the presence of a Notary Public and three (3) witnesses. If the testator hand writes the will then two (2) witnesses and the Notary Public are required.

(b) Attested Will - a will may be executed without a Notary Public if it is witnessed by the testator and four (4) witnesses. If it is not hand written by the testator then six (6) witnesses must attest to it. There are four requirements to the formation of a valid open will:

(i) The will must be dated indicating the place, day, the exact time (hour), month and year in which it is executed;

(ii) The will must be read by the testator or the Notary Public in the presence of the witnesses;

(iii) The will must be signed by the testator, the Notary Public, if necessary, and by the witnesses;

(iv) The will must be simultaneously executed.

(2) The Closed Will.

The closed will may or may not be in the testator's handwriting but is drafted in such a way so that the contents of the will are not disclosed to anybody but the testator, or drafter, if any.

The Civil Code requires that the closed will be executed following certain formal requirements. Once the will is signed by the testator it must be placed in an envelope and sealed. The envelope containing the will is then taken to a Notary Public who must draft a notarized writing on the envelope itself. The notarized statement must attest that a sealed envelope containing a will was handed to the Notary by the testator and that the testator has informed him as to the number of pages contained in the will. It must also indicate that the will was written and signed by the testator and whether it contains any annotations or smudges. The Notary Public must make a record of this proceeding in his protocol book and it must be signed by the testator and three (3) Witnesses. The sealed will is then returned to the testator and upon his death it is opened before a court tribunal in the jurisdiction where the will was executed.

(3) Foreign Language Wills

Both open and closed wills may be executed in a language other than Spanish if certain legal formalities are followed. In the case of a notarized will, it is not sufficient that the Notary translate the will since the law requires that at least two interpreters sign the will along with the testator to certify that the will was translated to the testator in a language they understand. If it is an un attested will (with no notary) then the will may be drafted in the language of the testator, English for example and it is valid if all the witnesses understand the language in which the will is drafted.

(4) Privileged Wills

The Code provides for certain wills executed by certain individuals under special circumstances to be recognized at law. The most common form is the maritime will and the military will. The military will allows military personnel to execute a will by a commanding officer and two witnesses. It is merely a carryover of Roman law which allowed its soldier's to manifest their testamentary intent when in danger of death.

The maritime will on the other hand, allows maritime crew to execute a will by the ship's captain (or officer in command) and two witnesses.

B. Testamentary Capacity

It is essential for the validity of a will that the person who is executing the will understand the nature of the act that he is doing. As such, the Civil Code requires that a testator have moral and legal capacity to execute a will.

By moral capacity, the Code contemplates that the testator be of sound mind. A test established in the Uniform Probate Code of the United States is helpful in understanding this concept. Pursuant to Section 2-501 of the Uniform Probate Code a testator has requisite capacity to make a will if: (1) he has actual knowledge of the act he is undertaking; (2) he knows the natural objects of his bounty; (3) he understands the nature and extent of his property; and (4) he understood the disposition he was making.

By legal capacity the Civil Code refers to those conditions imposed by law which would prevent testamentary intent, namely age. The Civil Code specifically provides that a person under the age of fifteen is incapable of testamentary disposition.

1.3 RESTRICTIONS ON THE POWER OF TESTATION

Many civil law jurisdictions impose forced heirship provisions which limit the individual's power of testamentary disposition. In a forced heirship jurisdiction the majority of a person's property at death passes directly to their descendants regardless of those persons wishes. Costa Rica does not have a forced heirship provision. However, the Civil Code places certain restrictions on the power to dispose of the estate which are designed to provide financial support to the family of the testator.

A. The Family Allowance

The Civil Code provides that a testator is free to dispose of their property as long as they have provided for: (i) the support of their minor children until the age of majority and if the child is disabled, for life; (ii) support for their parents and spouse as required. If the testator fails to provide for this support as required, the support amount will be deducted from his estate and the balance distributed pursuant to his will.

B. Community Property

Community Property is all property that is acquired by husband and wife during their marriage. The basis of the community property system is that the property acquired during the marriage was done so as the fruit of the common labor of both husband and wife and as such both should share equally upon the termination of the marriage. Costa Rica is a community property jurisdiction.

The Civil Code does not directly address the issue of community property as it relates to testamentary disposition. Since the Civil Code allows the testator the power to freely dispose of his property it creates a unique situation when the testator attempts to dispose of property that is considered community property. This is so because the Family Code specifically provides that upon the dissolution of marriage (which can arise as a result of death) each spouse acquires a half (1/2) interest in community property. As such, when this situation arises the spouse will take a share of the estate by way of community property and in addition may be entitled to the remaining portion of the estate by way of testamentary disposition.

As an example, assume that John and Cindy both reside in Costa Rica and their only asset is their community property home valued at $100,000.

They have two children from the marriage. If John dies without a will then the Costa Rican intestate law will distribute the estate as follows taking into account the community property distribution. The spouse, Cindy receives 50% ($50,000) of the community property. This leaves an estate for distribution worth $50,000 and which is distributed as follows: The spouse, Cindy is entitled to 50% ($25,000) of the estate under the Civil Code dispositions and each of the children share equally, 25% each in the remainder of the estate.

C. Testamentary Gifts to Charity

The Civil Code places restrictions on the right to make testamentary gifts to religious organizations. Any gift to a religious organization which exceeds 10% of the testator's estate will be held invalid. These restrictions were inherited from ancient law which was concerned that testators might be inclined to favor the church over the heirs, in wills made shortly before death, out of concern for increasing their chances in the afterlife. The government was also concerned that such a disposition would result in great accumulations of wealth for the church.

1.4 SATISFACTION OF LEGACIES

When the testator provides in his will that a specific person is to be given a specific piece of property or item then this creates a legacy. The Civil Code allows any type of property or right to be bequest as long as it does not extinguish with the death of the testator.

1.5 REVOCATION OF WILLS

A. Revocation by the Testator

Under the Civil Code the testator has the power to revoke their will at any time.

(1) Revocation by Subsequent Testamentary Instrument This revocation can be accomplished by the express actions of the testator in a testamentary instrument which explicitly states that it revokes an earlier will in whole or in part. The language used by the testator in revoking an earlier will must be clear and explicit. If the second will fails to explicitly refer to the intent to revoke the first will then the second will revokes the first will only to the extent that its provisions are inconsistent with the first will.

1.6 PROBATE AND ESTATE ADMINISTRATION

Estate administration refers to the process whereby the assets of the decedent are marshaled, the debts and liabilities discharged, and the remaining assets distributed according to the will or the law of intestacy. In general, the first step in the estate administration process is to open the probate proceeding. The will of the decedent is offered for probate and its execution and validity is proven. If the decedent did not leave a will then the intestate heirs are judicially determined.

In Costa Rica there are two ways in which to probate a will. There is a judicial probate proceeding and there is a Notary probate proceeding.

A. The Judicial Proceeding

The judicial proceeding must be initiated by an interested party which can be an heir, legatee or a creditor. The petition to open the probate proceeding must include the following:

(1) Name and description of the party filing the petition,

(2) Name and description of the alleged heirs,

(3) Statement if there are children outside the marriage,

(4) Set forth all minor or disabled children,

(5) Indicate if there is a will,

(6) Set forth a list of the property left by the deceased along with the approximate value of each,
(7) Attach the certified death certificate.

 The petition is filed before the civil court that has jurisdiction over the matter. The court reviews the petition and if all the requirements have been satisfied it will issue a ruling opening the probate proceeding.

During this proceeding the authority of the executor of the estate is established. An executor known locally as an *Albacea* is a person named in the will to serve as the personal representative of the estate. If no executor is named in the will then the heirs and surviving spouse must appoint one.

1. The Role of the Personal Representative

The personal representative *(Albacea)* is given broad powers and duties required to manage and preserve the decedent's assets. The Civil Code requires the personal representative to obtain special authorization from the court in order to carry out any of the following:

(i) to execute a lease of any property of the estate; (ii) if they intend to compromise or give up any rights to property valued in excess of ¢10,000; (iii) if they intend to mortgage any assets whose value exceeds ¢10,000; (iv) on decisions whether or not to carry on the decedent's business. This authorization must be provided by way of agreement between the interested parties or in the absence of such agreement, by the judge. The personal representative has the obligation to deposit in the court registry all the income derived from the assets of the estate. Every month, the personal representative must file a statement of accounting with the court. The personal representative is entitled to compensation for his services. If the will specifies the amount or rate of compensation for the personal representative then the will provisions are binding. If the will does not provide for his compensation then the Civil Code provides that the personal representative shall be compensated 5% of the first ¢10,000 and 2.5%

for the remainder of the value of the estate. Once appointed, it is the duty of the personal representative of the estate to file with the court an inventory list of all the property belonging to the estate. In order to establish the fair market value of the property of the estate the court names an appraiser to issue a valuation of all the estate property.

2. Creditors of the Estate

Creditors of the descendant must appear in the probate proceeding to have their debts recognized by the court. This process is known as Legalización de Creditos.

3. Partition of the Estate

In order to conclude the probate proceeding the court will issue a final ruling as to the rights of all those parties that appeared within the proceeding alleging an interest in the estate. If there are no minors as beneficiaries of an estate, it is possible for the parties to the proceeding to come to a private agreement as to the manner in which the estate should be divided. If the court approves the agreement it will order partition of the property according to the terms of the agreement.

In the absence of an agreement, the court will order the distribution of the estate. However, before the proceeding is concluded the personal representative must file an accounting statement with the court and the court must approve the final accounting of the property of the estate.

B. Notary Proceeding

Under certain circumstances Costa Rican law allows a Notary Public in Costa Rica to probate a Will. This is an option available in lieu of having a judge in a judicial proceeding probate the Will. This option is only available if there are no contested issues and no children or adults of diminished capacity as beneficiaries. It requires that all interested parties personally appear before the Notary Public and manifest their acceptance to the distribution of the property as set forth in the Will. The Notary Public then publishes in the official newspaper the manifestations of the parties and allows thirty days for third parties to appear in opposition. The property of the estate is inventoried and the Notary Public names an appraiser to assess the market value of the property. Once values are fixed the Notary Public carries out the partition of the estate by recording it in a Notary protocol book and making an extraction for the public record.

1.7 PROBATE OF FOREIGN WILLS IN COSTA RICA

It is increasingly common to find a situation where a citizen of one country, the United States for example has a will drafted in a particular state of the United States but has also acquired real estate property and other assets in Costa Rica. What happens to the Costa Rican assets when that individual dies and probate is initiated in the United States and disposition of his estate is sought according to the provisions of his United States Will.

The Costa Rican Code of Civil Procedure has a special provision which allows the recognition in Costa Rica of the ruling of a foreign tribunal on estate matters. If a foreigner has property in Costa Rica and their Will is probated abroad then Costa Rica will recognize the distribution, transfers and other legal acts carried out by the foreign Court where the Will was probated. In order to have the foreign judgment recognized in Costa Rica, it will be necessary to have it authenticated and legalized by the Costa Rican Consulate with appropriate jurisdiction.

The authenticated judgment will then have to be filed in Costa Rica before the First Chamber of the Supreme Court to obtain recognition. This procedure of judgment recognition is referred locally as "Exequatur". If the Supreme Court approves the judgment it will issue a ruling to one of the lower civil courts to carry out the distribution of the property located within Costa Rica. It is advisable in the foreign proceeding that the Court clearly identifies and describes the Costa Rican assets and names an executor for the Costa Rican property since the Supreme Court will simply "recognize" the foreign judgment and will not alter, amend or modify the foreign judgment. If the description and terms of the foreign judgment are vague or the assets not fully described it may hamper processing the judgment in Costa Rica.

Another alternative in estate planning is to have a separate Will in Costa Rica which would be limited to disposition of the assets located within Costa Rica. This way the local assets are probated with the local

Will avoiding the judgment recognition proceeding. This alternative must be carefully analyzed by your legal advisor in conjunction with the will you have executed in your home country since you do not want to create any inconsistency between the two documents that could lead to confusion at the time the Wills are probated.

2. TRUSTS

A trust is any arrangement whereby property is transferred with the intention that it be administered by a trustee for the benefit of another. Generally, such a trust arises from the expressed intention of the owner of the property to create a trust with respect to the property. The law governing trusts in Costa Rica is found in the Commercial Code which provides that a trust confers to a fiduciary (trustee) property rights which the fiduciary is obligated to use pursuant to the agreement.

2.1 LEGAL FORMALITIES IN CREATING A TRUST

In general, to have a trust there must be trust property that is transferred to a trustee who in turn manages and administers the property for the benefit of designated beneficiaries. In order to accomplish this purpose, the Commercial Code sets forth several requirements.

A. Creation of the Trust

In order to create a trust it must be in writing. The written instrument must be either an "inter-vivos" trust instrument, this means that it is created during the life of the proponent (settlor), or the trust can be created by a provision in a will. A trust created by will is known as a testamentary trust.

The Commercial Code specifically prohibits the creation of the following trusts:

(a) Any trust established with a secret purpose;

(b) Any trust instrument which provides for the substitution of beneficiaries upon their death unless the substitution is made to persons that are ascertained and living when the settlor dies;

(c) If the trustee is a corporate entity its duration may not exceed thirty (30) years unless the entity is a government, or charitable non-profit organization;

(d) Any trust which assigns commissions, income, or other economic benefits to the trustee.

B. The Trustee

An individual who is named as trustee must have the capacity to acquire legal rights and to enter into contracts. In the case of corporate entities, only those whose articles of incorporation specifically authorize it to receive by contract or will trust property may act as trustee. If for any reason the named trustee is no longer available then the settlor (property owner) must name a substitute trustee. If the settlor is unable to do so, then an interested party may petition the court to name a substitute trustee. A successor trustee is not liable to the beneficiary for breaches of trust committed by a predecessor trustee unless he (i) acquiesced to the illegal acts of his predecessor; (ii) took no steps necessary to remove trust property from his predecessor; (iii) fails to take the steps necessary to cure any breach of trust perpetrated by his predecessor.

The Commercial Code allows the settlor to appoint several trustees so that they can jointly carry out the intent of the trust. If more than one trustee is named then all decisions made must be by unanimous agreement among the co-trustees.

(1) Powers and Duties of Trustee

The Code lists specific duties and obligations which the trustee must follow:

(a) The trustee must take all reasonable steps necessary to comply with the intent of the trust;

(b) Identify and register all trust property and keep trust property separate from his personal property;

(c) The trustee must keep the beneficiaries of the trust informed by providing an accounting of trust property at least once a year, unless agreed otherwise;

(d) To collect trust income;

(e) To exercise all legal rights to defend the trust and trust property.

The Code imposes additional limitations on the trustee which pertain to the trust property as follows:

(a) The trustee must act as a prudent investor when investing trust property. As such, the trustee must reasonably diversify trust investments so that no more than 1/3 of the trust property is invested in one venture;

(b) The trustee may designate another person to execute a determined act of the trust but under no circumstance may the trustee delegate his function;

(c) Any loans made with trust funds must be backed by a first mortgage on the property. The loan amount must not exceed 60% of the appraised value of the property;

(d) The trustee must pay all taxes due on trust property. If he fails to do so, the trustee becomes personally liable for the taxes due;

(e) The trustee must not encumber trust assets without express authorization to do so.

2.2 TERMINATION OF TRUSTS

The Commercial Code provides that a trust is extinguished under any of the following circumstances:

(1) The trust has accomplished the purpose for which it was created or the impossibility to accomplish the purpose for which it was created;

(2) It expires as specified in the trust instrument;

(3) There is an express agreement between the settlor and the trustee to terminate the trust;

(4) If the trust by its terms is revocable, it may be terminated by the settlor at any time;

(5) A trust may fail for the lack of a trustee and the impossibility of appointing a substitute trustee.

Once the trust is extinguished, the trust property passes to the individual indicated in the trust instrument. If no person is specified, the property reverts to the settlor and in their absence, to their heirs.

CHAPTER 9

IMMIGRATION AND NATIONALITY LAWS

The year 2004 marked the beginning of a radical shift in immigration policy in Costa Rica. In the past Costa Rica was always characterized as very laid back in the enforcement of its immigration laws. Not anymore. Tourists frequently overstayed their visas with little or no consequences and the term "perpetual tourist" was entrenched in the culture with foreigners living in Costa Rica some for decades with no legal residency status at all.

However, the financial and social problems of many South and Central American countries such as Colombia, Venezuela, Argentina, Nicaragua and Peru triggered a large amount of immigrants from those countries to enter Costa Rica as tourists and then remain here illegally. In reaction to this trend the Costa Rican immigration policy has radically shifted and the country now wants to limit the amount of foreigners that reside in the Country and has been strictly enforcing the immigration laws by conducting immigration sweeps and deporting any foreigner that is caught with an expired visa or tourist permit.

The problem with the shift in policy is that Costa Rican authorities have lumped all foreigners in the same basket. As such, individuals from countries that have traditionally brought in the vast amount of tourism revenue and investment are in many instances treated the same as those that do not positively contribute to Costa Rica. Furthermore, press leaks and declarations by government officials have created a degree of uncertainty and confusion for foreigners wishing to reside in Costa Rica.

This combined with actions by the Department of Immigration in modifying internal policies and regulations without accurately informing the general public is counterproductive to a well organized and planned immigration policy. The Department of Immigration has been extremely inefficient in processing and renewing residency permits. Although the administration of President Oscar Arias has been diligent in overhauling the immigration procedures and weeding out corrupt officials it has certainly been a big challenge and the battle has not been won as of this edition.

1. THE IMMIGRATION LAWS

As of this edition, the Costa Rican laws which govern immigration are found in the General Law of Immigration No. 8487 which came into effect in August of 2006. The administration and enforcement of Costa Rican immigration laws rests with the Department of Immigration *(Dirección General de Migración y Extranjería)*. This department is under the direction of the Ministry of Public Security *(Ministerio de Seguridad Pública)*. The law also creates the National Immigration Council *(Consejo Nacional de Migración y Extranjería)* which is made up of one representative from the Ministry of Foreign Relations, Ministry of Government and Police, Ministry of Public Security, Ministry of Labor and Ministry of Justice and the Costa Rican Tourism Institute. The purpose of the immigration council is to (1) Propose the national immigration policy, (2) Carry out the immigration guidelines established by the executive branch, (3) Establish selection criteria for the admission of foreigners to Costa Rica, (4) To review and recommend on residency petitions filed before the Department of Immigration, (5) To propose modifications to immigration policy in order to improve it and adapt it to the needs of the country.

1.1 THE DUTIES OF THE DEPARTMENT OF IMMIGRATION

The General Law of Immigration defines the functions of the Department of Immigration as follows:

(1) The Department of Immigration is responsible for issuing entry visas to immigrants in accordance with the admission criteria established by law;

(2) It is responsible for granting extensions of stay to aliens who have entered the country;

(3) If an alien has entered the country under a temporary or non-resident category, the Department of Immigration has the authority to reclassify the immigration status of the alien;

(4) The Department of Immigration has the authority to legalize the

status of any illegal alien.

(5) It must document and tabulate the arrivals and departures of international passengers to and from Costa Rica;

(6) It has the authority to deny admission into the country to aliens as provided by law;

(7) If an alien cannot prove his lawful admission into the country, the Department of Immigration has the power to declare that individual's presence in the country as illegal;

(8) It may revoke or cancel an alien's status of "permanent resident" or "temporary residency" as provided by law;

(9) It may cancel the permit for entry and presence of aliens within Costa Rica as provided by law;

(10) It may order the deportation of any alien as provided by law; (11) It has the authority to issue exit and re-entry visas to aliens as necessary;

(12) It has the authority to issue passports and exit visas to Costa Rican citizens traveling abroad;

(13) It is in charge of issuing identity cards to aliens who have been legally admitted as permanent residents.

1.2 VISA PROCESSING

A visa is a permit to enter or exit the country. A visa to enter Costa Rica is required of all foreign citizens unless their country of origin is covered by bilateral treaties or international agreements that waive the visa requirement.

When a visa is required to be admitted to Costa Rica that visa must be applied for in the Costa Rican consulate abroad. Costa Rica has the following categories in granting visas.

(1) No Visa required and up to 90 day stays. The citizens of these countries may enter Costa Rica without a visa and can remain in the coun-

try as tourists for up to 90 days. Some of the countries included in this category are: United States, Canada, Germany, Great Britain, Argentina, Belgium, Brazil, France, Spain, Holland, Italy, Israel, Japan, Panama; Portugal, South Korea; Sweden, Switzerland.

(2) No Visa required and up to 30 day stays. As with the previous category these citizens do not require a visa to enter Costa Rica and remain as tourists for 30 days. Some of the countries included in this category are: Saudi Arabia, Australia, Belize, Chile, Taiwan, El Salvador, Philippines, Guatemala, Honduras, Mexico, Turkey and Venezuela.

(3) Visa required for 30 day stay. The citizens of these countries must apply for a visa at the Costa Rican consulate in their country prior to travelling to Costa Rica. If granted, the consulate will authorize their entry for 30 days. Some of the countries included in this category are: Colombia, Nicaragua, Ecuador, Egypt, Greece, India, Malaysia, Peru, and Thailand.

(4) Visa Required but Restricted. Visas to citizens of these countries are restricted and must be applied for in the Costa Rican consulate at the country of origin. Some of the countries included in this category are: Armenia, Bangladesh, Vietnam, Cambodia, Cuba, China, Iran, and Nigeria.

For a complete list of the visa requirements you can visit the internet web page of the Costa Rican Department of Immigration at www.migracion.go.cr.

A. Visa Categories

The Costa Rican government grants two types of entry visas. Category [A] visas are issued to individuals who seek either temporary or permanent resident status. A category [B] visa is issued to those not seeking resident status such as tourists.

(1) The Category A Visas:

Category [A] visas are subdivided into two main categories: permanent resident visas and temporary resident visas.

(a) Permanent Resident Visa Categories

Individuals who seek permanent resident status fall into four categories: A1 for Immigrant visas; A2 for Rentista and Pensioner status; A3 for Investor status; and A4 for alien relatives of a Costa Rican citizen (i.e. spouse, children, parents, and unmarried brothers and sisters).

(b) Temporary Resident Visa Categories

Individuals who seek admission to Costa Rica as temporary residents will fall into one of the following categories:

A5- This visa is for scientists, professional, technical and specialized personnel who are hired by corporations or institutions established in Costa Rica to carry out work within their specialty or trade.

A6-This visa category applies to executive and management personnel of national or international business enterprises.

A7 – This is a student visa.

A8 - Religious personnel.

A9 -This category applies to those individuals who have been granted political asylum or refugee status.

A10 – This is for the spouse and children of the applicant to visa categories A5 through A9.

(2) Category B Visas

Category [B] visas apply to those individuals who do not seek permanent or temporary residence in the country. Generally, stays in Costa Rica under this category are brief. The category [B] visas are subdivided into the following categories:

B1 - Tourists

B2 - Individuals with scientific, professional, cultural, economic, or political expertise who have been invited to the country by a governmental, public or private institution.

B3 - Travel agents (They may not take purchase orders or sell products while in the country.)

B4 - Commercial delegations.

B5 -Artists, athletes or participants of any public attraction or entertainment.

B6 - Passengers who are in transit.

B7 - The crew of international transport vessels.

B8 - Migrant workers.

1.3 THE RESIDENCY CATEGORIES

The current immigration law divides residency categories into either Permanent Residency or Temporary Residency.

A. Permanent Resident Status

The Permanent residency category means that you can live and work in Costa Rica since it is generally granted without limitations. Since 2006 there are only two ways to acquire permanent residency in Costa Rica:

(1) Family Unification. The foreigner who is related in the first degree to a Costa Rican citizen. This means the parents, minor children or children of the age of majority with a disability, minor siblings or siblings of the age of majority with disability, and those that are married to a Costa Rican citizen.

(2) Temporary Residents for Three Years. A foreigner their spouse and related family in the first degree that have held Temporary Residency status for three consecutive years.

B. Temporary Resident Status

The Temporary Residency category can be granted to those applicants that qualify for the status which allows them to reside in Costa Rica for a maximum period of two years. Upon expiration of the term an application for renewal of the status would have to file with the Department of Immigration. Those that are approved under the Temporary Residency category may own their own business but may not work for others without the written approval of the Department of Immigration.

Temporary Residency has the following subcategories under which a foreigner may apply:

(1) The spouse of a Costa Rican citizen.

(2) The executives, representatives, general managers or technical staff of companies which have set up operations in the Country in areas defined by the government as priority investment areas. This category will also extend to the spouse and child of the applicant. This category makes it easier for multinational companies to bring their management and technical staff to Costa Rica.

(3) Investors. This category is designed for individuals that come to Costa Rica to invest in the Country. Under the new immigration law the minimum investment required is US$200,000. Furthermore, the applicant must demonstrate that the investment made will provide an economic and social benefit to Cost Rica. The law specifically excludes personal investments such as purchase of home, lots or buildings to qualify for this status. To apply for this status you will have to provide financial statements audited by a Certified Public Accountant to document the financial investment plan that is proposed. The granting of this status is completely discretionary by the Department of Immigration. As such just because you apply there is no guarantee of approval.

(4) The Retiree (Pensionado) and Income Recipient *(Rentista)* Category

This immigration category dates back to 1971 when Costa Rica established the status in order to attract retirees to the country in order to help the country boost its foreign reserves and investment. The revised immigration law (Law 8487) repealed the 1971 program but maintained both of these categories in the new law.

A. Pensionado Status

Individuals who receive a fixed pension of at least six hundred dollars per month (US$600) qualify for the status of Pensionado. The pension can come from a government or private company.

B. Rentista Status

Those that do not have a fixed pension but have a permanent and stable source of income of at least one thousand dollars per month (US$1,000) can qualify for the status of Rentista. If you apply with your spouse for this category then you will have to demonstrate an income of US$2,000 per month. If you have minor children or students under the age of twenty five or with a disability they may also qualify as your dependents under this category if you demonstrate an additional five hundred dollars per month (US$500) per child

What qualifies as a permanent and stable source of income is up to the Department of Immigration. In practice the most common way to qualify is to provide the Department of Immigration with a letter from either a local or internationally recognized bank or financial institution stating that you have deposits or investments with them that generate at least the minimum required by the Costa Rican immigration law.

The Department of Immigration requires that the letter specifically state that the income generated is in a permanent and stable manner. It is important that you keep in mind that in order to renew the residency status under either the Pensionado or Rentista category the applicant must demonstrate that the income requirements were satisfied and that the funds were exchanged into Costa Rican currency in Costa Rica. Since this category is only good for two years you will need to ensure that the source of income that was the basis for your application is in place when you file your renewal. If you do not have the funds available to you at the time of renewal you may risk losing your immigration status.

• *Quick Reference:* Pensionado and Rentista Immigration Status

Pensionado: Income required US$600 per month
Rentista: Income required US$1,000 per month.
              If applying jointly with spouse then US$2,000 per month.

Length of Status: 2 Years and then must renew.

Residency Requirement: Must reside in Costa Rica at least 6 months.

(5) Other Temporary Residency Categories.

a. The representatives of those Religious organizations which have been recognized by the Ministry of Foreign Relations. This category is aimed at individuals that work or represent religious orders such as priests and nuns for example.

b. Scientists, Professionals and Technicians.

This category requires a letter from the Costa Rican Ministry of Labor indicating that the applicant will not displace a Costa Rican worker.

c. News and Press Agency Correspondents

d. Those that are married or have minor children or persons with a disability to any of the individuals that have Temporary Resi dency as set out in the law.

1.4 THE RESIDENCY APPLICATION PROCESS

All residency applications must be filed through the Costa Rican Embassy or Consulate located in your country of origin. For a complete list of the Costa Rican Embassies or Consulates located abroad you can visit the website of the Ministry of Foreign Relations at http://www.rree.go.cr/servicio-exterior/ The only exception to this filing requirement are applications for Permanent Residency under the family reunification status. Those applications can be filed directly in Costa Rica with the Department of Immigration.

Each category will have requirements which are specific for the particular status that you are applying for. However, regardless of the category the applicant must provide the following when applying for residency status.

1. Residency Application.   There is no specific form that is used as the application. The law requires the applicant to set out on paper the (a) The basis for the application and reasons for applying. (b) Full name of the applicant, nationality, date of birth, occupation, intended address in Costa Rica, full name and nationality of the Applicants parents. (c) Set forth an address for personal service within the judicial

perimeter of San Jose. (d) Date of the application.

The application must be signed and authenticated by either a Costa Rican Consular Officer or a Costa Rican Notary Public. Without the proper authentication the application will not be processed. You can represent yourself before the Department of Immigration or hire an Attorney to do it for you. If you hire an Attorney you will need to confer to them a Special Power of Attorney so that they can represent you before the Department of Immigration.

   2. Supporting documents. Your residency application must be accompanied by your supporting documents. All supporting documents must be certified and authenticated by the Costa Rican Consulate in the country where the document was issued. The typical process requires you to obtain an original or certified copy of the original document. With that document in hand you will then need to have the document certified by the appropriate agency or department. In the United States for example the certifying department is generally the Secretary of State for the particular state where the document was issued. Once your document has been properly certified then you can deliver it to the Costa Rican Embassy or Consulate with proper jurisdiction that will then proceed with the authentication process. You're not done yet! From there the documents must be presented to the Costa Rican Ministry of Foreign Relations in Costa Rica who will authenticate the Consular certifications.

   (a) Certificate of Birth. Your application must contain your birth certificate as well as those of any of your dependents that area applying for status as well. The birth certificate must be certified and authenticated by the Costa Rican consulate in the country where it was issued.

   (b) Police Certificate. You must provide a Police Clearance Certificate which indicates that you do not have a criminal record. The police certificate can come from your local police department. The police certificate must also be authenticated by the Costa Rican consulate abroad and is only good for three months from the date of issue. After three months, the Department of Immigration will not accept it and you will have to provide a new one.

   (c) Marriage Certificate. If you are married and applying for dependent status for your spouse then you must provide a certified marriage certificate and have it authenticated by the Costa Rican consulate where the certificate was issued.

(d)   Fingerprints. The applicant will be fingerprinted in Costa Rica by the Ministry of Public Security and the prints will be sent to Interpol for a background search on the applicant.

(e) Passport Copy. You must provide a copy of the entire passport. The copies must be certified as authentic by wither the Costa Rican Consular Officer or a Costa Rican Notary Public.

(f) Proof of Income. If you are applying for Rentista or Pensionado Status you will need to provide a letter to prove either pension or investment income. If the letter is based on investment income then be sure that the wording of the letter complies with the requirements of the law. To do so, the letter must indicate that the applicant will receive the income in Costa Rican in a permanent and stable manner for five years.

(g) Photographs. The applications require three photographs facing front.

(h) Translations. All documents that you submit with your application indicated above must be translated into Spanish by an official translator. The Costa Rican Ministry of Foreign Relations has a list of authorized translators.

(i) Immigration Data Sheet *(Formulario de Filiación)*. This form can be downloaded from the Department of Immigration web site at www.migracion.go.cr The form must be filled out and attached to your application.

(j) Application fees. The application fee is US$30 which must be paid by direct deposit to the account of the Department of Immigration with Banco de Costa Rica. The Application must also pay documentary stamps *(especies fiscales)* which are 125 Colones on the application and 2.50 Colones for each page of the application.

The application and the supporting documents must then be filed with the Costa Rican Embassy or Consular Official with proper jurisdiction.

If the documentation is in order, the file is forwarded to the Department of Immigration who will assign a case file number to the application.

Depending on the basis for the application, it can take anywhere from five months to one year for the residency application to wind itself through the process. The time frame depends on the amount of applications that are pending at the time.

The application first goes before the legal department of Immigration which reviews all the documents to ensure they comply with the requirements of the law. If a document is missing or they want you to correct the wording on a document they will notify you of the errors that must be corrected. You must correct any errors or notices provided to you by the Department of Immigration in order for the processing of the application to continue.   Most notices sent by the Department of Immigration are time sensitive. The Department of Immigration has been enforcing a time deadline for correcting documents which ranges from fifteen to thirty days. If you do not respond to the request issued by the Department of Immigration in their notice they may close out the file and require you to file a new application all over again.

On the other hand, if all the documents are in order the legal department will forward the file to the Immigration Council (Consejo de Migracion) which meets at least once a month and votes on the application. If approved, the Immigration Council will issue a written resolution recommending the approval of the application and returning the file to the Director of Immigration who will in turn issue a ruling from the Department of Immigration conferring upon the applicant the residency status. Your status begins on the date the resolution is signed by the Department of Immigration. With the resolution in hand you must now appear before the Department of Immigration who will issue the residency identification card *(Cédula de Residencia).*

Prior to retrieving the residency card the applicant must deposit to the order of the Costa Rican government the sum of three hundred dollars ($300). This payment is nonrefundable and charged to cover the administrative costs

• *Quick Reference*- Document Authentication

   • Obtain a certified copy of your birth certificate, police certificate and marriage certificate, if applicable.

• Have the Secretary of State in the state where you reside authenticate your certified documents.

• Have the Costa Rican consulate in your jurisdiction authenti cate the signature of the Secretary of State.

• In Costa Rica have the Ministry of Foreign Relations authen ticate the signature of the Costa Rican consul.

All the original documents that you submit with your application become the property of the Department of Immigration and you will not get them back so keep this in mind when compiling your documentation.

In order to renew your Rentista or Pensionado card you will need to file a written request for renewal to the Department of Immigration and provide Proof that you have exchanged the required minimum from Dollars to Colones.

Under the current immigration law, after three years of residing in Costa Rica under the Pensionado or Rentista category the resident may request a change of status to permanent residency before the Department of Immigration. When switching status the applicant should be aware that he must qualify for the permanent residency requirements and be aware that he must also apply for the cancellation of the Pensionado/Rentista status. It is best to wait until the Permanent Residency application is ruled upon before cancelling the Pensionado/Rentista status.

1.5 RENEWAL OF YOUR RESIDENCY STATUS.

If you have Permanent Residency it is granted free of conditions and no renewal is required. Your identification card (*Cedula de Residencia*) would have to be renewed every 5 years.

If you have Temporary Residency it is valid for a maximum of two years which means you will have to file a written application to renew your status. In the past two years the government became so overwhelmed with renewal requests that it started issuing Executive decrees which automatically renewed all residency status for additional terms. The government claims that it is working on technology that will assist it with the renewal process. At the present time the renewal process is cumbersome and appointments given by the Department of Immigration to renew a status takes between 8 to 11 months.

1.6 COSTS AND LEGAL REPRESENTATION

You can certainly process your residency application on your own without legal assistance but many find that to be very frustrating and time consuming. An Attorney who has experience in immigration processing is essential if you want a smooth application process. Find an Attorney that will be up front regarding your options and qualifications for the available categories.

The fees charged by Attorneys vary significantly depending on the residency category you are applying for. The more complicated the category the more you will be charged. Fees range from $750 to $2,500 depending on the complexity involved. Be wary if you are asked to pay all the money up front without proof that your application has an assigned file number with the Department of Immigration.

1.7 RIGHTS AND OBLIGATIONS OF FOREIGN RESIDENTS

In general, foreign residents of Costa Rica are guaranteed the same individual and social rights as Costa Ricans. However, foreign residents are prohibited from interfering in the political affairs of the country and are subject to the jurisdiction of the Costa Rican authorities and courts unless an international treaty provides otherwise.

Foreign residents in Costa Rica who are legally authorized to work in the country are subject to the protection of Costa Rica's labor and social legislation.

1.8 CANCELLATION OF RESIDENCY STATUS

The Department of Immigration may cancel the residency status of any foreigner with the resulting loss in immigration status under any of the following conditions:

a) If the resident does not comply with the requirements and conditions imposed when their residency status was granted

b) f the resident participates in national political elections.

c) If the resident does contribute with taxes and public expenditures when he is obligated to do so.

d) If the resident enters or leaves the country without doing so
through official immigration border control posts.

e) If the resident has been convicted either in Costa Rica or abroad
for crimes punished under the Costa Rican criminal law including crimes against life, genocide, acts of terrorism, drug trafficking, human trafficking, fraud, conspiracy, weapons trafficking or illegal possession, sexual abuse of minors, trafficking in
cultural, ecological and archeological artifacts, tax evasion, domestic violence, crimes against minors the elderly or those with
a disability, Those associated with gangs or criminal organizations.

f) Permanent Residents that are absent from Costa Rica for more
than one consecutive year unless they have a justifiable reason
based upon health, educational, or family reasons.

g) Temporary Residents that are absent from Costa Rica for more
than six consecutive months unless they have a justifiable reason based upon health, educational, or family reasons.

h) If the Resident obtained their residency status by way of false
declarations or by presenting false or altered documents.

i) Are working for remuneration without authorization to do so.

j) Those that the Department of Immigration deem to compromise
Public Security, Public Order or the Costa Rican way of life.

k) Those that don't renew their immigration status within three
months of its expiration date unless the delay is properly justified.

l) If the residency was granted based upon marriage with a Costa Rican citizen and the marriage was done with the sole purpose of obtaining an immigration benefit.

1.9 EXCLUSION, DEPORTATION & EXPULSION

Exclusion occurs when an Immigration Officer at a point of entry denies a foreigner entry into Costa Rican by ordering the return of that individual to their point of origin. Costa Rican law authorizes immigration officers to exclude foreigners in the following cases: (1) When they do not arrive with the necessary documentation to authorize their admission, (2) Those affected by contagious diseases which could create a public health hazard, (3) Those recognized internationally as drug traffickers and those who are engaged in prostitution, (4) Those convicted of criminal offenses which according to Costa Rican law would carry a one year prison sentence. (5) Those that have been deported or expelled from the country (6) Those whose backgrounds may threaten national security or public order, (7) Those who enter the country attempting to avoid immigration controls, (8) Those that appear on the Department of Immigration's undesirable list. There are no appeals to an order of exclusion issued by a Costa Rican immigration official.

A deportation is an act by which the Department of Immigration places a foreigner located within Costa Rica outside of its border. Before the foreigner can be deported the Department of Immigration must open an administrative deportation file which shall contain all the facts, investigations, interrogations and witness statements to substantiate the request for deportation. The following situations allow the deportation of the individual: (1) Entering Costa Rica illegally, (2) Entering the country or obtaining residency by giving false statements or providing false documents, (3) Remaining within the country after the expiration of the entry visa or authorized time limit, (4) Remaining within the country after the residency status has been cancelled. The deportation proceeding is a summary proceeding and the Immigration Police are authorized to carry out all orders of deportation.

An Expulsion action is an order issued by the Ministry of Public Security against a resident of any category or status ordering the individual to leave the country because their presence and activities pose a national security risk or alter the tranquility and public order of the country.

2. NATIONALITY

The laws governing Costa Rican citizenship and nationality are found in the Costa Rican Constitution and the Law of Naturalization No. 7033 of August 4, 1986.

2.1 COSTA RICAN CITIZENSHIP

The Costa Rican Constitution provides that Costa Rican citizenship may be acquired by birth or by naturalization.

A. Citizenship by Birth

The following individuals acquire Costa Rican citizenship at birth:

(1) A child born in Costa Rica of a Costa Rican father and mother;

(2) The child of a Costa Rican father and mother who is born abroad and registered in the National Registry by his parents while he is a minor or if the child registers himself prior to his 25th birthday;

(3) The child born in Costa Rica whose parents are foreigners, if the child is registered by his parents as a Costa Rican while he is a minor, or if the child registers himself prior to his 25th birthday;

(4) The child who is deemed abandoned and found in Costa Rican territory.

B. Citizenship by Naturalization

The following individuals are eligible to acquire Costa Rican citizenship by naturalization:

(1) Those who have acquired citizenship by virtue of prior laws;

(2) Nationals of other Central American countries, the citizens of Spain and other Ibero Americans by birth who have resided in Costa Rica for five years and comply with other requirements of law;

(3) Central Americans, Spaniards, Ibero Americans not by birth and other foreigners who have officially resided in Costa Rica for a min-

imum of seven years and also comply with the requisites established by law;

(4) Women who have lost their citizenship by virtue of marriage;

(5) Any foreigner who has lost their nationality by having married a Costa Rican citizen. Also, a foreigner who has been married to a Costa Rican citizen for at least two years and has resided in Costa Rica for two years and who manifest their desire to acquire Costa Rican citizenship.

(6) Recipients of honorary citizenship as conferred by the Legislative Assembly.

2.2 THE NATURALIZATION PROCESS

In order to initiate the naturalization process, the petitioner must draft an application for naturalization which certifies that the applicant is:

(1) More than 21 years of age;

(2) That he has been a resident of Costa Rica and complied with the residency requirements imposed by Article 14 of the Constitution. This can be proven by documentation and the sworn testimony of four witnesses;

(3) That the petitioner is of good conduct and has a profession and or assets that will enable him to support himself and his family, if any;

(4) That he has not been convicted for criminal offenses while residing in the country. This must be done by providing a police certificate to that effect;

(5) That he is current in his tax liabilities;

(6) That he intends to continuously reside in the country and is willing to renounce his prior nationality if required.

The written petition for naturalization must be signed and authenticated and filed with the naturalization section of the Civil Registry Office. The Civil Registry gives public notice of the petition for naturalization by publishing it for ten working days. During this time anyone opposed to the naturalization may file a statement in opposition. If a statement in opposition is filed the petitioner has eight days in which to provide testimony and proof to contradict the opposition. Once this time has elapsed the Civil Registry must issue its final decision either granting or denying the petition for naturalization. Once the petition for naturalization is approved and signed, the registry will indicate the change in nationality by way of a written document signed by the Director of the Civil Registry.

2.3 DUAL CITIZENSHIP

The Costa Rican Constitution was amended in 1996 to recognize dual citizenship. As modified, a Costa Rican citizen may not resign or lose their nationality. This modification came about as a result of an administrative proceeding initiated by the Department of Immigration which took away the Costa Rican citizenship of Dr. Franklin Chang, scientist and NASA Astronaut because he had become a citizen of the United States of America. Dr. Chang who is a local icon was born in Costa Rica, but became a citizen of the United States of America. Since the existing legislation specifically prohibited dual citizenship, the Department of Immigration stripped Dr. Chang of his Costa Rican citizenship. This action by the government created a public backlash and criticism. In response, the Costa Rican Legislature first restored Dr. Chang's Costa Rican citizenship and subsequently repealed the provisions of the Constitution which prohibited dual citizenship in order to avoid a similar circumstance from occurring in the future.

CHAPTER 10

INTELLECTUAL PROPERTY LAWS

Intellectual Property are ideas, inventions, creative expressions or information which have a commercial value and are thus given protection by law to ensure those property rights.

Intellectual Property is divided into: (1) Artistic and literary property, (2) Industrial property and (3) Commercial and Industrial Secrets. Since Costa Rica joined the World International Property Organization (WIPO), a specialized agency of the United Nations whose mandate is to promote the protection of intellectual property worldwide it has been under pressure to implement the guidelines established in the WIPO treaties namely the WIPO Copyright Treaty and the WIPO Performances and Phonograms Treaty. You can view the WIPO treaties at their internet web site www.wipo.org.

To that end, in 2000, the Costa Rican legislature ratified the World International Property Organization treaties and extensively modified its intellectual property laws to comply with those international treaty agreements by passing the following laws related to Intellectual Property. (1) Law No. 7968 Approving the WIPO Treaty on Copyright Law (WCT), (2) Law No. 7967 Approving the WIPO Treaty on Performances and Phonograms (WPP). (3) Law No. 7979, Law Reforming the Copyright Law and Law on Industrial Property and Inventions. (4) Law No. 7978, Law of Trademarks and other distinctive Marks. (5) Law No. 7982, Approval of the Central American Treaty on the Protection of Industrial Property. (6) Law No. 7975, Law on Trade and Commercial Secrets. These six laws came into effect in the year 2000 and shall be discussed in more detail in the following sections.

1. ARTISTIC AND LITERARY PROPERTY

The protection of artistic and literary property includes written material such as books and articles as well as recordings and other forms of artistic expression

1.1. COPYRIGHT PROTECTION

Copyright refers to the right granted by law to an author or originator of certain literary or artistic productions, whereby that individual is invested, for a limited period, with the sole and exclusive privilege of multiplying copies of the same and publishing and selling them.

In Costa Rica, copyright law is governed by Law No. 6683 of October 14, 1982, *Ley de Derechos de Autor y Derechos Conexos,* and its amendments, the most recent of which came into effect in February of 2000 by way of Law No. 7979 to comply with the World Intellectual Property Organization Treaty and Law No. 7968 which approved the World Intellectual Property Organization Treaty on Copyright Law and came into effect on February 1, of 2000.

Copyright protection extends to expressions and not to ideas, procedures, methods of operation, or mathematical concepts as such. In general terms, copyright protection can be requested to protect literary works, musical compositions, photographic work, graphic and sculptural works, motion pictures, computer programming, and sound recordings among others.

A. How to Apply for a Copyright

The copyright process is initiated by filing an application for registration with the copyright office which is located in the National Registry in the capital city of San José. The copyright application must contain (1) the name and address of the author or their legal representative if any; (2) name and address of the author, publisher and printer; (3) the title, description of the work to be copyrighted and place and date of publication; (4) a detailed description of the work. In the case of computer programs, the law requires a copy of the program, description and program manuals. The application must be authenticated by an attorney and contain the documentary stamps required by law.

(I) Deposit Requirements

The law provides for special deposit requirements for many types of works as follows:

(1) Published Works: The law requires that any work reproduced

in print or by magnetic, electronic, electromagnetic or other means, must deposit a copy with each of the following institutions no later than 8 days after the initial publication: The University of Costa Rica; The State University for Distant Studies, National University; the library of the Legislative Assembly; The National Library; The library of the Ministry of Justice; the National Archives; The Costa Rican Technological Institute, and the Copyright Registry.

(2) Unpublished Works: A work may be registered in unpublished form by providing one typewritten copy signed by the author and authenticated by an attorney to the Registry of Copyright office.

(3) Artistic Works: Deposit for artistic works such as paintings, sculptures, drawings or other three dimensional works, may be done by providing a detailed description of the characteristics of the work together with photographs of the work.

(4) Architectural Plans, Maps etc.: To register plans, sketches, maps, photographs, and phonograms, a copy must be placed on deposit with the Registry of Copyrights.

(5) Computer Programs: To register computer programs the author must provide a copy of the computer disk containing the program along with a sworn statement attesting to the contents of the disk.

(6) Motion Pictures: If the work is a motion picture, the deposit requirement is one complete copy of the script, dialogue, scenery and music and a copy of the film footage.

(II) Notice and Certification of Copyright

Once the application for copyright registration has been accepted by the Copyright Registry, the Registrar shall order the publication of notice of the copyright application in the official newspaper, La Gaceta. The publication will run for thirty (30) days and if no opposition is voiced during that time the copyright registration is deemed effective. Proof of copyright registration may be obtained by requesting a certificate of registration from the Registry of Copyright. This registration constitutes proof that the work is registered in the name of the certificate holder.

B. The Duration and Protection of the Copyright

1. Copyright Duration

The Costa Rican copyright law provides that an author retains the personal inalienable and perpetual right in their copyrighted work. The work is automatically protected for a term enduring for the author's life, plus an additional seventy (70) years after the author's death in the case of physical persons. If the copyright holder is not a physical person then the copyright lasts for seventy years (70) from the end of the year in which the work was originally published or disseminated to the public. In the case of a joint-work prepared by two or more authors the seventy year period begins to run upon the death of the last surviving co-author.

During this time frame, the copyright law gives the owner of the copyright the exclusive right to do and to authorize others to (a) edit the copyrighted work, (b) reproduce the copyrighted work, (c) translate the copyrighted work to other languages or dialects, (d) the adaptation of the copyrighted work to phonograms, video, movies or other audiovisual sources, (e) communicate or transmit the copyrighted work directly or indirectly to the public, (f) make available the copyrighted work to the public, (g) the distribution of the copyrighted work, (h) the transmission of the copyrighted material by radio or other public transmission including cable, fiber optics, microwave, satellite or any other means, (i) import into the country of copyrighted material without authorization (j) utilize any other means or process on the copyrighted material known or which may be known in the future.

2. Copyright Protection

In the past the major complaint of copyright holders has been the inability to effectively enforce their rights against third parties within the Costa Rican judicial system. In order to bring the enforcement procedures in line with those of the World Intellectual Property Organization Treaties signed by Costa Rica, the legislature passed Law No. 8039 on October 12, 2000, Law for the Procedures to Protect Intellectual Property Rights *(Ley de Procedimientos de Observancia de*

Los Derechos de Propiedad Intelectual). The law provides for administrative and civil remedies for copyright violations including criminal sanctions. In addition, the law confers upon the Intellectual Property Office the power to order precautionary actions including injunctions prohibiting the dissemination and reproduction of copyrighted material and confiscation of false or illegal merchandise.

Criminal penalties including prison for up to three years may be imposed for those adjudicated guilty of any of the following: (1) Communicating or disseminating to the public literary or artistic works that are copyrighted. (2) Communicating or disseminating to the public phonograms, video grams or transmissions including satellite transmission. (3) Copyrighting or publishing works that belong to others. (4) Adapting, modifying, translating protected works. (4) Manufacturing, importing, selling or leasing satellite decoders, (5) Altering the electronic information recorded to protect the copyright holder.

2. TRADEMARKS AND COMMERCIAL NAMES

2.1 TRADEMARKS

A trademark is generally synonymous with a brand name. That is, trademarks and brand names identify a certain product or service as coming from a particular company. In Costa Rica the law on trademark protection is governed by Law No. 7978 Law on Trademarks and Other Distinctive Signs *(Ley de Marcas y Otros Signos Distintivos)* which came into effect on February 1, 2000, through the Protocol to the Central American Agreement on the Protection of Industrial Property and the Paris Convention for the Protection of Industrial Property.

A. What is a Trademark

The law defines a trademark as any word, name, symbol, or any other graphic or material means which uniquely distinguishes the products, goods, or services of one person or entity from those of the same class but belonging to another. As such, the critical element in a trademark is that it identifies and distinguishes one product from another.

The law is also applicable to trade names and slogans. A trade name is a name used to identify a particular commercial business or enterprise. A slogan is any phrase, design, or print which is used to attract the attention of the public to a particular product, company, or service.

B. What can be Registered

The law allows the registration of any word, name, symbol, or any other graphic or material means which uniquely distinguishes the products, goods, or services.

1. Trademarks That Cannot be Registered

The law prohibits the registration of some of the following as trademarks:

(a) A form which confers a functional or technical advantage to a product or service; (b) a sign or indication which in the common language or the commercial use of the country is a common designation for the product or service involved; (c) a color when viewed independently; (d) a letter or digit when considered independently; (e) if the requested mark does not have sufficient distinctiveness in relation to the product or service to which it applies;(f) if it is contrary to morals and public order; (g) if it has elements which may offend or ridicule persons, ideas, religions or national symbols; (h) if it may cause confusion as to the geographic origin or nature of production of the product; (i) if it is identical or similar to a trademark which may have expired and not renewed during the 6 month priority period after expiration;(j) if it reproduces, imitates in any manner the emblems, signs, denominations or abbreviations of any governmental or international organization without their authorization; (k) if it reproduces, imitates in any manner the official sign or stamp to signify quality control adopted by any governmental or public entity; (l) if it reproduces the coin or currency of any country or territory including negotiable instruments, commercial documents, seals, and stamps; (m) if it includes or reproduces any medals, awards, diploma's or other elements that may lead one to believe that those awards have been conferred to the product or service unless officially authorized; (n) if it is made up of any plant variety protected in Costa Rica or other foreign country.

C.   The Trademark Application Procedure

In order to request a trademark registration the applicant must file a trademark application with the Intellectual Property Office of the National Registry. If the applicant is not located within Costa Rica they can confer a Special Power of Attorney to be represented in Costa Rica during the registration process.

The application should contain the following: (a) Name and address of the applicant. (b) Place of incorporation and residence if the applicant is a corporate entity. (c) Name of the legal representative, if applicable. (d) If the applicant does not have a domicile or commercial establishment in Costa Rica they must provide the name and address of their local representative. (e) The name of the trademark which is being requested. (f) If the trademark includes a graphic design, logo and color then the application must be accompanied by fifteen color copies of the trademark design. (f) A translation into Spanish of the trademark is requested when it is in a language other than Spanish. (g) A list of the names of the products or services for which the trademark is being used or will be used setting forth the international classification for which trademark protection is being applied for. (h) Any authorizations, if applicable for the particular trademark. (i) If the trademark is already registered in another country or countries then provide an official certification from the Intellectual Property office in the country of origin. (j) Proof of payment of the application fee.

The fee is based upon the base salary of a level I government employee. Since the wage scale changes so will the fees and as such you should consult with the Intellectual Property Office to determine the applicable fee when your application will be submitted. *(See Appendix 29 for Sample Trademark Application)*

Once the application is filed at the Intellectual Property Office it is reviewed by the Registrar to which it was randomly assigned who must ensure that the application complies with the applicable law and that the trademark protection requested is not prohibited by law. If defects are found in the application, the Registrar will notify the applicant of them in writing and the applicant will have fifteen (15) days from the date of service to correct any defects or the application will be deemed abandoned. If the application and supporting documentation are in order, the Registrar will authorize the applicant to publish notice of the trademark application in the official newspaper, *La Gaceta*, for three (3) days during a two week period.

Anybody who wishes to oppose the registration of the trademark may file an opposition in writing before the Intellectual Property Office within two (2) months after the first publication. The notice of opposition must set forth the legal basis to substantiate a denial of the registration process. The opponent to a trademark application must present evidence within thirty (30) days of filing the written opposition. The applicant is then given sixty (60) days in which to reply to the opponent.

Once all the writings are received and reviewed by the Registrar they will issue a written decision as to their findings and conclusions. The decision of the Registrar may be appealed to the head of the Department and that decision may in turn be appealed to the Administrative Court *(Contencioso Administrativo)*.

D. Effect and Duration of the Registration

The registration of a trademark is granted for ten (10) years from the date of registration. The registration may be renewed for additional ten year periods. Once a certificate of registration is issued, it establishes ownership of the trademark, trade name, or slogan. The owner then acquires the right to prohibit its use by third parties, to prohibit the importation or goods bearing the mark and to request enforcement and damages for the infringement of their mark.

E. Licensing and Enforcement

The owner of a trademark may enter into contracts with others by granting permission to use the trademark. In order for these contracts to be effective against third parties they must be registered with the Registrar of Industrial Property. The same is true for any document that purports to assign rights in a trademark.

2.2 INTERNATIONALLY RECOGNIZED TRADEMARKS

The current trademark law added a layer of protection which was lacking from previous legislation. The current law recognizes and extends trademark protection to trademarks and brands that are well known in the international market place. In order to prevent the unlawful use of well recognized trademarks and brands the law authorizes the Registrar to reject or cancel the registration and prohibit the use of any trademark, trade name or service mark that constitutes a reproduction, imitation or translation of a well recognized name which is being used to promote identical or similar products and services which would be susceptible to confusion among the public.

2.3   REGISTRATION OF A COMMERCIAL NAME

A business or company that establishes in Costa Rica a commercial activity may register with the Intellectual Property Office their commercial name. The exclusive right to a commercial name is acquired by its use in the commercial market place and expires with the extinction of the company or commercial establishment that uses it. By registering the commercial name the holder has the right to take action against any third party that uses any sign in commerce which identifies the commercial name which is protected.

3. PATENTS AND INDUSTRIAL DESIGNS

3.1 PATENTS

A patent is a contractual agreement between an inventor and a government, in this case the Government of Costa Rica. Through it, the government grants the inventor the exclusive right to make, use and sell his invention for a specific term of years. In return for the patent rights, the inventor discloses the complete invention to the public in order to promote the progress of science. In Costa Rica, the law of patents is set forth in Law No. 6867 of April 25, 1983 on Patents of Invention, Industrial Designs and Utility Models which was reformed by Law No. 7979 effective January 31, 2000.

A. CATEGORIES OF PATENTS

Costa Rican law recognizes three types of patents:

(1) Patents for Inventions - These patents are for inventions that are new, have an inventive level and have industrial applications. This type of patent is granted for a term of twenty (20) years from the date they are granted.

(2) Improvement Patents - These patents are granted for improvements of a prior patent. However, the law grants the original patent holder the exclusive right to introduce improvements during the first year following the grant of the original patent.

(3) Confirmation Patents -This refers to patents which are granted for inventions that have already been patented abroad. The law allows one to obtain a confirmation patent for the period remaining on the foreign patent.

A. Duration and Expiration of the Patent

As stated above, patents for inventions are issued for a period of twenty (20) years.30 The law does not allow for the extension of the term of the patent and it expires as provided by law.

The law requires that the patent be commercially exploited in a permanent and stable manner in Costa Rica so that it will meet market demands within four (4) years from the date the application is submitted or three (3) years from the date the patent is granted, whichever is longer. If the supply to the market is interrupted for a period of a year or more, then this will be grounds for expiration of the patent.

B. INVENTIONS THAT MAY NOT BE PATENTED

The law does not consider the following to be inventions and as such will not issue a patent for them:

(1) discoveries, scientific theories, mathematical methods and computer programs when looked at as an isolated matter.

(2) Esthetic creations and literary or artistic works.

(3) economic or business plans, principles or methods for purely mental or intellectual activities, and game rules;

(4) The combination or variation of known and recognized products unless the combination or fusion produces and industrial product that would not be obvious to a qualified technician in the field.

The law also specifies that the following are excluded from being patented:

(1) Inventions whose commercial exploits must be prevented to protect public order, morality, and the health and welfare of human or animal life or to preserve vegetation and avoid grave danger to the environment.
(2) methods of surgical or therapeutic treatment, and diagnostic procedures and methods (however products or devices to carry out the foregoing may be patented);

(3) Plants or animals.

(4) Procedures which are essentially biological in nature for the production of plants and animals.

3.2 THE PATENT APPLICATION PROCESS

An application for a patent may be filed by the inventor or his assignee. There is no citizenship requirement; so a Costa Rican or foreigner may apply. However, if the applicant has his residence outside of Costa Rica, then he must appoint a Costa Rican Attorney as his agent. Costa Rica does recognize international reciprocity.

The patent application must be filed in the Registry of Industrial Property and must contain the following information:

(1) Name of the inventor;

(2) A detailed description of the invention. This includes the specifications and claims (5 copies) which will set forth its industrial applicability;

(3) Drawings (5 sets) that are clear and concise;

(4) In the case of inventions relating to medical products a certificate from the Ministry of Health is required. For agro-chemicals, a certificate from the Ministry of Agriculture is required.;

(5) If the application is for a foreign patent then a certified copy of the foreign patent must be provided indicating the expiration of the foreign patent.

Once the application is submitted and accepted, notice is provided by publishing an announcement of the application for three (3) consecutive days in the official newspaper La Gaceta. Opposition to the application may be filed within one month after the first publication. The person opposing the application must submit evidence to support their opposition within one month after his notice of opposition is filed. The applicant has one month to reply. If the application is approved, the Industrial Property Registrar will register the patent and issue a patent certificate and publish in the official newspaper the resolution granting the patent.

The law provides for both civil and criminal penalties for infringement and/or fraud of a patent registration.

4. INDUSTRIAL AND COMMERCIAL SECRETS

A law to protect industrial and commercial secrets in Costa Rica is a relatively new concept. The law addressing this topic came into effect in January of 2000 with the publication of Law 7975, Law on Confidential Information *(Ley de Información No Divulgada)*. The purpose of the law is to protect non public information regarding commercial and industrial secrets from being passed on, acquired or used by third parties without consent. The information must be within the parameters established by the law to be protected. The law does not cover information which is in the public domain or information which is obvious to a technician well versed in the subject matter. The law allows confidentiality agreements to be entered into between parties to a commercial relationship to prevent disclosure of confidential information.

5. REGISTRATION OF INTERNET DOMAIN NAMES

The Costa Rican internet domain extension is .cr which is administered by the Costa Rican National Academy of Sciences *(Academia Nacional de Ciencias)* under the NIC- Internet Costa Rica banner. The user can obtain information about domain names and registration procedures at their web site which is www.nic.cr.

NIC-Internet Costa Rica will register domains with any of the following extensions:

.cr / .co.cr is Commercial registration

.fi.cr is Financial Entity registration
.go.cr is Government registration
.or.cr is Organizations registration
ed.cr is Educational registrations
sa.cr. is Health related registrations

The cost for a commercial registration with NIC-Internet Costa Rica is US$25 per year for its third level domain extension such as .co.cr or fi.cr extension For the second level domain extension .cr the cost is $80 per year.

CHAPTER 11

THE TAX SYSTEM

1. THE TAX SYSTEM IN GENERAL

The Costa Rican tax system is constantly in transition as Costa Rica grows out of an agriculturally based economy where tax collection was low and tax evasion a cultural way of life. The Costa Rican tax system is made up of Personal Income Taxes, Corporate and Business Income Taxes, Sales Tax, Customs Taxes, Transfer Taxes and a host of other smaller taxes that are levied on specific activities.

The major overhaul of the tax system occurred in 1995 when the Tax Justice Law *(Ley de Justicia Tributaria No. 78535)* and the Tax Adjustment Law *(Ley de Ajuste Tributario No. 7543)* were passed. These laws created severe administrative fines, penalties, and for the first time, criminal prosecution for serious offenders.

The tax laws can be complicated to understand because there are several separate laws addressing taxation. As of this edition the Costa Rican Tax Laws are made up of the following laws and their corresponding regulations: (1) Law For Tax Simplification and Efficiency *(Ley de Simplificación y Eficiencia Tributaria)*1; (2) Tax Procedure and Standards *(Codigo de Normas y Procedimientos Tributarios)*; (3) Income Tax Law *(Ley del Impuesto Sobre La Renta)*; (4) Sales Tax Law *(Ley de Impuesto General Sobre Las Ventas)*; 5) Selective Consumption Tax Law *(Ley de Consolidación de Impuestos Selectivos de Consumo)*; (6) Regulations for Closing Business Establishments *(Reglamento de Cierres de Negocio)*; Regulations for Tax Collection and Audits *(Reglamento General de Gestión y Recaudación Tributaria)*.

The fiscal year in Costa Rica begins on October 1 and ends on September 30 of each year. The tax returns are due by December 15th of each year.

In the past several years several legislative bills have been introduced in an attempt to increase the tax base and the power of the Costa Rican

Department of Revenue. To date none of these proposed bills have passed in the Legislature.

Any modification to existing tax laws and new regulations are posted on the web page of the Costa Rican Treasury Department at www.hacienda.go.cr Likewise, the reader can obtain information on updates at www.costaricalaw.com

2. THE INCOME TAX

2.1 INCOME TAX LAWS

Costa Rican income tax law is found in Law No. 7092 of April 2, 1988 *(Ley del Impuesto Sobre La Renta)* and the tax regulations found in Executive Decree No. 18455-H of September 9, 1988 *(Reglamento a La Ley de Impuesto Sobre La Renta)* As modified in 1995 the revised law imposes severe monetary fines by Costa Rican standards and introduces criminal penalties for various tax related offenses. At the time, such an enforcement mechanism in the tax arena was new to Costa Rican legislation.

2.2 WHO IS THE TAXPAYER

The Costa Rican tax law provides that all individuals or legal entities that carry on a business or trade activity for profit within Costa Rica are subject to a tax on their income. Costa Rica abides by a limited territoriality concept in taxation. This means that Costa Rica only taxes income that is derived from a Costa Rican source and does not levy a tax on foreign source income. The tax regulations specify who shall be considered a resident of Costa Rica for tax purposes as follows:

(1) Physical persons that are citizens of Costa Rica that derive income from a Costa Rican source.

(2) Physical persons that are foreigners but who have resided or been present in Costa Rica for at least six (6) continuous months during the fiscal year.

(3) Physical persons that represent or have official positions abroad and are paid by the government.

(4) Legal entities which are inc rporated in Costa Rica as well as de facto corporations that operate within Costa Rica.

(5) The branch offices, agencies or other permanent establishment in Costa Rica of persons not domiciled in Costa Rica.

(6) The trusts or fiduciary agreements formed pursuant to Costa Rican law.

(7) The estate located in Costa Rica regardless of the nationality or domicile of the deceased.

(8) Limited Liability Companies or corporations that carry out activities within Costa Rica.

(9) Any and all persons or legal entities which are not expressly indicated above but which carry on a business or trade for profit within Costa Rica.

A. Entities Exempt From Income Taxation

The tax law provides that the following are tax exempt:

(1) The government, municipalities and autonomous and semiautonomous governmental entities that are specifically excluded by law;

(2) Political Parties and Religious institutions - irrespective of their credo;

(3) Enterprises that are approved under the Free Trade Zone Law (Law No. 7210 of November 23, 1990).

(4) Labor organizations and solidarity associations.

(5) Cooperatives recognized by law.

(6) Employee solidarity associations.

(7) The insurance fund of the National Magistrate Association and the Teacher's credit union.

(8) Civic associations of small and medium agricultural farmers whose purpose is to provide technical assistance and subsidize the purchase of agricultural tools to those farmers.

(9) National (State) Universities

(10) Free Zone Enterprises

(11) Foundations

(12) Associations which are declared of public utility and whose funds are destined solely to public goals or charity.

2.3 WHAT IS TAXABLE INCOME

Taxable income in Costa Rica is based upon net income. In order to arrive at net income it is necessary to establish the gross income derived by the taxpayer and deduct from that the necessary business expenses and the deductions specifically authorized by the tax law.

A. Gross Income

The Costa Rican tax law defines gross income as the total income and profits received or earned during the taxable year which is derived from a Costa Rican source. This includes income derived from real property, investment of capital (deposits or negotiable instruments) and other business activities. Gross income also includes any increase in net worth during the taxable year which cannot be justified by declared or registered income.

(1) Items Excluded from Gross Income: The tax law excludes the following items from gross income:

(a) Capital contributions in cash or kind;

(b) The revaluation of fixed assets, except in the case of depreciable fixed assets which will be considered to establish depreciation allowances if approved by the tax administration;

(c) Profits, dividends, participation's and any other form of distribution of benefits paid or credited to the taxpayer;

(d) Any income derived as a result of contracts or agreements made on goods or capital which is located abroad, even if the contract or negotiation was executed in Costa Rica;

(e) Capital gains obtained from the transfer of real or personal property so long as this income does not constitute a habitual transaction. For purposes of the law a habitual transaction is defined as a person or entity which predominantly engages in this activity in a public and frequent manner.

(f) Inheritances, legacies, community property;
(g) Prizes from national lotteries;
(h) Gifts - charitable donations which are approved.

B. Deductions

As previously stated, various deductions may be subtracted from gross income in order to arrive at the taxable income. In order to be allowable deductions the taxpayer must demonstrate that they were necessary to produce taxable income. The tax law specifically sets forth the following deductions from income:

(1) Costs - Any costs incurred which are necessary to produce the income may be deducted. (i.e. raw materials, parts, components or services needed to produce the goods or services);

(2) Salaries - Wages, bonuses, gifts, benefits actually paid out are deductible as long as the income tax of the recipient has been withheld and paid to the Treasury;

(3) Taxes - Any taxes levied against the goods or services or transactions carried out in the ordinary course of business are deductible;

(4) Insurance Premiums - Insurance Premiums for policies which cover fire, theft, earthquake or similar risks is tax deductible;

(5) Interest - Is an allowable deduction subject to the following restrictions: (a) No deduction allowed for interest payable to shareholders of limited liability companies; (b) That portion of the interest rate which exceeds the established market rate; (c) If you intend to deduct interest payments which equal 50% of your net income,

a special form and documentation must be provided to the tax authority; in order to allow the interest deduction there must be a connection between the interest paid and taxable income.

(6) Bad Debts - Bad debts are deductible if they relate to the transactions in the ordinary course of business of the taxpayer and all legal efforts have been exhausted to collect the debt;

(7) Depreciation - A depreciation deduction is allowed for the exhaustion, wear and tear, or obsolescence of property which is used in the trade or business. The tax law establishes the maximum depreciation amounts allowed;

(8) Business Losses - A deduction is allowed for business losses. Losses incurred in one taxable year may be carried over for 3 years (*5 years for agricultural enterprises);*

(9) Social Security Contributions - The social security contributions established by law and paid to the employee are deductible;

(10) Board of Director Remuneration - A deduction is allowed for remuneration, wages, commissions, honoraria, paid to members of the board of directors who are located abroad;

(11) Payments made to entities not domiciled in Costa Rica for technical and financial support, as well as for the use of patents, trademarks, franchise fees, or royalties are an allowable deduction. If these payments are made to an agent or subsidiary of a firm which is permanently established in Costa Rica then the deduction cannot exceed 10% of the annual gross sales of that company. A deduction is also allowed for payments to person's or entities not domiciled in Costa Rica which provide news services; production, distribution or other form of service related to films, television shows, videotapes, records, novels and other image related material and sound mediums.

(12) Travel Expenses - Allowable deductions for travel expenses may not exceed 1% of the gross income declared.

(13) Royalties - a deduction is allowed for payments or credits made to entities not domiciled in Costa Rica for consulting as well as royal-

ties and for the use of patents, trademarks, etc.;

(14) Start up Expenses - A business deduction is allowed for all expenses incurred in organizing the enterprise. This refers to expenses necessary to initiate production of taxable income;

(15) Advertising - Advertising and sales promotion expenses incurred in Costa Rica or abroad are deductible;

(16) Casualty losses - A deduction is allowed for casualty and theft losses which are not covered by insurance;

(17) Gifts made to the State.

2.4 INCOME TAXES ON RESIDENT INDIVIDUALS

The Costa Rican tax law distinguishes between employment income and self-employment income. The law imposes different tax rates for each category of income. The amount of income that is subject to each different tax rate varies from year to year based upon inflation and the price index established by the Central Bank. You can check any changes in the income thresholds established at the internet web page of the Costa Rican Department of Revenue *(Direccion General de Tributacion Directa)* http://dgt.hacienda.go.cr/tramosytarifas/Paginas/ *(See Appendix 30 for Sample Income Tax Form D 101)*

A. Employment Income

For those individuals who derive employment income, it is the responsibility of the employer to withhold on a monthly basis the estimated income tax due. According to the tax law employment income includes salary, prizes, bonuses *(except the Christmas bonus which is exempt),* overtime which an employer pays to an employer. Employment income for salaried individuals as specified above is subject to a progressive tax rate of 10% and 15% as follows:

Monthly Income (Colones)	Tax Rate
0 to ¢ 586,000	Exempt
¢ 586,000 to ¢ 879,000	10%

(1) Tax Credits - An employee is allowed a tax credit in the amount of ¢ 1,110 per month for each dependent child and another credit in the amount of ¢ 1,460 per month for a spouse.

B. Self Employment Income

Those who carry on a business or trade for profit as self employed are subject to income tax rates which range from 10% to 25% as follows:

Annual Income (Colones)	Tax Rate
• From 0 to ¢2.599.000	Exempt
• From ¢2.599.000 hasta ¢3.880.000	10%
• From ¢3.880.000 hasta ¢6.473.000	15%
• From ¢6.473.000 hasta ¢12.972.000	20%
• Greater Than ¢12.972.000	25%

C. Imputed Income

The tax law may impute income to individuals, limited liability companies or professional associations if they do not file a tax return or their financial transactions are not properly logged in authorized books when so required by law. The imputed income formula is based upon the base salary of a mid-level government employee as published in the annual budget. *(Oficinista I, según fijado en la Ley de Presupuesto Ordinario de la Republica)*

Under the imputed income provision, doctors, dentists, architects, engineers, lawyers, accountants, economists, realtors are presumed to have earned 335 times the base salary if they do not file an income tax return. For appraisers, private accountants, technicians, and all other professionals and technicians in general, the imputed salary is 250 times the base salary.

2.5 CORPORATE TAXATION

In Costa Rica the tax law provides that corporations (stock corporations, general and limited partnership, professional companies, trust companies, foreign branches) are to pay income tax at a flat rate of 30% on net profits. The tax law provides a tax break for small companies and enterprises pursuant to the following schedule:

Gross Income Amount (Colones)	Tax Rate
If Gross Income is up to ¢38.891.00	10%
If Gross Income is up to ¢78.231.000	15%
If Gross Income is Greater Than ¢78.231.000	30%

The tax year for corporations runs from October 1 to September 30 and tax returns must be filed by December 17 of each year.

Corporate entities are also subject to a stamp tax for education and culture *(Timbre de Educación y Cultura)*. This stamp tax was created by Law No. 5923 of August 18, 1976 and the proceeds generated from this stamp are destined for the University of Costa Rica, the University of Distance, the National Museum, the Board of Education and the Costa Rican Printing Office. This stamp tax must be paid when (1) A corporation records its articles of incorporation in the National Registry, (2) A corporation records any modifications or documents which by law require public registration in the Mercantile Section of the National Registry, and (3) on an annual basis and the amount is based upon the capital stock of the corporation as follows and is due on March 31st of each year.

Item	Amount Due
Incorporation and subsequent registrations	¢750,00
Capital Stock up to ¢250.000.00	¢750,00
From ¢ 250,000 to ¢ 1,000,000	¢ 3,000
From ¢ 1,000,000 to ¢ 2,000,000	¢ 6,000
Greater than ¢2,000,000	¢ 9,000

Note: The income thresholds set forth in the income charts discussed herein are established in Costa Rican currency, the Colon. The Treasury Department adjusts the income thresholds on a yearly basis in order to account for inflation and monetary devaluation.

2.6 SIMPLIFIED TAX OPTION FOR INDIVIDUAL BUSINESS OWNERS

The law simplifies the income and sales tax reporting requirements for sole proprietorship's, which are those business enterprises that are owned by individuals. The law establishes a simplified tax option which establishes a flat tax for both income and sales tax. (Regimen de Tributación Simplificada). In order to qualify for this option the following criteria must apply: (1) It is only available to physical persons not corporate entities. (2) The business must fall into one of the following categories to be eligible:

(a) Bars, taverns or similar establishments, (b) retailers, (c) photographic studios, (d) shoe artisans, (e) Furniture manufacturers, (f) Ceramic, porcelain or clay makers, (g) Structural metal works, (h) Florists, (i) Bakeries, (j) Restaurants, cafes, sodas and other similar food and beverage establishments. (k) fishermen. (3) The business may not have more than fifteen million Colones of annual purchases in materials and supplies necessary to produce the finished product. (4) The total number of employees necessary to carry out the operations may not be more than three excluding the owner of the business. (5) The option is not available to franchise type establishments or to those that have more than one establishment.

Those that meet the criteria must apply for this option to the revenue department *(Tributación Directa)*. Once approved the business owner must file a simplified return *(Declaración Jurada Régimen de Tributación Simplificada)* every trimester to pay for both the income and sales tax due for that trimester. The amount to be paid is the result of a formula which multiplies the total purchases made by the business owner during the trimester and multiplied by an income factor and sales factor established by the tax department as follows:

ACTIVITY	INCOME FACTOR	S A L E S FACTOR
Bars, Taverns or similar establishments	0,02	0,040
Retailers	0,01	0,020
Photographic Studios	0,01	0,020
Shoe Artisans	0,01	0,026
Furniture Manufacturers	0,01	0,065
Ceramic, Porcelain, Clay Works	0,01	0,020
Structural Metal Works	0,01	0,052
Florists	0,01	0,058
Bakeries	0,01	0,020
Restaurants, Cafes and Sodas	0,02	0,040
Fishermen (small)	0,025	

For those businesses that can qualify for this option it is well worth exploring with your accountant since it significantly reduces your paperwork and tax filing requirements.

2.7 TAX REPORTING REQUIREMENTS

In addition to filing a tax return at the end of the fiscal year, the taxpayer is also obligated to file a form D-151 titled Summary of Clients, Providers and Specific Expenses (Resumen de Clientes, Proveedores y gastos especificos) All public entities and taxpayers that must file tax returns are obligated to file this form when applicable. The form requires the taxpayer to provide information to the tax department regarding (1) All sales or purchases of goods or services to one single person or entity which exceeds 2.5 million Colones. (2) Sales or purchases for whatever amount for transportation, repairs and maintenance of machinery or equipment, publicity, merchandising in general and equipment and furniture. (3) Services related to leases, commissions, professional services and interests which exceed 50,000 Colones per year. The information which is provided on the D-151 form is used by the tax authority to cross reference the tax return filed by the taxpayer.

Likewise, all credit card processing agencies in Costa Rica must fill out form D-154 which is a summary of all credit and debit card trans-actions that they process *(Resumen de Tarjetas de Credito Empreas Afiliadas).*

For example if you have a retail business and you have a credit card merchant account with a local processor then all your credit card transactions are automatically reported to the Costa Rican Revenue Department and the sales tax portion of the credit card charge is auto-matically deducted by the merchant account processor and paid to the Costa Rica treasury directly.

2.8 INVESTMENT INCOME WITHHOLDING TAX

There is a withholding tax of 8% on any income generated from an investment in any Costa Rican financial instrument such as mutual funds, stock transactions on the Costa Rican stock exchange. The tax is automatically deducted from the interest or gain earned by the finan-cial entity that issues or administers the financial instrument that in turn must pay the tax to the government Treasury. For example if you purchase a Certificate of Deposit from a Costa Rican bank it will de-duct 8% of the interest earned and pay that amount to the Treasury.

3. TAX ON FOREIGN REMITTANCES

Income or financial benefits derived from a Costa Rican source which is destined to or sent abroad is subject to a Tax on Foreign Remittances (Impuesto Sobre Remesas al Exterior) The law is applicable to Costa Rican source income which is generated from (1) Goods located within Costa Rica, (2) Capital which is used within Costa Rica, (3) Civil, Com-mercial, Banking, Industrial, Services provided or developed in Costa Rica, (4) Bonuses paid abroad, (5) Payments for the use of patents, formulas, trademarks, privileges, franchises, re-insurance and insur-ance premiums. The law also mentions specific cases which are subject to the foreign remittance tax.

Those are (1) Payments to public officials abroad, (2) Payment to crew members of Costa Rican vessels, (3) Interest and commissions on loans invested in or used in Costa Rica, (4) Revenue from exports, (5) Revenue from local distributors for overprices and or hiring of ser-vices, (6) News agencies providing news services to local residents, (7) Negotiations on transmission and or dissemination of images and sound. (8) Payments to corporate directors that act abroad, (9) Payments or credits for technical consulting provided abroad for persons or entities domiciled in Costa Rica.

Under this law it is the obligation of the payor to withhold the foreign remittance tax from the payment that is made. The payor then has the obligation to submit the payment to the Costa Rican treasury department.

Activity Tax Rate	Foreign Remittance
Transport and Communications	8.5%
Reinsurance and Bonding	5.5%
Movies, Audio and Dissemination of Sound or Images	20%
Profit Sharing or Dividends	5% to 15%
Radio and TV Soap Operas	50%
Technical or Financial Assistance and Franchising	25%
Personal Consulting Services	15%
Pensions and Salaries	10%
Leasing of Capital Goods, Interest, Commissions, And other financial expenses	15%
Other Witholdings	30%

4. SALES TAX

Costa Rica applies a sales tax (value added tax) on certain goods and services known locally as Impuesto de Ventas. The current rate is 13% and it is applied to the net sales price to all products which are not exempted.

There are exempted products and the Legislature periodically modifies the list which generally is made up of items deemed basic necessities, such as basic foodstuffs, medicines, school supplies and agricultural supplies.

It is the responsibility of the business that makes the sale to collect the sales tax at the source and pay it to the government treasury on a monthly basis by filing with the revenue department a sworn declaration of the sales tax collected for that month.

Under the sales tax law there are three forms of payment and collection of the sales tax for business enterprises. The first one is the "traditional" method *(Sistema Tradicional)* which is applicable to persons or corporate entities that carry on a business or services in a habitual manner. The second method is the "purchase" method *(Sistema de Compras)* which is only available to retail commercial establishments whose sales do not exceed one million two hundred thousand Colones.

These enterprises pay a flat tax which is based upon the applicable sales tax (13%) multiplied by the percentage of the profit margin which the revenue department has established for that particular business. The third method is the "simplified" method *(Sistema Simplificado)* which was discussed in the previous section.

According to the sales tax law the following services are subject to the sales tax: (1) restaurants, (2) bars, (3) nightclubs and social entertainment or recreational establishments and the like, (4) hotels, motels, bed and breakfasts and pensions whether for transitory patrons or not, (5) automobile repair and body shop establishments, (6) repair and reconditioning shops of any kind, (7) parking lots, (8) telephones and cable, (9) warehousing and storage services, (10) public entertainment in general, (11) television, cable and satellite transmission services as well as video rentals, (12) customs agents services, (13) real estate brokerage services, (14) international moving services, (15) insurance.

Failure to comply with the sales tax law by not issuing a receipt, not withholding the applicable sales tax, failing to pay the sales tax to the revenue department for two consecutive months or concealing the sales tax withheld can result in the revenue department closing down the business. If you are going to establish a business enterprise that will require collecting the sales tax it is wise to retain the services of an accountant to register your business with the Revenue Department and take responsibility for filing all the necessary sales tax forms for you on a monthly basis.

5. CONSUMPTION TAX

In addition to the sales tax discussed above, the government also levies a consumption tax on selected items. The tax, referred to as the Selective Consumption Tax *(Impuesto Selectivo de Consumo)* ranges from 8% to 10%. Most imported goods are charged this tax, taking the products' cost, insurance and freight as the tax base.

6. TRANSFER TAXES

In Costa Rica, the sale of real property and the sale of movable property such as vehicles, planes or boats trigger a transfer tax which must be paid simultaneously when the title is recorded to transfer ownership from the seller to the buyer. On real property, (i.e. sale of a home or raw land) the transfer tax *(Impuesto de Traspaso)* is 1.5% of the value indicated in the transfer deed or registered tax value of the property whichever is higher. The tax must be paid when the title deed is recorded otherwise the deed will not be accepted for registration at the National Registry. For vehicles, the transfer tax is 2.5% of the tax base

The tax base is established by the Department of Revenue for every vehicle in Costa Rica. As such, if you sell an automobile for US$25,000 the vehicle transfer deed must pay 2.5% of that amount, US$625 to the revenue department as transfer tax. The vehicle tax base maintained by the Department of Revenue can be consulted via the Internet at www.hacienda.go.cr/autohacienda/Autovalor.aspx to determine the tax base for a particular vehicle. Without this payment the deed will not be accepted for registration in the National Registry.

7. PROPERTY TAXES

Property Taxes in Costa Rica are imposed and collected by the Municipal Government where the property is located. The Property Tax Law *(Ley de Impuesto de Bienes Inmuebles)* places the burden on each local municipal government to create their property data base, conduct property appraisals and collect the corresponding property tax.

The property tax is typically paid on a quarterly basis. The current property tax rate is 0.25% of the recorded property value. The property value may be modified by the Municipal government automatically when the property is either sold or mortgaged. When either of these events occurs the Municipal government will adjust your property value upward to the amount set forth in the property transfer deed or the amount set forth in the mortgage deed. If, for example, your property is on the Municipal tax rolls at a base of $55,000 but you borrow $75,000 on the property and the lender records a mortgage deed on the property; then the Municipal government will automatically increase the property tax base to the amount of the mortgage recorded on the property which is $75,000.

The Property Tax law requires property owners to file every five years a declaration of value *(Declaración de Bienes Inmuebles)* with the Municipal government setting forth the value of their property. *(See Appendix 32 for sample municipal property declaration form)*

Since there is no sanction for failure to file it depends on the property owner whether they voluntarily file or not. However, the risk for not filing is that the Municipal government will send out their own appraiser to set the tax base for your property. This may result in a higher value being established on your property. Some Municipal governments have been more open than others in working with the property owner to voluntarily agree on a property value which is still well below actual market value. If you can work with your Municipal government it may be to your benefit to file the declaration since it will fix your property taxes for five years from the date of filing.

CHAPTER 12

ENVIRONMENTAL LEGISLATION

Costa Rica has tried to create a balance between development and the environment. To that end the Costa Rican Constitution has been amended twice to include constitutional protections for its citizens to guarantee a safe and ecologically balanced environment. Specifically, Article 50 of the Costa Rican Constitution was amended in 1994 and states that "every person has the right to a healthy and balanced environment" and Article 46 of the Constitution was amended in 1996 to include a constitutional protection for health and environment. In addition to the constitutional protections indicated, Costa Rica has a series of laws that address particular subject areas but all of which are aimed at environmental protection and planning.

As of this edition, the laws and regulations covering environmental matters are (1) Environmental Protection Law *(Ley Organica del Ambiente # 7554 de 1995)* (2) Wildlife Conservation Law *(Ley de Conservacion de la Vida Silvestre # 7317 de 1992)* (3) Bio-Diversity Law *(Ley de Biodiversidad #7788 de 1998)* (4) General Health Law *(Ley General de Salud # 5395 de 1973)* (5) Water Law *(Ley de Aguas #276 de 1942)* (6) Forestry Law *(Ley Forestal # 7575 de 1996)*.

The governmental entity responsible for the oversight of the environmental protection laws is the Ministry of the Environment and Energy known locally as MINAE *(Ministerio del Ambiente y Energía)*. The Ministry has a web site available at www.minae.go.cr

1. ENVIRONMENTAL PROTECTION LAW

The Environmental Protection Law *(Ley Organica del Ambiente)* was passed by the Legislature in November of 1995. In passing this law the intent of the Legislature was to provide the government with the necessary legal structure to oversee the rational use of the nations' natural resources and reduce the damage to the environment.

1.1 ENVIRONMENTAL IMPACT STATEMENT

Pursuant to the law, any activity which will impact or alter the environment or which will generate residues or toxic, dangerous materials will require an environmental impact statement *(Evaluación de Impacto Ambiental)*. The law created a specialized technical office, the Technical Environmental Administration, *(Secretaria Técnica Nacional Ambiental-SETENA)* responsible for evaluating the environmental impact of those activities or projects required by law to present environmental impact statements. In those cases where the impact statement is required no authorization for the activity or project will be given unless SETENA has completed a review of the environmental impact of the project and approved it by issuing a written resolution setting forth the basis and foundation for the decision.

It seems that the criteria and regulations which specify what projects require an Environmental Impact Statement are constantly evolving. Likewise, we have witnessed a trend at the local municipal government to require certain type of developments to provide an environmental impact statement before they will issue a construction permit. The law had exempted certain types of projects from this requirement but the Constitutional Chamber struck down the exemption provision and since then those exempt projects are now being required to provide Environmental Impact Statements. This process has become so tedious and time consuming that it is best to hire a professional firm that specializes in this field to assist with the project.

A. The Preliminary Environmental Evaluation Form

The first step in obtaining approval from the office of SETENA is by completing and filing the Preliminary Environmental Evaluation Form *(Formulario de Evaluacion Ambiental Preliminar FEAP)*. The SETENA will review the information contained in the FEAP form and then make a determination if the project may proceed without the need for a full Environmental Impact Study.

B. Projects subject to a Preliminary Environmental Evaluation or Environmental Impact

The law requires an environmental impact evaluation based upon either the type of activity involved or the location of the project or both.

As previously indicated the exemptions are not in force. The law requires the following activities to apply for a preliminary environmental evaluation: (1) Commercial or service related projects that will utilize more than 3,000 m2 (32,291 sq.ft.) of covered area. (2) Agricultural Projects such as (i) Pig, beef, sheep farms depending on the density and the size of the farm, (ii) Poultry farms, (iii) Commercial Forestry plantations, (iv) Fish hatcheries with more than 1 hectare (2.47 acres) in surface area. (3) Tourism projects which occupy more than 2,000 m2 (21,527 sq.ft.) or have more than 50 rooms. (4) Housing developments built on more than 10,000 m2 (2.47 acres) of land. (5) Condominiums whose total are will be more than 5,000 m2 (1.24 acres). (6) Agro-industrial projects, (7) Industrial Projects with any of the following criteria (i) employ more than 40 workers, (ii) Use more than 25 cubic meters of water per day, (iii) Use more than 500 Kw of electricity per hour per day. (iv) Generate more than 500 Kg (1,339 lbs.) of solid waste per day, (v) any other project that uses hazardous material as part of is process. (8) Electrical generation projects that generate less than 2,000 kw per hour. (9) Educational facilities that will have a capacity of more than 100 students, (10) Any project or activity that will occur on land that does not have more than a 15% slope for filtration. (11) Commercial or office space with a covered area between 3,000 and 5,000 m2. (12) Housing and residential developments whose total land area is between 10,000 m2 and 12,000 m2. (13) Educational facilities whose capacity is between 100-250 students.

In addition, the law also requires environmental evaluation for projects that will be located in a specific type of area. (1) Projects located in areas zoned as Protected Areas which can include Parks, Forestry reserves, Wildlife Refuge (2) Projects that will be located near the coast line. (3) Projects which are to be developed on land with a different zoning requirement than is established in the zoning plan. (4) Projects located near any water resource as defined by the Costa Rican Water Company (AyA) and the Subterranean Water, Irrigation and Drainage Service (SENARA). (5) Projects located in areas which are classified by the National Emergency Committee as high risk for natural disasters. There are other laws which also impose an environmental evaluation as a requisite for the development of a particular activity some examples are mining, electrical generation, public works projects, and marinas so check carefully with the appropriate governmental agency before embarking on a project.

1.2 AIR, WATER, AND SOIL

The Environmental Law states that the government shall make all efforts possible to reduce the level of contamination in the air, water, and soil. The Environmental Law does not go into specifics on how it intends to accomplish this goal but does indicate that the government must formulate policy and plans to carry this out. Nevertheless, Costa Rica has slowly been addressing air quality issues by eliminating leaded gasoline and instituting mandatory emission testing of all vehicles in the country on a yearly basis. As to water use and protection there is a specific law, the Water Law *(Ley de Aguas)* which addresses the use of water resources; it shall be discussed in further detail in this chapter.

1.3 PROTECTION OF MARINE, COASTAL AREAS, AND TROPICAL FORESTS

The Environmental Law provides that marine and coastal areas as well as tropical forests are of public interest. The law allows the Ministry of Environment and Energy to delineate certain coastal and tropical forests as protected zones. In the areas that are so designated the law prohibits any activity which may contaminate and interrupt the natural cycle of the ecosystem.

1.4 ADMINISTRATION

The Environmental Law creates the National Environmental Council *(Comisión Nacional Ambiental)* which will be in charge of formulating and implementing environmental policy. The Environmental Council is made up of members from the Ministry of National Planning, Ministry of the Environment and Energy, Ministry of Health, Ministry of Agriculture, Ministry of Education, Ministry of Science and Technology and the President of the Republic.

In order to supervise enforcement of the new environmental regulations created by this law, the position of Environmental Comptroller was established *(Contralor del Ambiente)*. The Comptroller is named by the Ministry of the Environment and Energy. The law also created an Environmental Administrative Tribunal *(Tribunal Ambiental Administrativo)* which is basically the administrative court responsible for hearing and ruling upon complaints alleging violations of the Environmental Law. The ruling of this administrative tribunal exhausts the administrative process.

2. WILDLIFE CONSERVATION

In Costa Rica there are two bodies of laws aimed at protecting wildlife. The Wildlife Conservation Law *(Ley de Conservación de La Vida Silvestre)* passed by the legislature in 1992 and the Law on Biodiversity *(Ley de Biodiversidad)* passed in 1998.

2.1. WILDLIFE CONSERVATION

The Wildlife Conservation law prohibits hunting, fishing, extraction and export or import of any fauna or flora which is near extinction and identified as such on the endangered list by the Department of Wildlife *(Dirección General de Vida Silvestre).*

A. Wildlife

1. Hunting

The Wildlife Conservation Law in conjunction with regulations issued by the Ministry of the Environment and Energy (MINAE) contain stringent requirements for hunting. The regulations establish four hunting "zones" and set forth the species and seasons in which those species may be hunted. The law prohibits hunting without a license issued by the Department of Wildlife. Only Costa Rican citizens and permanent residents are allowed a general license to hunt. Nonresident hunting licenses carry restrictions, including a limitation that they hunt only on Saturday, Sunday, or legal holidays.

2. Fishing

The law authorizes both non-residents and Costa Ricans to fish as long as they abide by the regulations established by law and have a valid fishing license which is issued by the Department of Wildlife and valid for one year for residents and sixty days for non residents.

Check for applicable regulations related to fishing which are issued by the Department of Wildlife.

3. Wildlife Refuge

The Executive Branch of the government has the power to declare any area a wildlife refuge. Once an area is declared a wildlife refuge, the extraction of any flora or fauna from that area is prohibited.

B. Flora

In order to preserve the natural flora of the country, the law regulates the collection and extraction of plants and flowers *(flora)* by requiring a license. In order to export native flora, its products or by-products, a permit from the Department of Wildlife is required plus payment of an export tax equal to 5% of the F.O.B. value of the shipment.

C. Violations

The law provides for both civil and criminal penalties for violation of the Wildlife Conservation Law. Hunting or fishing within protected zones can result in monetary fines convertible to prison sentence from 4 to 8 months and forfeiture of the equipment used. Likewise, the extraction or destruction of flora from protected areas can result in a fine or prison sentence of 2 to 8 months.

2.2 BIO-DIVERSITY

In 1998 the legislature passed the Law on Bio-diversity to extend protection and establish policy on the use and conservation of all living organisms regardless of the ecosystem they reside in. The general principles which the law establishes as a framework are: (1) Respect for life in any form regardless of actual or potential economic value, (2) Bio-diversity is of strategic importance to the development of the country, (3) Respect and protection of cultural diversity specially indigenous populations and other cultural groups (4) Rational and balanced use of biological resources to ensure its use by future generations.

A. National Conservation System

The law authorizes the creation of a national conservation system which is made up of conservation areas divided by territorial location and which are under the supervision of the National Conservation Council *(Consejo Nacional de Areas de Conservación)* which is a division of the Ministry of Environment and Energy (MINAE). The conservation council is responsible for enforcing applicable environmental legislation to each specific geographic conservation area.

B. Sustainable Ecosystem

In order to preserve the ecosystem which the law mandates is the "duty of the State and its citizens" the Bio-diversity law requires that technical standards be adopted to ensure conservation of the ecosystem by requiring evaluations, studies, environmental impact statements, permits, licenses and/or incentives to accomplish the task of maintaining the ecosystem. The law also requires that human activities be adjusted to the technical specifications approved by the Ministry of Environment and Energy to ensure protection of the ecosystem.

When environmental damage occurs in an ecosystem, the law authorizes the applicable governmental agencies to take all necessary steps to restore, recover or rehabilitate the damaged area including the ability to freely contract with educational institutions, public or private enterprises and scientific organizations that may be necessary to restore the damaged ecosystem.

3. THE FORESTRY LAW

The Forestry Law *(Ley Forestal)* was passed in 1990 and its goal was to establish as a national priority the efficient and rational use of the country's forestry reserves. In order to do so, the law created a Forestry Department *(Oficina Nacional Forestal)* which is the entity responsible for establishing the national forestry policy and strategy. Among its other functions, the Forestry Department must (1) develop programs to study the forestry reserves of the country and provide for their efficient administration and utilization; (2) preserve the soils and fight erosion to prevent the deterioration of the forestry reserves; (3) establish forestry reserves, protected zones, and wildlife refuge.

3.2   FORESTRY RESERVES AND PROTECTED AREAS

In addition to regulating the forestry reserves owned by the government the law imposes use restrictions and establishes protected zones which are also applicable to private property. The law declares the following areas to be protected zones: (1) The area which borders a natural spring is protected for a 200 square meter (2,152 sq. ft.) radius; (2) 10 square meters (107.6 sq.ft.) on the side of each river is considered a protected zone. These increases to 50 square meters (536 sq. ft.) for hilly terrain; (3) on lakes, the shores are protected up to 100 square meters (1,076 sq. ft.).

When public or private land is labeled a protected zone the law prohibits the cutting of any trees and carrying out any activity on the land which would affect its vegetation.

3.2 LUMBER INDUSTRY

The Forestry Law is also aimed at eliminating illegal lumbering activities by authorizing inspectors of the Department of Forestry to enter and inspect land to ensure compliance with the Forestry Law. Timber which has been illegally exploited will be seized along with the machinery used to cut and transport it.

3.3 VIOLATIONS OF THE FORESTRY LAW

The Forestry Law provides for prison sentences of up to 3 years for those that invade a protected zone or conservation area and exploit forestry resources from those areas. When a corporate entity commits an illegal act in any of the protected forestry areas the civil responsibility for the damages caused may be pursued personally against the corporate representative. The law also imposes imprisonment for any of the following offenses: (1) Use of one or several forestry products on private property without the permit from the Department of Forestry; (2) Those who purchase or processes forest products without following the guidelines established by law; (3) Carry on activities which modify the use of the land and soil in forestry areas without authorization to do so; (4) Unauthorized extraction and transportation of forestry products from private or public lands; (5) Those that build roads or paths through forestry land.

4. WATER RESOURCES

Costa Rica has a Water Law *(Ley de Aguas)* which governs the water resources of the country. The law provides that all the following are waters of public domain (1) The oceans (2) Lagoons and estuaries that are permanently or intermittently linked to the ocean;(3) The rivers and their tributaries; (4) water extracted from mines; (5) underground water that has not been tapped by a well; (6) surface runoff waters; (7) marshland. Waters that has been established as private domain includes underground water that is pumped by a well and thermal and mineral waters that naturally surface upon private property.28 The law allows property owners to drill a well for water upon their land for private use without the need of applying for a governmental concession to do so. The use of any water deemed public domain requires a governmental permit prior to its exploitation and use.

4.1 WATER POLLUTION

Within the Wildlife Conservation Law *(Ley de la Conservación de la Vida Silvestre)*, the legislators inserted a regulation which prohibits pollution of the country's oceans, lakes, and rivers. The regulation requires manufacturing and agro-industrial facilities to install treatment plants to prevent waste and contaminants from polluting and destroying the wildlife.

Failure to comply with the law can result in monetary fines and imprisonment for up to two (2) years. The Public Health Law *(Ley General de Salud)* also states that it is prohibited, either directly or indirectly to contaminate the surface, ground and maritime waters. It specifically prohibits the discharge by drains or other means of liquid or solid waste that may endanger public health or land and aquatic fauna.

5. THE PUBLIC HEALTH LAW

The Public Health Law *(Ley General de Salud)* provides that the State must oversee public health and designates the Ministry of Public Health as the entity responsible for setting the agenda on public health issues.

5.1 HEALTH CARE PROVIDERS

The Public Health Law imposes certain restrictions and affirmative duties on health care providers which it defines as Pharmacy, Medical, Microbiology, Dentistry, Veterinary, and Nursing professionals. Medical facilities which provide services to the public are also regulated by the Public Health Law. These regulations may impose requirements on those facilities regarding physical installations, equipment, organization and personnel depending on the type of medical facility that is involved.

5.2 PHARMACEUTICAL PRODUCTS AND MEDICATIONS

The Public Health Law also regulates the manufacture and import of all pharmaceutical products and medications. In order to import or distribute medications the company must be registered with the Health Department and the Board of Pharmacy. The law defines as "medication" any substance or natural product, synthetic or semi-synthetic and any combination of these products which are used in the diagnosis, prevention, treatment or care of any illness or abnormal physical condition or their symptoms. Also included are diet supplements, foods or cosmetics that have any medicinal substance added to them. If you intend to import any type of pharmaceutical or medicinal product then check with the Ministry of Health first to determine that the product is authorized to enter the country.

The law stipulates that the Costa Rican Customs Department may not authorize the importation of said products unless they are authorized by the Ministry of Health.

5.3 REGULATIONS FOR FOOD MANUFACTURERS

All products destined for human consumption must abide by the regulations of the Public Health Law and require a health permit.36 Likewise, any business that dispenses food products to the public must be inspected by the health department before it will be allowed to operate. The health permits must generally be renewed on a yearly basis.

5.4 RESTRICTIONS ON INDUSTRIAL FACILITIES

All industrial and manufacturing facilities must have the permission of the Ministry of Health before they can begin operations. The law defines industrial establishment as any place whether open or covered that is destined to the transformation, manipulation of products whether natural or artificial by way of physical, chemical, biological, manual, machine or instruments. The law prohibits any other governmental agency from granting these types of facilities an operational permit or license without having the consent of the Ministry of Health. In order to issue the permit, the applicant must demonstrate that the area where the facility is located is in an area where such an activity is permitted according to the applicable zoning plan. In Costa Rica not all Municipal governments have zoning plans in place and you should consult with your local Municipal government to determine if there is a plan and if not what are considered the industrial zones within their jurisdiction.

5.5 HOUSING AND DEVELOPMENT REGULATIONS

Those that intend to build a house or develop a housing development or urbanization must ensure that the development plans comply with applicable regulations established by the Ministry of Health. As part of the construction permits requirements the law requires that the Ministry of Health approve the construction, repair, modification of any structure destined for human habitation.

Likewise, all housing construction must ensure that they have properly designed and implemented a system for the disposal of both liquid and solid waste. The property owner is responsible to ensure that the waste disposal system for their property is property maintained. The use of a public sewage disposal system in Costa Rica is quite limited. As such many of the homes rely on septic systems. When purchasing a home be sure to understand the layout of your septic system to avoid problems after you have purchased.

CHAPTER 13

LEGAL REPRESENTATION

1. ATTORNEYS

Finally everybody's favorite topic – Lawyers.   The first reaction is to try and avoid them. However in Costa Rica you will find that you can't live without them.

In Costa Rica the Bar Association *(Colegio de Abogados)* is responsible for drafting guidelines regarding the legal profession. To be admitted to the Costa Rican Bar as an Attorney, the applicant must have either graduated from or have a foreign law degree accredited by one of the Costa Rican law schools. Although there have been several attempts by the Bar Association to implement a bar admission examination to test the competence of the applicants, these attempts at regulation have been struck down by the Constitutional Chamber of the Supreme Court. As such, there is no bar examination for admission to the Costa Rican Bar.

For many years the University of Costa Rica's School of Law held a virtual monopoly on law school education in Costa Rica. The proliferation of private universities which began in the mid 1980's has increased access to legal education and there are currently more than a dozen law schools in Costa Rica. The quality of the education varies significantly from school to school since the Costa Rican Bar Association does not have a supervisory role in the law school curriculum being taught at the University level.

In Costa Rica, students who choose to study law enter law school directly upon completing high school. The law school programs in general are quite formal and theoretical requiring students to study the exact text of each of the legal codes. The length of time required to graduate from law school differs significantly from school to school. The proliferation of these law schools and the lack of an admission examination have resulted in an unprecedented growth in the number of Attorneys who now number more than fifteen thousand.

The Attorneys must adhere to the law which created the Bar Association, *Ley Organica del Colegio de Abogados,* the regulations of the Bar Association, Reglamento Interior del Colegio de Abogados and the Moral Code, Codigo de Moral. Complaints against Attorney's are handled by a Tribunal of the Bar Association which includes the President of the Bar Association and two other members. The Bar Association maintains at website at www.abogados.or.cr

1.1 ATTORNEYS FEES

The Executive Branch and the Ministry of Justice establishes the minimum fees that are to be charged by licensed Attorneys and Notaries Those are set forth in Executive Decrees No. 32493 which has been in effect since 2005.

The information which is provided should be used as a guideline since the actual cost of legal representation can vary significantly based upon the complexity of the legal issue and the experience and reputation of the Attorney. Likewise the Executive Decree sets forth the minimum that Attorneys can charge and allows them to charge more than the fee schedule stipulates so long as the client has agreed to the fee that is being charged. Also, keep in mind that the fees charged by an Attorney for legal representation are distinct and separate from the fees charged by an Attorney when they are acting in their capacity as a Notary Public *(Notario Publico).* Notary fees are discussed in the following section.

Pursuant to the fee schedule, Attorney's fees rendered in the areas of civil, commercial, tax, agrarian, or administrative law may be based upon a percentage of the disputed amount so long as the disputed amount can be predetermined. This scale which is based on percentages is referred to as the standard rate *(Tarifa General)* and it applies to legal actions which are deemed ordinary. The minimum percentages can range from 10% to 25% of the disputed amount and higher than that if agreed upon between the Attorney and client; but the law prohibits the Attorney from charging less than the established fee schedule.

According to the fee schedule the following are some of the minimums established for particular causes of action.

• Landlord-Tenant Eviction = 50% of the monetary estimation of the lawsuit (the estimation is 3 months rent).

• Mortgage Foreclosure = The minimums can range from 6% to 12.5% of the amount of the mortgage that is being foreclosed.

• Probate and Estate Proceedings = The minimums can range from 6% to 12.5% of the value of the estate.

Given the fact that many litigated proceedings in Costa Rica can take years to be litigated in the Costa Rican court system it is rare for Attorneys to work on a contingency only basis. Most will require an advance payment to represent you in a litigated matter.

In addition to a percentage fee schedule the Decree on Attorney's fees also sets forth the minimum flat fee rates that may be charged by an Attorney. These amounts vary depending on the area of law. You can also retain an Attorney on an hourly basis and these fees can range anywhere from $40.00 to $300.00 per hour.

2. THE PUBLIC NOTARY

In common law countries such as the United States and England, the role of the Notary Public is limited. They generally authenticate signatures on legal documents but they may not draft or interpret legal documents. This is not the case in Costa Rica where the Notary Public has extensive powers to act on behalf of the State.

In order to be licensed as a Notary Public in Costa Rica you must be an Attorney. In Costa Rica, the Notary is delegated powers to act on behalf of the State. They may draft and interpret legal documents, authenticate or certify the authenticity of documents and attest to the existence of certain facts. Since Notaries exercise a public function, they are under the direct supervision of the Supreme Court of Justice. In order to organize, supervise and control the activities of Notary Public's in Costa Rica the Notary Code created the National Directorate of Notaries *(Dirección Nacional de Notariado)* which is a branch of the Judicial Department and responsible for Notary registration and

The Notary Public makes a public record of their sworn attestations by recording them in a registry book known as a Protocol. The Protocol book is issued to the Notary by the National Directorate of Notaries and it consists of two hundred (200) pages. When the document that is logged in the Protocol book requires recording in the National Registry the Notary Public prints an extract of the document, known as a Testimonio, and adheres a Notary security ticket (Boleta de Seguridad) to the document and files it for registration. *(See Appendix 33 for sample Notary security ticket)*

For example, if you purchase a vehicle the law requires that the transfer of title to the vehicle from the seller to the buyer be carried out and recorded by a Notary Public. As such, both the seller and the buyer will personally appear before the Notary Public who will prepare the vehicle title transfer deed *(Escritura de Traspaso)*. Once the document is transcribed in the Notary Protocol book the Notary will have both parties to the transaction sign in the presence of the Notary and after having requested proof of identification to sign in the Protocol book. The Notary then prints an extract of the deed and adheres to it his security ticket. The document is then presented for filing at the National Registry where it is processed and the transaction recorded.

When the Notary completes the protocol book they must file it with the National Archives where it will be bound and stored for public record.

The fee schedule for Public Notaries is found in Executive Decree No. 32493. The general table of fees is as follows:

NOTARY PUBLIC FEE SCHEDULE	
First 10 Million Colones	2%
Excess of 10 to 15 Million Colones	1.5%
Excess of 15-30 Million Colones	1.3%
Excess of 30 Million Colones	1.0%

The general table is applicable as a percentage of the transaction amount for mortgage transactions, property sales deeds, segregation and sale of lots, automobile sales deeds, and certain types of contracts. The regulations allow a Notary to charge an additional 50% from the general table if an act or contract is of a complex nature. In the case of option contracts or buy-sell agreements the regulations state that the fee is half of the general table.

CHAPTER 14

POWERS OF ATTORNEY

A Power of Attorney is an instrument that allows or authorizes another person to act as one's agent. In Costa Rica, Powers of Attorney are governed by Title VIII, Chapter I of the Civil Code. Powers of Attorney can either be Special or General.

1. THE GENERAL POWERS OF ATTORNEY

Costa Rican law recognizes two distinct kinds of General Powers of Attorney. The Poder Generalisimo and the Poder General. In order to be valid the General Powers of Attorney must be recorded in the National Registry. As such, they must be issued and subscribed before a Notary Public who in turn must log the document in the Notary protocol book as a public instrument and record it in the National Registry. General Powers of Attorney do not become binding as to third parties until they are recorded in the National Registry.

(1) *Poder Generalisimo:* The Poder Generalisimo is quite broad in scope and hence I refer to it as the Unlimited General Power of Attorney. Unless the document specifies otherwise, the law confers the agent broad powers to buy, sell, mortgage, lien, and or encumber the property of the Principal. The agent is authorized to enter into contracts and to legally bind the Principal. *(See Appendix 34 for sample Poder Generalismo.)*

(2) *Poder General:* The Poder General which I shall refer to as a Limited General Power of Attorney is limited in the sense that the law specifically sets forth the acts which the agent may perform. Those enumerated powers are: (a) To perform any act which will preserve the condition of the assets, (b) To take legal action to ensure possession and which could interrupt the running of any statute of limitations on such actions, (c) To lease or rent real or personal property for terms of up to one year, (d) To sell the output or product produced which are destined for sale and avoid their deterioration or loss, (e) To collect debts and issue corresponding receipts, (f) To carry out all acts

related to the operation of a business when such acts are intrinsically tied to the nature of the business. Any act not contained in the list falls beyond the scope of the powers conveyed. The General Power of Attorney may be canceled by the Principal at any time. The cancellation must be recorded in the National Registry. The Principal may also indicate a termination date in the Power of Attorney. In the absence of either a termination or a cancellation, the General Power of Attorney expires at the death of the Principal.

2. SPECIAL POWERS OF ATTORNEY

The Special Power of Attorney authorizes an agent to carry out a specific task. The agent is only authorized to carry out the specific act or acts which are set forth in the document. The Special Power of Attorney ends when the acts authorized have been carried out by the agent.

The law does not require that the Special Power of Attorney be registered in the National Registry. The Special Power of Attorney is valid if the document contains the signature of the principal and the signature is authenticated by a Costa Rican notary public. However, if the Special Power of Attorney is to be used to transfer title to property, real estate or vehicles then the law requires that the Special Power of Attorney be executed before a Costa Rican Notary Public and logged in their Protocol book or before a Costa Rican Consular Officer and logged in the Consular Protocol book. *(See Appendix 35 Special Power of Attorney to sell Automobile.)*

3. POWERS OF ATTORNEY ISSUED OUTSIDE OF COSTA RICA

Situations often arise where an individual that does not permanently reside in Costa Rica but maintains a business or property in Costa Rica, requires an agent in Costa Rica to act on their behalf. These individuals often want to accomplish this mandate without having to leave their country of origin.

The fastest way to accomplish this task is to appear before a Costa Rican Consul in the country of origin. By law, Costa Rican consular officials act as Notary Public in the jurisdictions where they serve. *(See Appendix 36 for List of Costa Rican Consulates Abroad.)* As such, the Principal may personally appear before the Costa Rican Consul to grant a General or Special Power of Attorney. The instrument is then sent to Costa Rica where it is authenticated by the Ministry of Foreign Relations. Once the authentication is completed and the fees have been paid, the General Powers of Attorney may be filed in the National Registry of Costa Rica

There is another option for those individuals that reside in one of the countries that are a signatory of the "Interamerican Convention of the Legalization of Powers of Attorney Issued Abroad". Pursuant to the treaty, member countries will recognize Powers of Attorney issued in one of the member countries before a Notary Public of that country if they meet the following criteria: The Power of Attorney must be issued by way of a public instrument and the signature of the notary public that issued the document must be authenticated by either the Costa Rican consul in that country or the Supreme Court of Justice of the member country. As of this writing, the countries which have ratified the treaty are Argentina, Bolivia, Brazil, Costa Rica, Chile, Ecuador, El Salvador, Guatemala, Honduras, Panamá, Paraguay, Peru, Dominican Republic, Uruguay, Venezuela and México.

Those that reside in the United States and Canada and do not have access to a Costa Rican Consulate have another option. This option is only available for granting Special Powers of Attorney. Since the law does not require that the Special Power of Attorney be a Public Instrument, it is possible to appear before a notary public duly commissioned in your state or province and subscribe the Special Power of Attorney. It will then be necessary to have the county or provincial court to authenticate the signature of the notary public. The entire original document is then mailed to the nearest Costa Rica consulate, which will in turn certify the existence of the court which authenticated the document, and return the documents to you. The final step requires that the Special Power of Attorney be filed with the Costa Rican Ministry of Foreign Relations for final authentication. The Ministry of Foreign Relations generally takes two days to complete the authentication.

CHAPTER 15

AUTOMOBILES

This chapter addresses most of the situations that you will encounter regarding the licensing and ownership of an automobile in Costa Rica.

1. BUYING AN AUTOMOBILE AND RECORDING THE TRANSFER OF TITLE

All legally registered vehicles in Costa Rica are recorded in the Vehicle Section of the National Registry. If you purchase a new vehicle from the local dealership in most cases they will handle the recording of title and registration.   If you purchase a used vehicle then, the first step is to have a thorough title search done in the National Registry. The information contained in the National Registry will let you know the name of the record owner of the vehicle and whether there are any liens, encumbrances, or judicial annotations which may affect title to the vehicle. This information can be obtained from the web site of the National Registry.

In order to transfer title to a vehicle in Costa Rica, it is necessary to execute a formal bill of sale before a Notary Public. The bill of sale must be recorded in the protocol book of the Notary Public and include the following information: (a) name, identity card (or passport in case of foreigners) and the exact address of both buyer and seller; (b) price, make, style, year, color, engine number, license plate number, fuel type, and the cubic centimeter displacement of the engine; (c) time, date, place, and the name of the Notary Public which executes the bill of sale.

The Notary Public will issue a bill of sale document *(Escritura de Traspaso)* which sets forth the information contained in the protocol book. This document must be filed in the National Registry by the buyer to ensure that the sale is annotated and subsequently registered in the National Registry. *(See Appendix 37 for Sample Automobile Trans-*

fer Deed.) It is very important to record the sale as soon as possible since the doctrine of first in time, first in right which was previously discussed in property transfers is also applicable to vehicle transfers. Furthermore, since the government is quite eager to collect the transfer tax due at the time of sale it imposes severe monetary fines for vehicle transfers which are not presented to the National Registry within thirty days of the date of sale.

Once the bill of sale deed is presented to the National Registry it takes approximately thirty to sixty days to process the registration and have it recorded. When the registration process is completed the National Registry will issue a Certificate of Title *(Certificado de Propiedad)* in the name of the new owner of the vehicle. *(See Appendix 40 Certificate of Title to an automobile.)*

Avoid purchasing any vehicle that has any type of judicial annotation, traffic infractions or liens without having the seller clean up these encumbrances before you pay in full. If you insist on purchasing a vehicle with encumbrances then make sure you withhold enough money to ensure that the seller is motivated to clear up the registration problems. The National Registry will halt the registration of any vehicle that has pending encumbrances and this means that the title to the vehicle will not be registered in your name until those encumbrances are lifted.

1.1 AUTOMOBILE TRANSFER TAXES AND FEES

When you transfer title of a vehicle in Costa Rica this triggers a 2.5% transfer tax that must be paid to the national government at the time the transfer deed is filed in the National Registry. The transfer tax is based upon the tax base of the vehicle as established by the Costa Rican Revenue Department. The valuation done by the Revenue Department is generally based upon a combination of market averages and the National Automobile Dealer Association (N.A.D.A.) blue book value. The National Registry will ignore the sales price that you put on the bill of sale if it is less than the fiscal value indicated by the Department of Revenue and charge you based upon the fiscal value of the vehicle and not on the lower sales price. The fiscal value of all vehicles can be viewed in the title report of the vehicle that is issued by the National Registry. The typical closing costs for an automobile sold for ten thousand dollars ($10,000) would look as follows:

Sales Price: $10,000	
A. Transfer Tax (2.5%)	$ 250.00
B. National Registry Fee (.05%)	$ 50.00
C. Documentary Stamps	
National Archive Stamp	¢ .09
Bar Association Stamp	$ 5.76
Red Cross Stamp	¢ .38
Agrarian Stamp	$ 20
National Park Stamps	¢ .96
Subtotal Taxes and Fees	$ 327.19
D. Notary Fee (sliding fee schedule)	$ 200.00
TOTAL CLOSING COSTS	**$ 427.19**

Due to the expenses involved in transferring a vehicle, many luxury automobiles are titled in the name of a Costa Rican corporation so that at the time of sale the prospective buyer acquires the entire capital stock of the corporation which owns the car. Since the buyer is acquiring corporate stock no transfer of title has occurred and thus the transfer taxes are not triggered. The buyer, however, should be cautious that the corporation they acquire does not have any hidden liabilities which could be passed on to the new owner.

2. AUTOMOBILE LICENSING

In order for an automobile to legally circulate in the streets it must be registered in the Vehicle Section of the National Registry and have a valid vehicle registration certificate *(Tarjeta de Circulación)*. The registration certificate is valid for one year and expires on December 31 of each year for every vehicle. The registration certificate must be carried in the vehicle at all times. Along with the registration certificate the vehicle owner is also provided with a window sticker *(Marchamo)* that must be placed on the front windshield and certifies that the registration for that particular year is up to date. (See Appendix 39 for Sample Registration Card.) The renewal of the registration card can be done through several different agents authorized by the government, including private banks and insurance agents. The annual vehicle registration is divided into different components that are all billed on one statement. Those include: (1) The mandatory personal injury insurance *(seguro obligatorio)*, (2) Annual road tax *(impuesto a la propiedad de vehiculos)* (3) Road safety commission *(Consejo de Seguridad Vial)* (4) Municipal flat tax *(impuesto a favor de las Municipalidades)* (5) Wildlife preservation stamp *(timbre fauna silvestre)* (6) Funding for specific groups pursuant to Law No. 7088 and the (7) sales tax *(impuesto de ventas)*. In addition to these charges if the driver had any fines for either moving violations or parking meters during the year that were not paid, these will be billed on the annual registration card. See Figure I below for typical annual vehicle registration charges:

Figure I Breakdown of the Annual Vehicle Registration Fees

ITEM	AMOUNT
Mandatory PI Insurance	13,475
Road Safety Commission	4,447
Annual Road Tax	161,290
Municipal Tax	200
Wildlife Preservation Stamp	104
Law No. 7088	1,238
Sales Tax (13%)	1,752
TOTAL DUE	*182,506*

Note: This calculation is for a 2001 Toyota 4x4 with a fiscal value of 8,510,000 Colones

The most expensive portion of the annual vehicle registration is the road tax which is imposed by the government and is based upon the recorded value of the vehicle in the National Registry. Vehicles which are valued at less than nine million Colones pay an annual road tax that is based upon a combination of percentages that range from 1.2% to 3 % of exceeding amounts. On the other hand, vehicles valued at more than nine million Colones pay a 3.5% annual road tax without limits as to the amount. The schedule for the road tax is set forth below. Each year you can check the amount due on your vehicle by visiting the web site of the National Insurance Institute. At their site www. marchamo.ins-cr.com you enter your vehicle plate number and it will calculate the annual registration that must be paid for that year.

Figure J The Annual Vehicle Road Tax

Up to ¢580.000,00	¢19.500,00
Excess of ¢580.000,00 and up to ¢2.300.000,00	1,2%
Excess of ¢2.300.000,00 and up to ¢ 4.570.000,00	1.5%
Excess of ¢ 4.570.000,00 and up to ¢6.850.000,00	2.0%
Excess of ¢ 6,850.000,00 and up to ¢ 8.560.000,00	2.5%
Excess of ¢ 8.560.000,00	3.0%
Excess of ¢ 10.280.000,00	3.5

3. VEHICLE INSPECTIONS

All vehicles in Costa Rica must pass a general inspection *(Revisión Tecnica)* as a prerequisite to receiving the annual registration.

The government has given the general inspection task to a private company known as RITEVE. Riteve has established testing centers throughout the city of San Jose and other major provincial cities. If the vehicle passes the computerized inspection, it is issued an emissions certificate sticker commonly referred to as the RTV sticker. The sticker must be posted on the windshield. Vehicles which do not have a validly issued Riteve sticker will not be allowed to renew their annual registration.

If your vehicle is older than 5 years then the vehicle must be inspected annually. If the vehicle is less than 5 years then the inspection is good for two years. The date on which you are required to have your vehicle inspected depends on the last digit number of the license plate number of the vehicle. *(See Figure K below for the inspection dates).*

Figure K   Vehicle Inspection Dates

Month	Last Digit of License Tag
January	1
February	2
March	3
April	4
May	5
June	6
July	7
August	8
September	9
October	0

4. THE DRIVERS LICENSE

The driver's license in Costa Rica for automobiles and light duty trucks up to half a ton is the B-1 license. In order to obtain a B-1 license for the first time, the applicant must be at least eighteen years old (18). The applicant must pass a basic driver's education course, pass the medical exam and a driving test. The first license issued is valid for two years, and after that it is renewed every five years.

Costa Rica allows foreigners to drive in Costa Rica with a foreign drivers license for a three (3) months and renewable for an additional three months. As a foreigner on Tourist status your license is only good as long as your tourist visa status is valid.

The law authorizes the Ministry of Transportation to issue Costa Rican driver's license to those foreigners who have a valid foreign license and have passed the Costa Rican medical exam. The Medical Exam is available from Doctors who set up mobile offices near the licensing department and issue the medical certificate required by the License Bureau.

The procedures for granting non-resident foreigners licenses are arbitrary. Sometimes internal regulations have required proof that the applicant is either a resident of Costa Rica or demonstrates proof that they have applied for residency. The best chance for a "tourist" to obtain a Costa Rican driver's license is to apply for one before the expiration of the tourist visa since the license department will scrutinize your passport to establish your entry date into the country. If you have legal residency status in Costa Rica then you will have no problem obtaining your Costa Rican driver's license by showing a valid driver's license from your country of origin.

5. CAR INSURANCE

5.1. MANDATORY PERSONAL LIABILITY INSURANCE

Costa Rican law mandates that every vehicle maintain "no fault" personal liability insurance referred locally as *Seguro Obligatorio*. Since this insurance is mandatory, it is automatically billed to your annual vehicle registration certificate. As such, when you renew your vehicle registration at the end of each year you are paying for the mandatory no-fault coverage.

The premium payments for this no-fault coverage are established by the National Insurance Institute *(Instituto Nacional de Seguros)*. The insurance only covers personal injury or death of individuals involved in a traffic accident. The policy limits are established on a yearly basis but are generally very low. The policy coverage limits are 3,000,000 Colones for personal injury or death. As you can see from the policy limits for this mandatory coverage it is advisable to carry additional insurance coverage for third party liability.

5.2 VOLUNTARY CAR INSURANCE

The National Insurance Institute (I.N.S), which as of this edition was the only authorized insurer in Costa Rica, also sells supplemental automobile insurance policies covering a variety of risks. The Insurance monopoly of the National Insurance Institute is gradually opening as a new law now authorizes other private insurance companies from entering the market.

A. Personal and Property Damage

In order to supplement the mandatory personal liability policy which has very low policy limits, it is possible to purchase additional personal liability coverage from the insurance company. This coverage *(Cobertura A)* would provide personal liability coverage to an insured party that has been determined "at fault" in a traffic accident. Coverage is generally extended after the mandatory insurance policy limits have been exhausted. There is no deductible for this coverage. The typical policy limit for this policy is set forth below:

Coverage	Amount
Personal Injury or Death	50,000,000 Million Colones per person
	150,000,000 Million Colones per accident

The property damage policy *(Cobertura C)* covers property damage caused by the insured party to the property of third parties. Generally this coverage applies when the insured party damages either a vehicle or personal property of a third party. The typical policy limits for this policy is up to twenty million colones. The deductible on this policy is 20% .

B. Collision and Theft

Collision coverage *(Cobertura D)* ensures that any damages sustained by your vehicle as a result of a traffic collision will be paid by the insurance company if the other driver has no insurance or if you are at fault in the accident. Many who frequently drive in San José comment about the hazards involved. The rate of traffic accidents in Costa Rica is high and as a result so is the cost of collision insurance. The premium is calculated based upon the market value of the vehicle as established by the Insurance Institute. The deductible on this policy is 20%.

The theft coverage *(Cobertura F)* insures against the loss caused by the theft of the insured vehicle. As in the collision coverage, premiums are based upon the market value of the vehicle. The deductible on this policy is 20%.

C. What Does it All Cost ?

Assume you are the owner of a 2001 four wheel drive vehicle valued at nine million Colones and you want to insure it with all the coverage that we have indicated above. The premium payments per semester would be as follows:

Value of the Vehicle: 9,000,000 Colones. Premium payment per: Semester			
Insurance	Coverage	Premium	Deductible
Personal Liability (Coverage A)	50 per person /		
	150 per accident	C 7,566	0
Property Damage (Coverage C)	20 million per accident	C 20,773.020	20 %Min 60k
Collision (Coverage D)	9,000,000	C 258,127.00	20 % Min 90k
Theft (Coverage F)	9,000,000	C 86,850.00	10% Min 30k
Additional Risks (Coverage H)	9.000,000	C19.979.00	20% Min 90k

Based upon the assumptions that we have indicated, it would cost 393,295 Colones per semester or 786,590 Colones per year, which is approximately US$1,440 Dollars at the current rate of exchange.

6. TRAFFIC ACCIDENTS

6.1 WHAT TO DO IN AN ACCIDENT

Costa Rica has one of the highest per capita traffic accident rates in the world. Costa Rican drivers are notorious for driving fast and with complete disregard for others on the road. When you drive in Costa Rica do so defensively and be ready for the unexpected or unpredictable.

If you have the misfortune of getting into traffic accident do not move the position of the vehicle until you are told to do so by the Traffic Police. You can contact the Costa Rican Traffic Police *(Transito)* by calling 911 and they will dispatch an officer to the scene. At the same time, if you have automobile liability insurance then you must call the National Insurance Institute *(INS)* so they can send an accident inspector to the scene of the accident. The telephone number for the National Insurance Institute accident line is 800-800-800. Once the insurance accident inspector arrives they will complete the accident report and tell you what to do next.   If you don't report the accident to the National Insurance Institute it may deny coverage for your claim.

At the scene the Traffic Police Officer *(Oficial de Transito)* will prepare an accident report and issue a traffic summons and any traffic citations where appropriate. The summons is a green piece of paper which contains the summons number which will in turn become the case reference number with the traffic court.

Do not assume responsibility or agree to side deals with the other party involved since it may affect your insurance coverage. If there are witnesses to accident try and get their names, addresses and phone numbers since you may need them if the case goes to Traffic Court.

6.2 TRAFFIC COURT

All matters related to the Transit Law including infractions and accidents fall within the jurisdiction of the traffic courts. There are six traffic courts for the judicial circuit of San José and six courts for the rest of the country.

The transit police officer that arrives at the scene will issue both drivers involved in the accident a traffic summons *(boleta de citación)*. The transit officer then files a copy of the accident report they have prepared along with the traffic summons with the traffic court that has jurisdiction over the accident.

The place where the accident occurred will determine the jurisdiction for the traffic court. Both drivers have eight (8) working days from the date the traffic summons is issued to appear before the traffic court and enter a plea. The driver has the option of either entering a plea or rendering a statement of facts or he can enter a plea but abstain from rendering a statement.

 If the traffic accident resulted in injuries which produce an incapacity to work to a driver, passenger or pedestrian, the case becomes a criminal and not civil matter so it is crucial that it be handled by an Attorney. The Attorney should accompany you to render your statement since that statement will be used as evidence in trial.

During the traffic court process the Court will automatically place a Lis Pendens *(notice that a traffic case is pending)* on both vehicles involved in the accident. The Lis Pendens will be recorded against the vehicle in the National Registry and will not be lifted without a court order.

This measure ensures that the value of the vehicle will be available to cover any award of damages since this Lis Pendens will be converted to a lien on the vehicle and against the party that is found liable.

Once the traffic court has recorded the plea of both parties it will set a time and date for the trial to take place. Depending on the traffic court involved it could take up to two years to get a trial date. At trial both parties present their respective witnesses, and experts if needed. All the evidence is evaluated by the judge who enters a judgment setting forth their findings of fact and conclusions of law. The judgment will include (a) the degree of fault of each party; (b) license suspensions, if applicable and, (c) the award of money damages and court costs to the prevailing party. The Traffic Court will submit an Order to the Vehicle Section of the National Registry to place a lien for the amount of the judgment against the vehicle of the party at fault.

7. IMPORTING AN AUTOMOBILE

So you have found a nice little gem of an automobile up north that you want to bring with you to Costa Rica. How do you do it ? The process begins when you deliver your vehicle to the shipping company that will in turn ship it to Costa Rica. Your shipper will prepare a Bill of Lading indicating the merchandise that is being transported and the name of the person it is consigned to. If you intend to be in Costa Rica to receive the vehicle, you can have it consigned to yourself. You must have the original Bill of Lading in your possession in order to retrieve the vehicle from the port authorities in Costa Rica. The vehicle that you import must have a valid vehicle emissions certificate issued by the country where it is licensed. The emissions certificate must be authenticated by the Costa Rican Embassy or Consulate where the vehicle is being shipped from. Once the vehicle has arrived in Costa Rica you have two options. You can pay the import duties on the vehicle and thus have it nationalized or you can request a temporary importation permit as a tourist.

7.1 THE TEMPORARY IMPORT PERMIT

The law allows a tourist to import a vehicle and drive it in Costa Rica on a temporary basis for a maximum of six months. These temporary permits can only be applied for in the port of entry of the vehicle. The port of entry grants a three (3) month permit which can be renewed for an additional three months. No further extensions are allowed and the vehicle must either leave the country or pay the import taxes. If you are caught driving a vehicle that has an expired import permit then the law allows the authorities to seize the vehicle.

If you ship a vehicle with the intent of taking it out from customs with a temporary permit be sure that you follow these guidelines to minimize your difficulties with customs at the port of entry. Bring an original certificate of title for the vehicle. The title should be in the name of or endorsed to the individual that is applying for the temporary permit. The same holds true for the vehicle registration. Be sure the vehicle has a valid license plate from the country of origin and have your passport and driver's license with you. The temporary permit is granted to tourists who have a valid tourist visa. If you have overstayed your tourist visa you will run into problems and will most likely not be allowed to take the vehicle out from customs at the port of entry. The process is very bureaucratic so have patience and plan to be in the port for most of the day to complete all the procedures.

7.2 NATIONALIZING THE VEHICLE

Your other option is to pay the import duties and have the vehicle nationalized. In order to nationalize a vehicle it is highly recommended that you seek out a reputable customs broker to assist you in the process. It is best if you contact the customs broker before you ship the vehicle so that you can provide them with all the detailed information about the vehicle.

Based upon the information that you provide, the customs broker will be able to provide an estimate of the import duties that the vehicle will pay. This will avoid any surprises after the vehicle has already arrived in Costa Rica.

If you intend to nationalize the vehicle you have the option of paying the import taxes at the port of entry or you can request that the vehicle be "redestined" to a bonded warehouse in the capital city of San Jose and the nationalization process can be carried out there. The first step is for the Department of Revenue to appraise the value of the vehicle and then calculate the import duties that must be paid. Once the import duties are established you will have to pay that amount to the national treasury. The customs broker that you retain to assist you with the process will then provide you with a certified customs declaration form (poliza de desalmacenaje) which authorizes the release of the vehicle from the bonded warehouse or the port facility. Once the vehicle is released from customs it must be inspected by the Ministry of Transportation. The inspection facility is located in Alajuela close to the international airport.

The inspection process is referred to locally as *Revision Técnica*. Depending on the time of the year be prepared to spend a couple of hours at the inspection facility. If the automobile passes inspection a certificate is issued. Now you are ready to petition for the registration of your vehicle in the National Registry.

This is done by presenting a notarized written request for registration of the vehicle to the Vehicle Section of the National Registry. The request must be accompanied by the inspection certificate, the certified custom's declaration, and a notary security ticket *(boleta de presentación)*. While the request for registration is being processed, a temporary registration and license tag is issued for the vehicle. Once registered you will be provided a certificate of title for the vehicle along with a registration card and the metal license plates for the vehicle.

CHAPTER 16

INCENTIVES TO TOURISM AND BUSINESS ENTERPRISES

1. TOURISM

Since the mid 1980's Costa Rica has placed considerable emphasis in developing the tourism industry, which in the past few years has surpassed agriculture as the main source of foreign income. The number of international arrivals to Costa Rica increased from 435,000 in 1990 to over a 2 million in 2008 and numerous businesses and industries have developed to cater to the tourists. At the present time tourism in Costa Rica is at a crossroad. The original focus of the Costa Rican tourism policy was eco-tourism which has meant low impact development which preserves the natural vegetation of the country. However, in the past couple of years there has been a shift towards the large development projects with condominiums, hotels, and golf courses catering to mass tourism.

1.1 TOURISM DEVELOPMENT INCENTIVES

The key piece of legislation that initiated the growth in the investment of tourism related projects was the Tourism Development Incentive Law (*Ley de Incentivos para el Desarrollo Turístico*) passed in 1985 and amended in 1992. The law declares the tourism industry to be in the public interest of Costa Rica.

The law provides incentives to those companies that establish any of the following type of projects within Costa Rica: (1) Hospitality services, (2) Receptive tour and travel services, (3) Vehicle rental companies, (4) Domestic and international air transportation of tourists, (5) Water related transportation or recreational activities for tourists, (6) Food and entertainment services.

Those companies that qualify are provided incentives which range from exemptions from import duties on items deemed indispensable for their particular enterprise to income and property tax exemptions. Many of the incentives previously offered have been eliminated since the Tourism industry is fully developed in Costa Rica to date and the government felt that incentives were no longer needed. Coinciding with this were also some publicly documented cases where incentives were abused.

Since the existing benefits and incentives vary depending on the scope of the particular project, it is best to contact the Incentives Department at the Costa Rican Tourism Institute (ICT) and obtain a preliminary opinion based upon the particular circumstances and scope of your project to determine what is currently available.

1.2 APPLICATION AND QUALIFICATION PROCEDURES

The regulations require that any individual or corporate entity interested in obtaining the benefits provided by the Tourism Development Incentive Law must first have their activity or project declared and or qualified as a tourism related enterprise (*Declaración de Interes Turistico*) by the Costa Rican Tourism Institute *(Instituto Costarricense de Turismo)* In order to obtain this qualification statement, a formal application must be filed with the Tourism Services Department of the Costa Rican Tourism Institute. The application must set forth in detail, information about the applicant and the project which they intend to establish. The application must also include a police clearance certificate for each of the company representatives and a sworn statement by the applicant that the sole purpose of the company is to engage in tourism related activities. In addition, depending on the category the following are also required:

(1) Hospitality Services. Certificate from the national registry of the property where the project will be located. Must include a certified property survey map.

(2) Receptive tour and travel services: A Notary certification that the capital stock of the corporation is at least three million Colones. Proof that the company has correspondent relationships with at least three foreign travel agencies.

(3) Domestic and international air transportation of tourists: A certification issued by the Costa Rican Civil Aviation Administration that the company has permission to operate aircraft services.

(4) Water related transportation or recreational activities for tourists: A certification issued by the Municipal government where the activity

will take place authorizing the watercraft to dock at the appropriate facilities. If there are no docking facilities, the applicant must obtain the authorization of the Tourism Institute to provide alternative facilities.

(5) Food and entertainment services: Must have a rating from the Tourism Department as well as the health permit and a Municipal business license.

Once the Costa Rican Tourism Institute has issued its declaration that your particular project is "tourism" related then you can proceed with your application for the Tourism Contract (*Contrato Turistico*). The approval of the Tourism Contract is the document which actually sets forth the benefits and incentives which the applicant shall receive in accordance with the Tourism Development Incentive Law. The applications are reviewed by a tourism regulatory commission (*Comisión Reguladora de Turismo*) which is made up of one representative from each of the following: Tourism Institute, the Minsitry of Revenue and Taxation, the Ministry of Industry, Energy and Mines, and two representatives from private enterprise. If the commission approves the Tourism Contract, it will instruct the Tourism Institute to sign the contractual obligation with the applicant. The contracts are generally valid for six years and are renewed automatically if all the conditions established are complied with.

It is also common to run across advertisements offering the sale of existing tourism contracts. Since most of these are in the name of a Costa Rican corporation, the buyer simply purchases the stock of that corporation and in effect becomes the owner of the tourism contract.

Since tourism contracts are generally approved with a specific project in mind, caution and extensive research and investigation should be done before purchasing an existing tourism contract. You will need to determine if the existing contract and corporation can be used for your particular project.

Also, determine the amount of incentives that have actually been used by the corporation and whether the company has complied with the legal reporting requirements before the Tourism Institute.

2. INCENTIVES TO BUSINESS ENTERPRISES

2.1 THE FREE TRADE ZONES

In an effort to entice foreign business from establishing manufacturing and service facilities in Costa Rica, the legislature authorized the creation of industrial parks that would operate according to Free Trade Zone Legislation. This legislation provides manufacturers and service companies with several financial benefits and tax incentives. Since Costa Rica ratified the World Trade Organization agreements to eliminate fiscal incentives, some of the incentives currently available under this program are due to be phased out by 2015.

A. Enterprise Classification

The Free Trade Zone Law allows enterprises to apply for free trade zone status if their minimum investment in fixed assets in Costa Rica will be $150,000. These companies must set up their facilities in one of the legally authorized free trade zone parks. If the investment in fixed assets exceeds two million Dollars then the company can set up its facility outside of a free trade zone park.

The parks currently authorized to operate under the Free Trade Zone status are: 1. Parque Industrial Zona Franca Zeta Cartago: located in Cartago; 2. Parque Industrial Zona Franca Montecillos: located in Alajuela; 3. Parque Industrial-Zona Franca La Valencia: located in Heredia; 4. Parque Industrial- Zona Franca Alajuela (*Saret*): located in Alajuela; 5. Parque Indutrial Zona Franca Metropolitana: located in Barreal De Heredia; 6. Parque Industrial Zona Franca Bes: located in Alajuela; 7. Centro De Ciencia Y Tecnología Ultrapark: located in Heredia; 8. Parque Industrial Zona Franca Saret Puntarenas: located in Santa Rosa, Puntarenas; 9. Parque Industrial Zona Franca Fórum: located in Santa Ana 10. Parque Industrial Zona Franca Las Américas: located in San Francisco de Heredia. 11. Parque Global, S.A. located in la Aurora de Heredia. 12. Parque Industrial Coyol de Alajuela. For more information on Free Trade Zone parks you can visit the web site of their Association which is www.azofras.com

Free trade zone status is available to those companies that meet the minimum investment requirements set forth above and engage in any of the following activities: (1) Industries which produce, process, or package products for export or re-export; (2) Non manufacturing commercial enterprises which simply distribute or re-package no traditional export or re-export products; (3) Service oriented enterprises or companies which provide services to those companies established in the Free Trade Zone; (4) Enterprises dedicated to scientific research which will increase the technology of the industrial, agro industrial and commercial activities of Costa Rica; (5) Shipbuilding enterprises that operate docking facilities for the construction, repair or maintenance of ships.

B. Financial Benefits and Incentives.

For those enterprises that qualify the law provides the following incentives:

(1) Import duty exemptions on raw materials, component parts, packaging materials, and any other goods which are necessary for the operation of the manufacturing facility; (2) Import duty exemptions on machinery, equipment and vehicles which are necessary for the operation, production, administration and transportation of the manufacturing facility; (3) Exemption from any taxes associated with the export or re-export of products manufactured in the Free Trade Zone facility; (4) A ten year exemption from the payment of taxes on net capital assets. This provision also exempts the facility from the payment of property taxes and property transfer taxes for ten years. (5) Exemption from local sales and consumption taxes on the purchases of goods and services. (6) Exemption from taxes on the repatriation of capital; (7) Tax exemption on any profits generated by the manufacturing facility including exemption on dividends paid to shareholders according to the following table: (a) 100% exemption for eight years and 50% for the following four years for facilities located in areas which are deemed of standard economic development. (b) 100% exemption for twelve years and 50% for the next six years if the area is deemed low economic development; (8) Exemption from the payment of Municipal occupational licenses for a period of ten years; (9) Exemption of import and export duties on the commercial or industrial samples which are either imported or exported. Requires prior approval of the Free Trade Zone Commission; (10) Enterprises operating pursuant to the Free Trade Zone legislation are free to enter into contractual

agreements in foreign currency and may freely hold and transact with foreign currency. This facilitates the repatriation of capital; (11) Facilities which establish operations in areas which are deemed of low economic development by the Ministry of Commerce are entitled to receive a 15% bonus based upon the sum total of the company annual payroll as certified by the Social Security Administration. This benefit shall be paid out for a period of five years.

C. Employee Training

In addition to the financial and tax incentives already indicated, the Free Trade Zone law establishes provisions which can assist facilities located with the free trade zone parks with training of the local labor force. The facility may request that the Free Trade Zone Corporation provide assistance in training employees that will work in the Free Trade Zone.

These training programs are developed and coordinated by the National Training Institute (*Instiuto Nacional de Aprendizaje I.N.A.*).

D. Application Procedures

All applications for Free Trade Zone status must be submitted to the Corporación de La Zona Franca de Exportación, S.A. whose main offices are located in the Commerce Department building in San Jose. This corporation was created by the Free Trade Zone Law to administer the requirements and regulations established by law.

The application for Free Trade Zone status must contain the following information: (1) Name of applicant; (2) Type of application (i.e. free zone or temporary admission); (3) Nature of the business of the applicant; (4) Type of operation which will be carried out in the country; (4) Office and plant facility location; (5) Total investment required; (6) Date that operations will begin, (7) Personnel which will be required to carry out the operation. (*See Appendix 40 for Free Trade Zone application form*).

Once the application is filed with the Free Trade Zone Corporation, the latter will present the application within eight days to the Board of Directors for review. The Board of Directors will evaluate the application and issue a final determination as to the application. If approved, the Free Trade Zone Corporation forwards the file to the Executive Branch of the government so that the Executive Decree which confers the benefits of the free trade zone can be passed.

2.2 DRAWBACK INDUSTRY

The Costa Rican Customs Law (*Ley de Aduanas*) provides incentives to the drawback industry. Under the law, Régimen de Perfeccionamiento Activo, a company may import into Costa Rica raw materials without paying import duties on those raw materials if they will be used in a product that will be re-exported. The raw materials must be transformed, repaired, rebuilt, assembled or incorporated into a finished product that will be exported. In order to request this benefit the company must file an application with the Costa Rican Commercial Promotion office (PROCOMER). If approved the Ministry of Foreign Commerce will issue a written resolution conferring the benefit to the applicant.

CHAPTER 17

ESTABLISHING A BUSINESS ENTERPRISE

Going into business in Costa Rica is not for everyone. The business practices, customs, and the bureaucratic procedures involved take a lot of patience and persistence.

The World Bank rates Costa Rica 25/32 for ease of doing business and 22/32 for ease in starting a new business.

The procedures that will be required to establish a business vary depending on the nature of the business. The information that follows will be the basic steps required of most business enterprises that intend to sell a product or provide a service to the public.

The first decision to be made is whether to operate the business as a sole proprietorship or in the name of a corporate entity (*Sociedad Anonima or Sociedad de Responsabildad Limitada*).

You will probably be better off to set up as a corporate entity since any liabilities of the corporation are limited to the capital contribution of the shareholders. (*See Chapter on Corporate Formation.*)

1. THE MUNICIPAL BUSINESS LICENSE

Now that you have set up your corporation and signed a commercial lease for your business enterprise you need to begin the process which legally allows you to operate the business. The license to operate a business in Costa Rica is known as a *Patente Comercial*. The license must be applied for before the Municipal government where the business establishment is located.

The information which follows are the requirements established by the Municipality of San José. Although similar to most municipal requirements, check with your local municipal government for any variations.

Before you can file for the business license, the Municipality will require a zoning certification known as a Certificado de Uso de Suelo. To request the zoning certification you must fill out the appropriate Municipal form and attach to it a copy of the property survey map where the business will be located. The Municipality will review the zoning requested and if it falls within the authorized parameters for the particular zone will issue the certification.

While you wait for the Municipality to respond to the zoning use you should also fill out the Municipal Business License Application Form (*Solicitud de Patente y Declaración Jurada*). In this statement you are certifying to the Municipal government the type of business you will be engaged in. A copy of this application must be turned into the Department of Revenue who will stamp it as received on the original form. The form must have the Department of Revenue seal on it or the Municipal government will not accept it. (*See Appendix 41 for sample Municipal business license application form*)

Now that you have the two forms discussed above you can prepare the application for a business license. The Municipality of San José requires that the application be addressed to the licensing department (*Departamento de Patentes)* and set forth the following information: (1) Name of applicant; (2) Date the business initiated operations; (3) Specific description as to the nature of the business; (4) Commercial name of the business; (5) Exact location and telephone number of the business. The application must be signed by the applicant and the owner of the commercial local where the business is located. If the owner of the local does not sign the application you will need to attach a copy of the lease on the local where the business will be located. The name of the applicant for the business license must coincide with the name of the leaseholder. All signatures on the business license application must be authenticated by an Attorney.

In addition to the application, the zoning form (*Uso de Suelo*) and the license application (*Solicitud de Patente y Declaración Jurada*), the applicant must also prove that the company has a worker's compensation policy (*Poliza de Riesgos del Trabajo*) issued by the National Insurance Institute. Likewise, depending on the type of business involved, it may require authorization from the Department of Public Health who will issue a health permit (*Permiso Sanitario de Funcionamiento*). These certificates are issued by the regional office of the Public Health Department where the business is located and is required only for certain types of businesses. Generally, the Municipality will not accept an application unless all the required documents are attached to it. The length of time it takes to process an application varies for each Municipal government. Likewise, keep in mind that depending on the type of business involved there may be additional requirements from other governmental entities so research it well before you embark on this venture.

2. REGISTRATION OF THE BUSINESS WITH THE TAX AUTHORITIES.

Now that you are open for business, the law requires that you register with the Revenue Department (*Tributación Directa*) to collect the applicable sales tax. To that end, the tax authorities require that the sales invoices (*factura*) issued by each and every business in the country be printed with one of the authorized printers established by the Department of Revenue.

If the business will only issue cash register receipts then it must apply for this authorization. By law every business must issue its customer an approved invoice and collect the applicable sales tax.

Any business that is required to collect the sales tax by turning over the sales tax collected to the Department of Revenue on a monthly basis at the end of each month. The Department of Revenue is authorized by law to close any business that does not comply with the reporting and collection requirements.

3. BUYING AN EXISTING BUSINESS

The situation may arise when you would consider purchasing a business that has already been established and is in operation. The majority of such businesses are run as a corporation (*Sociedad Anonima*) and the purchase of the business would entail a purchase of the corporate stock, inventory, assets, and fixtures which belong to the corporation.

Extreme caution and thorough research is required before purchasing such a corporation. There is always the possibility that the corporation has hidden liabilities. Before any decision is made you need to carefully review the following documents: (1) Corporate minutes books:

The seller should provide you with the stockholders log book, the shareholders minutes book, and the minutes book for the board of directors. (2) Corporate articles of incorporation and by-laws: These documents will provide you with the detailed information of the corporation including the authorization of the corporate officers to act on behalf of the corporation. To ensure that you have all recorded documents available for review it is recommended that you photocopy the entire microfilm jacket from the Mercantile Section of the National Registry. All corporations recorded in Costa Rica have a microfilm jack which contains all the entries recorded for that corporation. (3) Corporate stock certificates: This will reveal the owners (shareholders of the corporation). It is important that the owners which appear in the share certificate also be registered in the shareholders log book and signed by the Secretary of the Corporation. (4) Corporate accounting books: By law, the corporation must have a Daily Ledger, Inventory and Balances, and General Ledger. You should have your accountant review the entries in the accounting books. (5) Corporate tax returns for the corporation: Make sure that the corporation which you are purchasing is in compliance with the applicable tax laws related to income, sales, property, and municipal taxes; otherwise you may inherit somebody else's tax mess; (6) Financial Statements: A business which has been well run and managed maintains accurate financial statements indicating revenue, expenses, and profits. (7) Business inventory: The seller should provide you with a detailed list of the inventory that is included in the sale of the business. (9) Commercial leases, if any: If the business you intend to purchase is located in a rented commercial local then you need to carefully review the lease agreement and inform the landlord of the proposed sale. (10) List of business suppliers and vendors: Request the seller to provide you with a list of the companies or individuals which supplied goods or services to the business and if there are any outstanding invoices. This can reduce the potential for undiscovered liabilities to suppliers. (11) Procure the telephone line (s): Be sure to include in the inventory of the corporation the telephone lines for the business. In Costa Rica it is often difficult to obtain phone lines and you don't want to purchase a business and then discover that the seller took the phone lines with them. (12) Review all permits and licenses: Request a copy of all the relevant permits and licenses which are applicable to your business and make sure that they are all valid and current. Depending on the nature of the business some relevant permits would include: Sanitation permit (*Permiso Sanitario de Funcionamiento*); business license (*Patente Comercial*); liquor license *(Patente de Licores)*; Gubernatorial permits as required *(Permiso de Gobernación)*. (13) Employee list: Request a list of the persons employed by the business. The list should set forth the complete name, identity card number, position, date employed and salary. Employees acquire rights after three months of employment and you should know your financial exposure if you assume their employment *(See Chapter 5 Employee-Employer relations for more information about labor laws.)* (14) Social Security and Workers Compensation policies: Depending on the nature of the business, the corporation may have an account at the Social Security Administration *(Caja Costarricense de Seguro Social)*. Be sure that payments are current. The same holds true for any workers compensation policies with the Instituto Nacional de Seguros. (15) Receipts for Utilities: Request that the seller provide you with proof of paid electrical, water, and telephone bills.

Once you have reviewed the required documentation and want to proceed with the purchase have an Attorney draft a sales contract for you to ensure a smooth transition of the business from the seller to the buyer.

The Costa Rican Commercial Code provides an alternative to purchasing an existing business which ensures that the buyer will not be liable for hidden liabilities. Titled the Purchase and Sale of Industrial and Commercial Establishments, Articles 478-489 of the Commercial Code sets forth the procedures that must be followed to purchase such a business enterprise. The law requires that the purchase price for the business be deposited with an independent Trustee. Notice is then published for three consecutive times in the newspaper requesting creditors or others having an interest in the business to file their claim within fifteen days from the first date of publication. Once the period to file a claim has expired a creditor committee is convened to establish the disbursement of the deposit among the creditors. If the creditors agree then the liquidation proceeds. If any of the creditors disagree they can file their claim in court. Once the process is complete, the fixtures, inventory, business records, patents and trademarks of the business pass on to the new buyer.

Due to the time frame and procedural requirements involved, the sale of a business pursuant to the Commercial Code sometimes becomes impractical. Which option is best for you should be determined after consultation with your Attorney.

APPENDIX

Appendix 1 - Key Government Offices of Costa Rica

Ministerio de Economía, Industria y Comercio
Ministry of Economy Industry & Comerce
Edificio del IFAM, Residencial Los Colegios, Moravia.
www.meic.go.cr
Telephone: 2235-2700, ext. 269
Fax: 2235-7325
Apartado postal: 10216-1000, San José, Costa Rica

Ministerio de Relaciones Exteriores y Culto
Ministry of Foreign Affairs
Avenida 7-9, Calle 11-13 San José
Tel. 2223-75-55
Apartado 10027-1000 San José, Costa Rica
www.rree.go.cr

Ministerio de Seguridad Pública
Minsitry of Public Security
Barrio Cordoba, Frente Liceo Castro Madriz
Teléfono: 2586-4000:
Apartado: 4768-1000 San José Costa Rica
www.msp.go.cr

Ministerio de Cultura y Juventud
Ministry of Culture & Youth
Calle 11 y 15 Avenida 3 y 7
Tel: 2255 3765 / 2255 3188 / 2255 3638
Apartado: 10227-1000 San José
www.mcjdcr.go.cr

Ministerio de Hacienda
Ministry of Finance
Tel:2284-5348 / 2284-5245
Apartado

www.hacienda.go.cr
Ministerio de Trabajo y Seguridad Social
Ministry of Labor and Welfare
Barrio Tournón, San José.
Central Telefónica 2542-0000.
Apartado 10133-1000. Costa Rica
www.ministrabajo.go.cr

Ministerio de Planificación Nacional y Política Económica
Ministry of National Planning & Economic Policy
Barrio Dent, San Pedro de Montes de Oca de Autos Subarú 200 mts. Al Norte,.
Teléfono: (506) 2281-2700
Apartado postal: 10127-1000 San José, Costa Rica
www.mideplan.go.cr

Ministerio de Agricultura y Ganadería
Ministry of Agriculture
San José, Sabana Sur, antiguo Colegio La Salle.
Apartado: 10094-1000 San José- Costa Rica
Tel: 2231-23 44
www.mag.go.cr

Ministerio de Ciencia y Tecnología
Ministry of Science & Technology
San José, Costa Rica
Apartado Postal: 5589-1000
Teléfono: 2248-1515
Dirección: 50 metros este del Museo Nacional, calles 19 y 17, Avenida 2da.
www.micit.go.cr

Ministerio de Obras Públicas y Transportes
Ministry of Transportation
Tel: 506 2523-2000, Sede Central
Apartado Postal 10176-1000
www.mopt.go.cr

Ministerio de Salud
Ministry of Health
Calle16, Avenida 6 y 8, San Jose, Costa Rica
Apartado: 104123-1000 San Jose
Tel: 2223-0333
www.ministeriodesalud.go.cr

Ministerio de Educación Pública
Ministry of Education
Teléfono (506) 256-8132.
Edificio Rofas, frente al Hospital San Juan de Dios.
www.mep.go.cr

Ministerio de Justicia
Ministry of Justice
Tel: 2256-6700
Calle 1era Avenida 12 y 14
Apartado 5685-1000 San Jose
www.mj.go.cr

Ministerio de la Presidencia
Ministry of Presidency
Tel: (506) 2207-9100
Fax:(506) 2253-1485
Apartado Postal: 520-2010 Zapote, San José
www.casapres.go.cr

Ministerio de Ambiente y Energía
Ministry of Environment & Energy
Tel: 2233-4533
Avenida 8 y 10, calle 25. Del Edificio de la Corte Suprema de

Justicia 200 E, frente a la Iglesia Votivo Corazón de Jesús.
www.minae.go.cr

Ministerio de Comercio Exterior
COMEX
Ministry of Foreign Commerce
Tel: (506) 2299-4700
Fax: (506) 2255-3281
Apartado 2297-1007 Centro
Colón, Costa Rica
www.comex.go.cr

Instituto Costarricense de Turismo ICT
Tel: (506) 2299-5800
Costado Este del Puente Juan Pablo II, sobre Autopista General Cañas
Apartado 777-1000 San Jose
www.visitcostarica.com/ict

PROCOMER
Foreign Commerce Promotion Office
Tel: (506) 2299-4700
Fax: (506) 2233-5755
Edificio Centro de Comercio Exterior. Avenida 3a. Calle 40. San José, Costa Rica.
Apartado Postal: 1278-1007 Paseo Colón, Costa Rica
www.procomer.com

Appendix 2
The Costa Rican Judicial System Contact Information

San Jose

JUZGADOS	TELEFONO
Civil 1	2295-3419
Civil 2	2295-3424
Civil 3	2295-3429
Civil 4	2295-3434
Civil 5	2295-3439
Civil 6	2295-3444
Penal I Cir	2295-3503
Penal II Cir	2247-9153
Labor II Cir	2247-9175
Admin II Cir	2247-9137
Family 1	2295-3473
Family	2295-3479

MENOR CUANTIA

Civil 1	2295-3152
Civil 2	2295-3156
Civil 3	2295-3160
Civil 4	2295-3164
Civil 5	2295-3168
Civil 6	2295-3172
Misdeamenor I	2295-3183
Misdeamenor II	2247-9241
Child Support I	2295-3199
Child Support II	2247-9175
Transit Court I	2257-0053
Transit Court II	2247-9271
Aserri	2230-3383
Escazu	2228-0453
Hatillo	2254-3234
Mora	2249-1026
Puriscal	2416-6151
Santa Ana	2282-6270
Acosta	2410-0134
Turrubares	2419-0210
San Sebastian	2227-0467
Alajuelita	2254-6184
Desamparados	2259-2708
Pavas	2247-9056

Alajuela

JUZGADOS	TELEFONO
Civil Court	2437-0437
Penal Court	2437-0415
Family & Juvenile	2437-0407

MENOR CUANTIA

Misdeamenor	2437-9380
Atenas	2446-5175
Grecia	2494-2760
Guatuso	2464-0229
Los Chiles	2471-1176
Naranjo	2450-0079
Orotina	2428-8004
Palmares	2453-3570
Poas	
San Ramon	2445-7181
San Mateo	2428-8361
Upala	2470-0150

Cartago

JUZGADOS	TELEFONO
Civil Court	2550-0448
Penal Court	2550-0456
Family & Juvenile	2550-0390

MENOR CUANTIA

Civil	2550-0398
Misdeamenor 1	2550-0457
Misdeamenor 2	2550-0385
Alvarado	2534-4051
Jimenez	2532-2254
La Union	2279-5064
Paraiso	2574-7249
Turrialba	2556-0756

Heredia

JUZGADOS	TELEFONO
Civil Court	2277-0462
Penal Court	2277-0431
Family & Juvenile	2277-0409

MENOR CUANTIA

Misdeamenor 1	2277-0388
San Isidro	2268-8009
San Rafael	2262-3804
Santo Domingo	2244-0197
Sarapiqui	2766-6238

Guanacastes

JUZGADOS	TELEFONO
Civil Court	
Cir Liberia- Cañas	2680-0194
Civil Court	
Cir Nicoya-Sta Cruz	2680-1072
Civ- Labor- Family	
Santa Cruz	2680-0049
Cañas	2669-0023
Nicoya	2685-5051
Penal	
Penal Liberia	2690-0176
Penal Cañas	2669-0201
Penal Nicoya	2685-5051
Penal Santa Cruz	2680-0446

MENOR CUANTIA

Liberia	2690-0164
La Cruz	2679-9145
Bagaces	2671-1016
Sta Cruz	2680-0076
Carrillo	2688-8096
Cañas	2669-0024
Abangares	2662-0158
Tilaran	2695-5021
Nicoya	2685-5051
Nandayure	2657-7113

Punta Arenas

JUZGADOS	TELEFONO
Civil Court	2630-0396
Penal	2630-0318

MENOR CUANTIA

Misdeamenor 1	2630-0340
Misdeamenor 2	2630-0318
Jicaral	2650-0050
Cobano	2642-0233
Esparza	2635-5032
Montes de Oro	2639-9009
Aguirre y Parrita	2777-0159
Garabito	2643-3659

Limón

JUZGADOS	TELEFONO
Civil Court	2799-1300
Penal Court	2799-1402
Juvenile Court	2799-1410

MENOR CUANTIA

Civil	2799-1377
Misdeamenor	2799-1377
Bribri	2751-0037
Matina	2718-6174
Siquirres	2768-9204
Pococi	2710-6362
Guacimo	2716-6463

Appendix 3

The Political Subdivisions of Costa Rica

PROVINCE OF SAN JOSE

CANTON N° 1 SAN JOSE: Size: 45 Sq. Km. Founded: December 7, 1848
Districts: 1 Carmen, 2 Merced, 3 Hospital, 4 Catedral, 5 Zapote,
6 San Francisco de Dos Rios, 7 Uruca, 8 Mata Redonda.

CANTON N° 2 ESCAZU: Size: 35 Sq. Km Founded: December 7, 1848
Districts: 1Escazu Central, 2 San Antonio, 3 San Rafael

CANTON N°3 DESAMPARADOS: Size: 126 Sq Km, Founded
November 4, 1862
Districts: 1 Desamparados Central, 2 San Miguel, 3 San Juan de Dios, 4
San Rafael, 5 San Antonio, 6 Frailes, 7 Patarra, 8 San Cristobal, 9 Rosario,
10 Damas, 11 San Rafael Abajo.

CANTON N°4 PURISCAL: Size 561 Sq Km. Founded August 7, 1868.
Districts: 1 Santiago, 2 Mercedes Sur, 3 Barbacoas, 4 Grifo Alto,
5 San Rafael, 6 Candelaria, 7 Desamparaditos, 8 San Antonio.

CANTON N°5 TARRAZU Size: 233 Sq Km, Founded August 7, 1868
Districts: 1 San Marcos, 2 San Lorenzo, 3 San Carlos.

CANTON N°6 ASERRI: Size: 182 Sq Km. Founded November 27, 1882
Districts: 1 Aserri, 2 Tarbaca, 3 Vuelta de Jorco, 4 San Gabriel,
5 La legua, 6 Monterrey.

CANTON N°7 MORA: Size: 161 Sq Km. Founded May 25, 1883.
Districts: 1 Colon, 2 Guayabo, 3 Tabarcia, 4 Piedras Negras, 5 Picagres

CANTON N°8 GOICOECHEA Size: 31 Sq Km. Founded June 8, 1891.
Districts: 1 Guadalupe, 2 San Francisco, 3 Calle Blancos, 4 Carmen,
5 Ipis, 6 Rancho Redondo, 7 Mata de Platano .

CANTON N°9 SANTA ANA: Size: 62 Sq Km. Founden January 1, 1907
Districts: 1 Santa Ana, 2 Salitral, 3 Pozos, 4 La Uruca, 5 Piedades,
6 Brasil

CANTON N°10 ALAJUELITA: Size 21 Sq Km. Founded April 5, 1909
   Districts: 1 Alajuelita, 2 San Josecito, 3 San Antonio, 4 Concepcion,
   5 San Felipe

CANTON N°11 VASQUEZ DE CORONADO: Size 215 Sq Km.
   Founded Nov 15, 1910
   Districts: 1 San Isidro, 2 San Rafael, 3 Jesus (Dulce Nombre)

CANTON N°12 ACOSTA Size: 342 Sq Km. Founded: October 27, 1910
   Districts: 1 San Ignacio, 2 Guaitil, 3 Palmichal, 4 Cangrejal,
   5 Sabanillas.

CANTON N°13 TIBAS: Size 9 Sq Km. Founded: July 27, 1917
   Districts: 1 San Juan, 2 Cinco Esquinas, 3 Anselmo.

CANTON N°14 MORAVIA: Size: 29 Sq Km. Funded January 8, 1914.
   Districts: 1 San Vicente, 2 San Jeronimo, 3 La Trinidad.

CANTON N°15 MONTES DE OCA: Size 16 Sq Km.
   Founded October 2, 1915
   Districts: 1 San Pedro, 2 Sabanilla, 3 Mercedes, 4 San Rafael.

CANTON N°16 TURRUBARES: Size 415.69 Sq Km. Founded July 31, 1920
   Districts: 1 San Pablo, 2 San Pedro, 3 San Juan de Mata.

CANTON N°17 DOTA: Size 483 Sq Km. Founded July 23, 1925.
   Districts: 1 Santa Maria, 2 El Jardin, 3 Copey

CANTON N° 18 CURRIDABAT: Size 16 Sq Km. Founded August 21, 1929
   Districts: 1 Curridabat, 2 Granadilla, 3 Sanchez, 4 Tirrases.

CANTON N° 19 PEREZ ZELEDON: Size: 1-800 Sq Km.
   Founded October 9, 1931
   Districts: 1 San Isidro del General, 2 GENERAL, 3 Daniel Flores,
   4 Rivas, 5 San Pedro, 6 Platanares, 7 Pejibaye, 8 Cajon.

CANTON N° 20 LEON CORTES: Size 120 Sq Km. Founded June 12, 1962.
   Districts: 1 San Pablo, 2 San Andres, 3 Llano Bonito, 4 San Isidro,
   5 Santa Cruz

PROVINCE OF ALAJUELA

CANTON N°1 ALAJUELA: Size: 389.14 Sq Km.
Founded December 12, 1848.
Districts: 1 Alajuela, 2 San Jose, 3 Carrizal: 4 San Antonio, 5 Guacima,
6 San Isidro, 7 Sabanilla, 8 San Rafael, 9 Rio Segundo, 10 Desamparados,
11 Turrucares, 12 Tambor, 13 Garita, 14 Sarapiqui.

CANTON N°2 SAN RAMON: Size 774.23 Sq Km.
Founded October 21, 1856.
Districts: 1 San Ramon, 2 Santiago, 3 San Juan, 4 Piedades Norte,
5 Piedades Sur, 6 San Rafael, 7 San Isidro, 8 Angeles, 9 Alfaro, 10 Voho,
11 Concepcion, 12 Zapotal, 13 Piedras Blancas.

CANTON N°3 GRECIA: Size: 217.38 Sq Km.
Founded July 24, 1867.
Districts: 1 Grecia, 2 San Isidro, 3 San Jose, 4 San Roque, 5 Tacares,
6 Rio Cuarto, 7 Puente de Piedra, 8 Bolivar.

CANTON N°4 SAN MATEO: Size 135 Sq Km. Founded October 7, 1868.
Districts: 1 San Mateo, 2 Desmonte, 3 Jesus Maria.

CANTON N° 5 ATENAS: Size: 125 Sq Km. Founded October 7 1868
Districts: 1 Atenas, 2 Jesus, 3 Mercedes, 4 San Isidro, 5 Concepcion,
6 San Jose, 7 Santa Eulalia.

CANTON N°6 NARANJO: Size: 128.31 Sq Km. Founded March 9, 1886.
Districts: 1 Naranjo, 2 San Miguel, 3 San Jose, 4 Cirri Sur,
5 San Jeronimo.

CANTON N° 7: PALMARES: Size 45 Sq Km. Founded July 30, 1888.
Districts: 1 Palmares, 2 Zaragoza, 3 Buenos Aires, 4 Santiago,
5 Candelaria, 6 Esquipulas, 7 La Granja.

CANTON N° 8 POAS: Size 68.56 Sq Km. Founded October 15, 1901.
Districts: 1 San Pedro, 2 San Juan, 3 San Rafael, 4 Carillos, 5
Sabana Redonda

CANTON N°9 OROTINA: Size: 130 Sq Km. Founded August 1, 1908.
Districts: 1 Orotina, 2 Mastate, 3 Hacienda, Coyolar, 5 Ceiba.

CANTON N°10 SAN CARLOS: Size 3.373-40 Sq Km.
Foundesd September 26, 1911.
Districts: 1 Quesada, 2 Florencia, 3 Buena Vista, 4 Aguas Zarcas,
5 Venecia, 6 Pital, 7 Fortuna, 8 Tigra, 9 Palmera, 10 Venado, 11 Cutris.

CANTON N°11 ALFARO RUIZ:Size: 129.29 Sq Km.
Founded June 29, 1915.
Districts: 1 Zarcero, 2 Laguna, 3 Tapezo, 4 Guadalupe, 5 Palmira,
6 Zapote.

CANTON N°12 VALVERDE VEGA: Size: 307.20 Sq Km.
Founded October 26, 1949.
Districts: 1 Sarchi, 2 Sarchi Sur, 3 Toro Amarillo, 4 San Pedro,
5 Rodriguez.

CANTON N°13 UPALA: Size: 1.780 Sq Km. Founded: March 17, 1970.
District: 1 Upala, 2 Aguas Claras, 3 San Jose, 4 Bijagua, 5 Delicias.

CANTON N° 14 LOS CHILES: Size: 1.264 Sq Km. Founded March 17, 1970.
Districts: 1 Los Chiles, 2 Caño Negro, 3 El Amparo, 4 San Jorge.

CANTON N°15 GUATUSO: Size 724 Sq Km. Founded March 17, 1970.
Districts: 1 San Rafael, 2 Buena Vista, 3 Cote.

PROVINCE OF CARTAGO

CANTON N° 1 CARTAGO: Size: 143.23 Sq Km.
Founded December 6, 1848.
Districts: 1 Oriental, 2 Occidental, 3 El Carmen, 4 San Nicolas,
5 San Francisco, 6 Guadalupe, 7 Coralillo, 8 Tierra Blanca,
9 Dulce Nombre, 10 Llano Grande.

CANTON N° 2 PARAISO Size: 287.22 Sq Km.
Foundesd December 12, 1848.
Districts: 1 Paraiso, 2 Santiago, 3 Orosi, 4 Cachi.

CANTON N° 3 LA UNION: Size: 48.00 Sq Km.
Founded December 7, 1848.
Districts: 1 Tres Rios, 2 San Diego, 3 San Juan, 4 San Rafael,
5 Concepcion, 6 Dulce Nombre, 7 San Ramon, 8 Rio Azul.

CANTON N° 4 JIMENEZ: Size: 345.65 Sq. Km.
Founded August 19, 1903.
Districts: 1Juan Viñas, 2 Tucurrique, 3 Pejibaye.

CANTON N° 5 TURRIALBA: Size: 1.644.57 Sq Km.
Founded August 19, 1989.
Districts: 1 Turrialba, 2 Suiza, 3 Peralta, 4 Santa Cruz, 5 Santa Teresita,
6 Pavones, 7 Tuis, 8 Tayutic, 9 Santa Rosa.

CANTON N°6 ALVARADO: Size: 152.62 Sq Km.
Founded July9, 1989.
Districts: 1 Pacayas, 2 Cervantes, 3 Capellades.

CANTON N° 7 OREAMUNO: Size: 32.32 Sq Km.
Founded October 17,1914.
Districts: 1 Sn Rafael, 2 Cot, 3 Potrero Cerrado, 4 Cipreses,
5 Santa Rosa.

CANTON N°8 EL GUARCO: Size: 194 Sq Km.
Founded July 7, 1939.
Districts: 1 El Tejar, 2 San Isidro, 3 Tobosi, 4 Patio de Agua.

PROVINCE OF HEREDIA.

CANTON N° 1 HEREDIA: Size: 282.51 Sq Km.
Founded December 7, 1848.
Districts: 1 Heredia, 2 Mercedes, 3 San Francisco, 4 Ulba,
5 Varablanca.

CANTON N° 2 BARVA: Size: 59.72 Sq Km.
Founded December 7, 1848.
Districts: 1 Barva, 2 San Pedro, 3 San Pablo, 4 San Roque,
5 Santa Lucia, 6 San Jose de la Montaña.

CANTON N° 3 SANTA BARBARA: Size: 73.50. Inni.
Founded: September 29, 1882.
Districts: 1 Santa Barbara, 2 San Pedro, 3 San Juan, 4 Jesus,
5 Santo Domingo.

CANTON N° 4 SANTO DOMINGO: Size: 31.01 Sq Km.
Founded October 28, 1869.
Districts: 1 Santo Domingo, 2 San Vicente, 3 San Miguel Sur, 4 Paracito, 5 Santo Tomas, 6 Santa Rosa, 7 Tures, 8 Para.

CANTON N° 5 SAN RAFAEL: Size:57.42 Sq Km.
Founded May 5, 1885.
Districts: 1 San Rafael, 2 San Josecito, 3 Santiago, 4, Angeles, 5 Concepcion.

CANTON N° 6 SAN ISIDRO: Size: 25.84 Sq Km.
Founded July 13, 1905.
Districts: 1 San Isidro, 2 San Jose, 3 Concepcion.

CANTON N° 7 BELEN: Size: 12.63 Sq Km.
Founded June 8, 1907.
Districts: 1 San Antonio, 2 Ribera, 3 Asuncion.

CANTON N° 8 FLORES: Size: 7.61 Sq Km.
Founded October 12, 1915.
Districts: 1 San Joaquin, 2 Barrantes, 3 Llorente.

CANTON N° 9 SAN PABLO: Size 8.50 Sq. Km.
Founded July 18, 1961.
Districts: 1 San Pablo

CANTON N° 10 SARAPIQUI: Size: 2.349.37 Sq Km:
Founded: November 8, 1970.
Districts: 1 Puerto Viejo, 2 La Virgen, 3 Horquetas.

PROVINCE OF GUANACASTE

CANTON N° 1 LIBERIA: Size: 1.567.65 Sq Km.
Founded: December 7, 1948.
Districts: 1 Liberia, 2 Cañas Dulces, 3 Mayorga, Quebrada Grande, 4 Nacascolo, 5 Curubande, Cereceda.

CANTON N° 2 NICOYA: Size: 1.316.00 Sq Km.
Founded: December 7, 1948.
Districts: 1 Nicoya, 2 Mansion, 3 San Antonio, 4 Quebrada Honda, 5 Samara.

CANTON N° 3 SANTA CRUZ: Size: 1.428.23 Sq Km.
    Founded: December 7, 1948.
    Districts: 1 Santa Cruz, 2 Bolson, 3 Veintisiete de Abril, 4 Tempate,
    5 Cartagena.

CANTON N° 4 BAGACES: Size: 1.019.61 Sq Km.
    Founded: December 7, 1948.
    Districts: 1 Bagaces, 2 Fortuna, 3 Mogote.

CANTON N° 5 CARILLO: Size: 601.57 Sq Km.
    Founded: June 16, 1877.
    Districts: 1 Filadelfia, 2 Palmira, 3 Sardinal, 4 Belen.

CANTON N° 6 CAÑAS: Size: 938.04 Sq Km:
    Founded: July 12, 1854.
    Districts: 1 Cañas.

CANTON N° 7 ABANGARES: Size: 662.75 Sq Km.
    Founded: January 1, 1989.
    Districts: 1 Las Juntas, 2 La Sierra, 3 San Juan, 4 Colorado.

CANTON N° 8 TILARAN: Size: 623.15 Sq Km.
    Founded: August 21, 1923.
    Districts: 1 Tilaran, 2 Quebrada Grande, 3 Tronadora, 4 Santa Rosa,
    5 Libano, 6 Tierras Morenas.

CANTON N° 9 NANDAYURE: Size: 586 Sq Km.
    Founded: October 15, 1961.
    Districts: 1 Carmona, 2 Santa Rita, 3 Zapotal, 4 San Pablo, 5 Porvenir,
    6 Bejuco.

CANTON N° 10 LA CRUZ: Size: 430 Sq Km.
    Founded: July 23, 1969.
    Districts: 1 La Cruz, 2 Santa Cecilia, 3 La Garita, 4 Santa Elena.

CANTON N° 11 HOJANCHA: Size: 215 Sq Km.
    Founded: November 11, 1971.
    Districts: 1 Hojancha.

PROVINCE OF PUNTARENAS

CANTON N° 1 PUNTARENAS: Size: 2.165.64 Sq Km.
Founded: December 12, 1984.
Districts: 1 Puntarenas, 2 Pitahaya, 3 Chomes, 4 Lepanto, 5 Paquera, 6 Manzanillo, 7 Guacimal, 8 Barranca, 9 Monte Verde, 10 Isla del Coco, 11 Cobano.

CANTON N° 2 ESPARZA: Size: 227.20 Sq Km.
Founded: November 6, 1851.
Districts: 1 Esparza, 2 San Juan Grande, 3 Macacona, 4 San Rafael, 5 San Jeronimo.

CANTON N° 3 BUENOS AIRES: Size: 2.260 Sq Km.
Founded: July 29, 1940.
Districts: 1 Buenos Aires, 2 Volcan, 3 Potrero Grande, 4 Boruca, 5 Pilas, 6 Colinas.

CANTON N° 4 MONTES DE ORO: Size: 176.70 Sq Km.
Founded: July 17, 1915.
Districts: 1 Miramar, 2 La Union, 3 San Isidro.

CANTON N° 5 OSA: Size: 2.262.20 Sq Km.
Founded: July 29, 1940.
Districts: 1 Puerto Cortes, Palmar 2 Palmar Norte, 3 Sierpe.

CANTON N° 6 AGUIRRE: Size: 496.60 Sq Km.
Founded: October 10, 1948.
Districts: 1 Quepos, 2 Savegre, 3 Naranjito.

CANTON N° 7 GOLFITO: Size: 2.292.30 Sq Km: Founded: June 10, 1949.
Districts: 1 Golfito 2 Puerto Jimenez, 3 Guaycara.

CANTON N° 8 COTO BRUS: Size: 967.00 Sq Km: Founded.
December 12, 1965.
Districts: 1 San Vitor, 2 Sabalito, 3 Agua Buena, 4 Limoncito.

CANTON N° 9 PARRITA: Size: 472 Sq Km. Founded: July 17, 1971.
Districts: 1 Parrita.

CANTON N° 10 CORREDORES: Size: 567 Sq Km.
Founded: October 19, 1973.
Districts: 1 Neilyr, 2 La Cuesta, 3 Canoas.

CANTON N° 11 GARABITO: Size: 350 Sq Km.
Founded: September 25, 1980.
Districts: 1 Jaco.

PROVINCE OF LIMON

CANTON N° 1 LIMON: Size: 1.756 Sq Km.
Founded: July 25, 1892.
Districts: 1 Limon.

CANTON N° 2 POCOCI: Size: 2.348Sq Km.
Founded September 19, 1911.
Districts: 1 Gaupiles, 2 Jimenez, 3 La Rita, 4 Roxana, 5 Cariari, 6 Colorado..

CANTON N° 3 SIQUIRRES: Size: 920.00 Sq Km.
Founded: September 19, 1911.
Districts: 1 Siquirres, 2 Pacuarito, 3 Florida, 4 Germania, 5 Cairo.

CANTON N° 4 TALAMANCA: Size: 3.004 Sq Km.
Founded: May 20, 1969.
Districts: 1 Bratsi, 2 Sixaola, 3 Cahuita.

CANTON N° 5 MATINA: Size: 770 Sq Km.
Founded June 27, 1969.
Districts: 1 Matina, 2 Batan, 3 Carrandi.

CANTON N° 6 GUACIMO: Size: 502.00Sq Km.
Founded: May 8, 1971.
Districts: 1 Guacimo, 2 Mercedes, 3 Pocora, 4 Rio Jimenez.

Appendix 4

Corporate Incorporation Form

NÚMERO CIENTO VEINTISIETE: Ante mí, PETER JUAN DOE, Notario Público con oficina abierta en San José (*quinientos metros oeste y ciento cincuenta sur de Multicentro Paco, San Rafael de Escazú*) comparecen FRANCISCO PEREZ PEREZ, mayor, soltero comerciante, vecino de San Jose, Barrio Don Bosco, veinticinco metros al sur de Purdy Motors Paseo Colon, con cédula de identidad número uno- quinientos veinte- trescientos cuatro y JOHN GILBERT, único apellido en razón de su nacionalidad Canadiense, mayor, casado una vez, empresario, vecino de San Rafael de Escazú, con pasaporte de su país número VH- cinco cinco cuatro dos nueve y DICEN: Que vienen a constituir una sociedad que se regirá por el Código de Comercio y sus reformas y por las siguientes cláusulas: **PRIMERA: La Denominación**: La sociedad se denominara: **EMPRESA INTERNACIONAL, SOCIEDAD ANÓNIMA**, siendo este nombre de fantasía, pudiendo abreviarse las dos últimas palabras "S.A.", **SEGUNDA**: Domicilio: El domicilio social será en la ciudad de San José, Sabana Oeste, de la Pops setecientos metros al Oeste y diez al sur sin perjuicio de tener sucursales o agencias en los demás lugares del país o fuera de él. **TERCERA: Plazo**: El plazo social de la compañía será de noventa y nueve años a partir de hoy. **CUARTA: Objeto**: El objeto de la sociedad será la industria, ganadería, agricultura, asesoría, consultoría, Bienes y Raíces y el comercio en general, la representación de casas extranjeras y nacionales, la importación y exportación de todo tipo de bienes y cualesquiera otros negocios relacionados de cualquier índole y podrá formar parte de otras sociedades así como vender, hipotecar, pignorar, arrendar, poseer y disponer, así como recibir toda clase de bienes muebles e inmuebles, derechos reales y personales, títulos valores y similares y enajenarlos o gravarlos conforme a sus necesidades y en general celebrar toda clase de actos o contratos para la debida explotación de la empresa, pudiendo formar parte de otras sociedades, abrir cuentas corrientes en cualquiera de los Bancos del Sistema Bancario Nacional o en el extranjero, pudiendo ser fiduciario, fideicomitente, fideicomisario o beneficiario. Podrá otorgar garantías fiduciarias o reales a favor de terceros, socios o extraños, cuando perciba retribución económica por ello, bastando la actuación para tener por existente la retribución así como otorgar toda clase de contratos, civiles, mercantiles, laborales. **QUINTA: Capital**: El capital social es la suma de **SESENTA MIL COLONES EXACTOS**, representados por SESENTA ACCIONES comunes y nominativas de MIL Colones cada una de ellas, íntegramente suscritas y pagadas por ambos socios por iguales partes, mediante dos letras de cambio numeradas UNO y DOS a favor de la compañía las cuales quedan depositadas en manos del Presidente de la compañía de lo cual da fe la suscrita Notario. Podrán emitirse títulos representativos de una o más acciones los que deberán ser firmados por el Presidente de la Junta Directiva. **SEXTA: Administración**: Los negocios sociales serán administrados, por una Junta Directiva formada por tres miembros socios o no quienes durarán en sus funciones todo el plazo que dure la sociedad, los cuales no son nombrados por votos acumulativos, reservándose la Asamblea de Accionistas el derecho de revocar los nombramientos en cualquier momento y elegir otros personeros y que son PRESIDENTE, SECRETARIO Y TESORERO. Corresponde al Presidente la representación judicial y extrajudicial de la compañía con las facultades de Apoderado Generalísimo sin límite de suma todo de conformidad con el artículo mil doscientos cincuenta y tres del Código Civil. Podrán otorgar toda clase de poderes a miembros de la Junta Directiva, accionistas, u otras personas, incluyendo los necesarios para operar cuentas bancarias, revocar los poderes conferidos, sustituir total o parcialmente su mandato sin que por ello pierdan sus facultades originales incluyendo las facultades que indica el artículo mil doscientos cincuenta y tres del Código Civil. **SÉTIMA: La Vigilancia**: La vigilancia de la sociedad estará a cargo de un Fiscal nombrado por el mismo período de la Junta y quien podrá ser o no socio y durará en sus funciones todo el plazo social de la compañía. **OCTAVA: Agente Residente**: Se nombrará un Agente Residente de conformidad con el inciso trece del artículo dieciocho del Código de Comercio. **NOVENA: Inventario y Balance**: La sociedad celebrará una Asamblea General Ordinaria de Accionistas dentro de los tres meses siguientes al cierre del año fiscal para conocer de los asuntos que indica el artículo ciento cincuenta y cinco del Código de Comercio. El balance se confeccionará de conformidad con la técnica contable imperante en la empresa y en él se estimarán los valores del activo por el precio del día, los créditos dudosos por su valor probable, no debiendo figurar en el activo los créditos incobrables. Los dividendos se pagarán y las pérdidas se absorberán en proporción a la acción o acciones de cada socio. **DÉCIMA: Convocatoria**: La convocatoria de los accionistas a la Asamblea se hará mediante aviso que deberá publicarse en la Gaceta con una antelación no inferior a ocho días, no contándose dentro del término ni el día de publicación o aviso, ni el de celebración de la Asamblea. Se prescindirá del trámite de convocatoria cuando esté presente la totalidad del capital social. **DÉCIMA PRIMERA: Disolución**: La sociedad se disolverá por cualquiera de las causas que enumera el artículo doscientos uno del citado Código de Comercio. **DÉCIMA SEGUNDA: Fondo de Reserva:** La sociedad creará un fondo de reserva que se regirá de conformidad con lo dispuesto en el artículo ciento cuarenta y tres del Código de Comercio.

DÉCIMA TERCERA: Liquidación: La liquidación de la sociedad se hará mediante un liquidador nombrado por la Asamblea General de Accionistas y en su defecto por un Juez Civil de San José que corresponda. **ASAMBLEA:** Constituidos los otorgantes en Asamblea General, acuerdan en firme hacer la siguiente integración de los Órganos Sociales así: **PRESIDENTE: FRANCISCO PEREZ PEREZ,** de calidades y cédula dicha; **SECRETARIO: JOHN GILBERT,** de calidades y cédula dicha; **TESORERO: DANIEL RODRIGUEZ PEREZ,** mayor, soltero, vecino de Heredia, San Antonio de Belen, cien al sur del Liceo, con cédula de identidad número cuatro- ciento veinte-seiscientos veinte, **FISCAL: CARLA FERNANDEZ FERNANDEZ,** mayor, soltera, de oficios del hogar, vecina de San Jose, calle treinta y seis y avenida central, con cedula de identidad numero uno- ochocientos uno-quinientos cincuenta y dos. El Presidente, Secretario y Tesorero aceptan sus nombramientos en este acto. El Fiscal acepta su designación mediante cartas de aceptación que se conservan en los expedientes sociales de la compañía. ES TODO. Expido un primer testimonio para los otorgantes, a quienes leído lo escrito, manifiestan que lo aprueban y firmamos todos en San José, a las diez horas del veinte de marzo del dos mil nueve. FRANCISCO PEREZP.- **JOHN GILBERT** – DANIEL RODRIGUEZ- PJDOE-*******LO ANTERIOR ES COPIA EXACTA DE LA ESCRITURA NUMERO CIENTO VEINTISIETE INICIADA AL FOLIO CIENTO CINCO VUELTO DEL TOMO NOVENO DE MI PROTOCOLO CONFRONTADA CON SU ORIGINAL RESULTO CONFORME Y LA EXPIDO COMO PRIMER TESTIMONIO, A SOLICITU DE LA COMPAÑÍA INTERESADA, A QUIEN LO ENTREGO EN EL MISMO ACTO DE FIRMARSE LA MATRIZ.

ENGLISH TRANSLATION OF CORPORATE ARTICLES OF INCORPORATION

NUMBER ONE HUNDRED TWENTY SEVEN: Before me, PETER JUAN DOE, Notary Public with offices in San Jose, personally appeared **FRANCISCO PEREZ PEREZ,** of legal age, single, business person, resident of San Jose, Barrio Don Bosco 25 meters south of Purdy Motors with identity card number 1-520-304 and **JOHN GILBERT,** no second surname on account of his Canadian nationality, of legal age, married once, business person, resident of San Rafael de Escazu with passport number VH 55429 and they state as follows: That they hereby appear to form a corporation which shall be governed by the Commercial Code and it's reformations and by the following clauses: FIRST: Name: The name of the corporation shall be **EMPRESA INTERNACIONAL, SOCIEDAD ANONIMA**, this name being a fantasy name and the last two letters may be abbreviated S.A. **SECOND: Domicile:**

The legal domicile of this corporation shall be in the city of San Jose, from Pops in la Sabana, 700 meters west and 10 meters south, the corporation may establish branch or subsidiary offices for the corporation in other parts of the country or outside the country. **THIRD: Term:** The Corporation is to exist for ninety- nine years beginning on this day. **FOURTH: Purpose**: The Corporation will engage in the business of industry, consulting and development and programming of computer applications and commerce in general. The corporation may represent foreign and local corporations and may import and export any kind of goods. It may establish business relationships of any sort and may form part of other corporations including the right to sell, mortgage, lease, own and dispose of any kind of tangible property, rights, and negotiable instruments. The corporation may enter into contracts, open banks accounts in local or foreign banks, and may guarantee the obligations of third parties when this results in a benefit to the corporation. **FIFTH: Capital:** The capital stock of the corporation is **SIXTY THOUSAND COLONES**. Which is represented by sixty shares of common stock of one thousand colones each share which have been subscribed and paid by the shareholders in equal parts by way of Promissory Notes number one and number two payable to the corporation and deposited with the President of the Corporation of which the undersigned Notary attests to. The corporation may issue Certificates of stock ownership for one or more shares which must be signed by the President of the Board of Directors of the Corporation. **SIXTH: Administration**: The Corporation shall be administered by a three member Board of Directors which shall consist of a President, Secretary and Treasure. The President of the corporation shall have an unlimited Power of Attorney over the corporation pursuant to Article 1253 of the Civil Code to act on behalf of the corporation. The President may issue powers of attorney to members of the board, shareholders, or third parties, including those necessary to operate accounts, to revoke previously issued powers of attorney and or partially substitute said mandate without losing the original powers conferred including those set forth in article 1253 of the civil code. **SEVENTH: Due Diligence**: An auditor shall be appointed who will be responsible for due diligence. The auditor may or not be a shareholder of the corporation and they shall serve for the same period as the Board of Directors. **EIGHT: Resident Agent**: The Corporation shall name a Resident Agent as stipulated in paragraph thirteen of Article eighteen of the Commercial Code. **NINTH: Inventory and Balances**: The Corporation shall hold a General Ordinary Shareholder Meeting no later than three months prior to the close of the fiscal year to review the items established by law in article 155 of the Commercial Code. The Shareholders meetings may be held at its legal domicile or outside of the country. The balances sheet must be prepared according to generally accepted accounting principles. The balance

sheet will set forth corporate assets at market value, bad loans which have been deemed uncollectable may not be included as assets. The dividends shall be paid or loses absorbed in proportion to the shares held by each shareholder. **TENTH: Calling and Notice of Shareholders Meeting**: A meeting of the shareholders may be called by publishing notice of the meeting in la Gaceta with no less then eight days prior notice. The date of publication of notice and the day of the meeting are not to be include within the eight days. The formal notice requirements for convening a shareholders' meeting may be waived if the entire capital stock of the corporation is present at the meeting and agrees to waive notice. **ELEVENTH: Dissolution**: The corporation may be dissolved pursuant any of the factors set forth in Article 201 of the Commercial Code. TWELFTH: Legal Reserve Fund: The Corporation shall establish a legal reserve fund which shall be governed by Article 143 of the Commercial Code. The corporation shall they can accept service of process on behalf of the corporation. **THIRTEENTH: Liquidation**: The Liquidation of the corporation shall be carried out by a liquidator named by the Shareholders or in its absence by a Civil Judge of San Jose. General Assembly: The shareholders hereby constituted in Quorum make the following designations to the Board of Directors: **PRESIDENT: FRANCISCO PEREZ PEREZ, SECRETARY: JOHN GILBERT, TREASURE: DANIEL RODRIGUEZ PEREZ**, of legal age, single, resident of Heredia, San Antonio de Belen, with identity card number 4-120-620 **AUDITOR: CARLA FERNANDEZ FERNANDEZ**, of legal age, single, resident of San Jose, street 36 between avenue 0 and 2, with identity card number 1-801-552. The President, Secretary and Treasure accept their positions in this act and the Auditor does so by way of letter of acceptance which is kept in the corporate books. THAT IS ALL. I issue this extract to the parties to whom I have read it and they accept it and we sing in the city of San José at 10:00 hours on the 20th of March 2009. FRANCISCO PEREZP- **JOHN GILBERT-** DANIEL RODRIGUEZ-
PJ DOE. ********
THE PRECEDING IS A TRUE COPY OF DEED NUMBER 127 INITIATED AT PAGE 5 OF BOOK 9 OF MY PROTOCOL BOOK. I ISSUE THE FOLLOWING AT THE REQUEST OF THE INTERESTED PARTY.

Appendix 5

Corporate Book Legalization Form

Appendix 6

Corporate Share Certificate

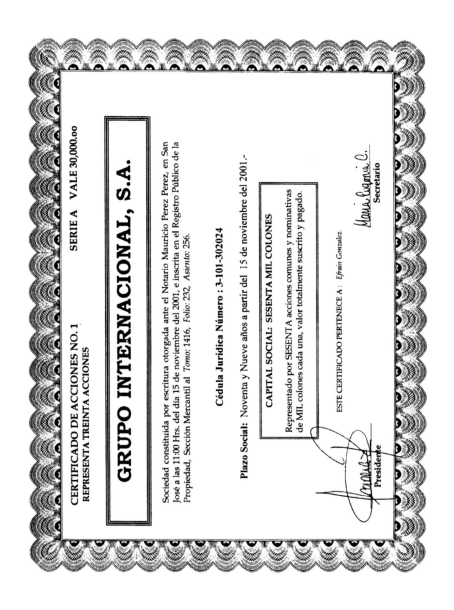

CERTIFICADO DE ACCIONES NO. 1   SERIE A   VALE 30,000.oo
REPRESENTA TREINTA ACCIONES

GRUPO INTERNACIONAL, S.A.

Sociedad constituida por escritura otorgada ante el Notario Mauricio Perez Perez, en San José a las 11:00 Hrs. del día 15 de noviembre del 2001, e inscrita en el Registro Público de la Propiedad, Sección Mercantil al *Tomo:* 1416, *Folio:* 232, *Asiento:* 256.

Cédula Jurídica Número : 3-101-302024

Plazo Social: Noventa y Nueve años a partir del 15 de noviembre del 2001.-

CAPITAL SOCIAL: SESENTA MIL COLONES

Representado por SESENTA acciones comunes y nominativas de MIL colones cada una, valor totalmente suscrito y pagado.

ESTE CERTIFICADO PERTENECE A : *Efrain Gonzalez.*

_____
Secretario

_____
Presidente

Appendix 7

Promissory Note

PAGARE   VALE POR ₡

VEINTICINCO COLONES   № 1334375-A

Conste que _____

promet ____ pagar incondicionalmente a la orden de _____

la suma de _____

(₡ _____)

pagadera _____

en _____ la cual devenga

intereses _____

Es garantía solidaria la fianza que otorga _____

_____ con autorización para conceder prórrogas.

Este título se rige por el Código de Comercio y se suscribe en _____

_____ el día _____ del mes de _____

de mil novecientos _____

DEUDOR _____

Cédula N° _____

_____

FIADOR _____

Cédula N° _____

Espacio para

Appendix 8

Bill of Exchange

Appendix 9

Labor Estimation Form

MTSS
MINISTERIO DE TRABAJO Y
SEGURIDAD SOCIAL

ESTIMACIÓN DE DERECHOS

Fecha **22 OCT 2001**

Señor: *Alicia Justina Jiménez L.*

A ruego suyo y basándome exclusivamente en las informaciones por usted suministradas, establecemos a continuación un detalle aproximado de los posibles derechos laborales, y del importe respectivo que pudiera corresponderle en relación con el caso consultado:

Profesión u oficio: _Servicio Doméstico_   7-4-99
Antigüedad: _2 años, 4 meses, 2 días_   9-10-01

a) Derechos estables con pocas variantes, adquirido por la sola prestación de servicios:

	DERECHO		IMPORTE
Vacaciones	*1 puedo + 5 días*	¢	*96.000*
Aguinaldo	*10 x /12*	¢	*123.600*

b) Derechos sujetos a prueba documental y al tipo de activad. Pueden disminuir los cálculos según firmas del consultante en documentos:

Horas extras: _____
Feriados: _____
Descanso semanal: _____
Salarios atrasados: _____
Unidad de salario: ¢ *96.000 x mes +50% Salario repuis ¢144.000*
Salario mínimo: ¢ _____
Diferencia de salarios: _____
Subsidio por: _____

c) Derechos discutibles -litigiosos en extremo- por lo que NO GARANTIZAMOS su existencia y la exactitud del monto del cálculo:

Preaviso:	*1 mes*	¢	*144.000*
Cesantía:	*54 días*	¢	*259.200*

Indemnización conforme al artículo 31 del Código de Trabajo:

TOTAL ¢ *622.800°°*

Los cálculos anteriores se hacen sin que el Ministerio asuma responsabilidad alguna por cuanto su exactitud depende de la veracidad de los hechos narrados por el consultante.
Advertimos, asimismo, para efectos de arreglo extrajudicial, trámite de la vía conciliatoria administrativa y en la vía judicial, que los extremos del grupo a) normalmente soportan rebaja, los del grupo b), tienden a bajar; y los del grupo c), podrían ni siquiera tenerlos el consultante.
Por lo anterior, no debe estimarse el total económico resultante, sino como guía para llegar a un arreglo.

Calidad de Artes Gráficas M.T.S.S.

FIRMA Y SELLO FUNCIONARIO RESPONSABLE

Appendix 10

Workers Compensation Policy Application Form

Appendix 11

Payroll Reporting Form

Appendix 12

National Registry Title Report Form

Consulta por Número de Finca - Registro Nacional-		
05/ene/2009	REGISTRO NACIONAL	PARTIDO DE SAN JOSÉ
11:15 AM	CONSULTA POR NUMERO DE FINCA	MATRICULA 205207---000

⇑ PROVINCIA: SAN JOSÉ FINCA: 205207 DUPLICADO: HORIZONTAL: DERECHO:000 ⇑

Title Report
Time and Date

Title Number

SEGREGACIONES: NO HAY

NATURALEZA: DE CAFE
SITUADA EN EL DISTRITO 1-ASERRI CANTON 6-ASERRI DE LA PROVINCIA DE SAN JOSÉ

LINDEROS

NORTE:	CALLE
SUR:	VICTOR MONGE
ESTE:	CLAUDINO NARANJO
OESTE:	VICTOR MONGE

⇐ Property Boundaries

MIDE: CUATROCIENTOS DIECINUEVE METROS CON TREINTA Y CUATRO DECIMETROS CUADRADOS
PLANO: NO SE INDICA

⇐ Property Size

LOS ANTECEDENTES DE ESTA FINCA DEBEN CONSULTARSE EN EL FOLIO MICROFILMADO DE LA PROVINCIA DE SAN JOSÉ NUMERO 205207 Y ADEMAS PROVIENE DE 2061-167-001

VALOR FISCAL: 1,462,000.00 COLONES   ⇐ Fiscal Valuation

PROPIETARIO:
ARACELLY MARIA ARCE MONGE
CEDULA IDENTIDAD: 1-0637-0866
ESTADO CIVIL: CASADO UNA VEZ
ESTIMACIÓN O PRECIO: MIL COLONES
DUEÑO DEL DOMINIO
PRESENTACIÓN: 0383-00001683-01
CAUSA ADQUISITIVA: DONACION
FECHA DE INSCRIPCIÓN: 22 DE NOVIEMBRE DE 1990

⇐ Property Owner Information

ANOTACIONES SOBRE LA FINCA: NO HAY

GRAVAMENES: NO HAY

⇐ Judicial Liens, Annotations or Encumbrances

Appendix 13

Property Survey Map – Plano Catastrado

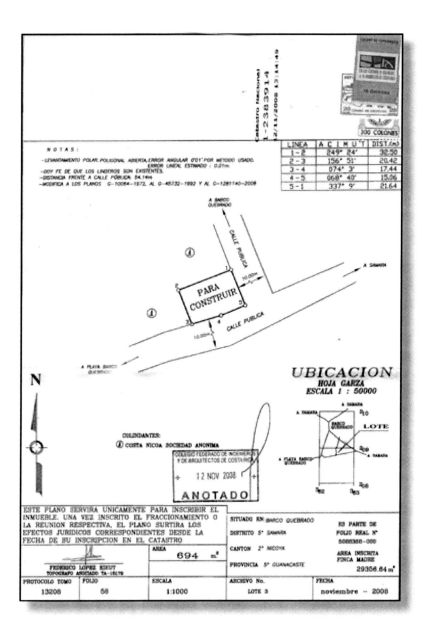

Appendix 14

Reciprocal Promise to Buy and Sell

RECIPROCAL PROMISE TO BUY AND SELL

Between us **JOHN DOE**, no second surname on account of his United States nationality of legal age, retired, married once, resident of Heredia, Costa Rica, and bearer of United States passport number 209267515 in his capacity as President with unlimited Power of Attorney for the corporation **COSTA RICA INTERNATIONAL, S.A.** corporate identity card number 3-101-0000 and whom shall hereinafter de referred to as the "SELLER" and **JOHN WHITE,** no second surname on account of his British nationality of legal age, business person, with United Kingdom passport number GB-101010101 and whom shall hereinafter be referred to as the "SELLER" have agreed to enter into the following Reciprocal Promise to Buy and Sell which shall be governed by the legislation of the Republic of Costa Rica and in particular articles 1053 and following of the Civil Code and by the following clauses:

FIRST: Legal Description of the Property and object of the Promise: The SELLER is the owner of real property which is recorded in the PROPERTY DIVISION, HEREDIA SECTION of the National Public Registry under title number SEVENTY SEVEN THOUSAND ONE ONE ONE -CERO CERO CERO [77111-000] and described as follows: Lot with one house located upon it. And located in District 6 San José de la Montaña, Canton-Two Barva of the Province of Heredia and which measures: TEN THOUSAND METERS SQUARED [10,000 m2], as fully identified in the title report of the National Registry attached herein as Appendix "A".

SECOND: The Property Survey Map: The SELLER manifests and warrants that the measurement of the property is as indicated in the property survey map of record for the property which is 4-100251-2005..

THIRD: The Reciprocal Promise: The SELLER hereby agrees to sell and the BUYER, agrees to buy the PROPERTY described above, free from any liens, encumbrances, annotations and with the municipal and property taxes paid to date.

FOURTH: The Sales Price: The sales price for the PROPERTY described above as a whole is TWO HUNDRED FIFTY THOUSAND DOLLARS [US$250,000].

FIFTH: Earnest Money Deposit And Payment Schedule. In this act the BUYER tenders an earnest money deposit of TWELVE THOUSAND FIVE HUNDRED DOLLARS [$12,500] and shall be held in escrow and governed by the escrow clause contained in this contract. The balance of the purchase price, TWO HUNDRED THIRTY SEVEN THOUSAND DOLLARS [$237,500] shall be paid to the SELLER in the following manner: (A) A Certified check issued from a Costa Rican banking institution payable to the SELLER for the sum of TWO HUNDRED THIRTY SEVEN THOUSAND DOLLARS [$237,500] which together with the earnest money deposit disbursed by the escrow agent to the SELLER shall make up a total of TWOHUNDRED FIFTY THOUSAND DOLLARS due to the SELLER at Closing. The final payment and closing of the transfer of the property must be done no later than JULY 15th, 2009 assuming all the conditions in the agreement are satisfied.

SIXTH: Earnest Money Escrow Agreement: Whereas both BUYER and SELLER agree to place the earnest money deposit indicated above in the possession of a third party Escrow Agent and whereas Escrow Company, S.A. is willing to hold said funds as Escrow Agent for the benefit of BUYER and SELLER the parties herein agree to the following regarding the earnest money deposit: (A) In the event of an alleged default or violation of the terms or clauses of this contract by the SELLER, the BUYER shall notify the ESCROW AGENT and the SELLER of such default in writing. If after FIVE working days, the SELLER has not cured the default then the ESCROW AGENT shall disburse the earnest money deposit to the BUYER. (B) In the event of an alleged default or violation of the terms or clauses of this contract by the BUYER, the SELLER shall notify the ESCROW AGENT and the BUYER of such default in writing. If, after FIVE working days, the BUYER has not cured the default then the ESCROW AGENT shall disburse the earnest money deposit to the SELLER. (C) In the event of a dispute between the parties hereto as to the facts of a default, the validity or meaning of the escrow instructions both parties agree to submit to binding arbitration as per the arbitration clause below. (D) In the event the BUYER does not complete the transaction by the agreed upon closing date in this contract the SELLER shall be entitled to keep the earnest money deposit as a fixed and definitive indemnification for damages caused by the default or violation of the BUYER. (E) Likewise, in the event the SELLER does not complete the transaction on the closing date agreed upon in this contract the Earnest Money Deposit shall be returned to the BUYER along with an additional US$2,000 as indemnification for damages. **SEVENTH: Conditions**: (1) **Liens and Encumbrances**: At the time of closing the property shall be free from any liens, encumbrances, and annotations. (2) **Property Boundaries**: The SELLER expressly manifests that he has walked the property boundary lines with the BUYER and the SELLER warrants to the BUYER that there are no disputes with neighbours regarding boundary lines nor any easements either apparent or implied which would allow third parties access through the property. (3) The condition of title to the property on the date of closing must be identical to the property title report attached herein as Appendix "A" and must be free from any judicial annotations and liens. (4) **Employees and Occupants.** Any employees of the SELLER must be liquidated and paid as set forth by the Costa Rican Labor Code and in compliance with all Social Security Payments for that employee in such a manner that the BUYER will not assume any liability for employees of the SELLER. If any employee is to remain on the property in the future as an employee of the BUYER that employee must have a signed work agreement with the BUYER. (5) **Risk of Loss or Damage**: The risk of loss for any damage of whatever kind, including acts of god to the residential dwelling that is located on the property shall be the sole responsibility of the SELLER from the date of this contract and up and until title to the property is effectively delivered to the BUYER and the BUYER is in physical possession of the property pursuant to the terms of this contract.

EIGHTH: Transfer of the Property: The escrow agent and the BUYER shall disburse the escrowed funds and remaining balance of the purchase price indicated above to the SELLER at closing simultaneously upon the signing of the property transfer deed (escritura de traspaso) transferring the title from the SELLER to the BUYER

NINTH: Property Taxes and Utilities: The SELLER must provide the following documentation at the time of closing: (a) **Property Taxes**: Certification issued by the Municipal authorities indicating that the SELLER is current in any municipal and property tax payments. The SELLER must provide the ORIGINAL CERTIFICATION and the receipt of payment shall not be acceptable. (b) **Municipal Tax Filings:** Copy of any filings with the Municipal government related to property valuation for property tax purposes (Declaración de Bienes Inmuebles) or a statement from the SELLER indicating that none has been filed through the date of closing. (c) **Utilities**: Electricity and Water: The last TWO paid receipts for electrical and water services which must be paid through, and including the date of closing. (d) **The Telephone Service**: The sale includes a telephone line currently installed on the property and which shall be in operation when the final payment is made. The telephone number is 2222-2222 The telephone service shall be paid in full at the time of closing.

TENTH: INVENTORY: The property is sold with the inventory set out in Appendix "B" all of which must be in the house and or on the property and ready for inspection by the BUYER at least 24 hours before closing and delivered to the BUYER on the date of closing.

ELEVENTH: Assignment to a Corporation: The BUYER may assign his rights pursuant to this contract to a Costa Rican corporation of his choosing.

TWELFTH: The SELLER hereby agrees not to sell, lien, or encumber the property in any manner.

THIRTEENTH: Closing Costs: (1) Costs related to the Reciprocal Promise to Buy and Sell: Each party shall pay their own Attorney for the time, preparation and review of this agreement. (2) Property Transfer Costs. The parties agree to equally split the closing costs for this transaction including the Notary Transaction fee. All transfer taxes and Notary Fees shall be those established by the Costa Rican government and the Notary Fees according to the fee schedule established by law.

FOURTEENTH: REAL ESTATE COMMISSION. The parties acknowledge that the Real Estate Agent in this transaction is Realtor, S.A. who shall be paid a commission by the SELLER of five per cent (5%) of the sales price. Said commission is due and payable at closing when title is transferred to the BUYER

FIFTEENTH: Modifications. Any modifications to the terms and conditions set forth in this contract must be in writing and signed by both parties. Both parties specifically rescind and thus leave with no effect any prior agreements whether oral, implied or in writing which relate to the purchase of the property as set forth above and acknowledge that the following is the full extent of their agreement.

SIXTEENTH: ARBITRATION AGREEMENT: The parties agree that this agreement shall be governed exclusively by the Laws of the Republic of Costa Rica. In the event that any conflict or dispute arises between the parties as to the facts of a default, or the validity, interpretation or meaning of this agreement; both parties agree to submit the final resolution of all disputes, claims and conflicts derived or somehow related to this agreement to arbitration before the Center for Arbitration and Dispute Resolution of the American Chamber of Commerce. Said arbitration shall be resolved by a single arbitrator in law appointed by both parties or, in lack of agreement by the appropriate procedures of the Center for Arbitration and Dispute Resolution of the American Chamber of Commerce, in accordance with its regulations. In all aspects of the procedures for arbitration the parties shall abide by the regulations of said arbitration center, which shall be in force at the time of initiation of arbitration.

SEVENTEENTH: Estimation: The parties estimate the value of this contract in the sum of two hundred fifty thousand dollars.

EIGHTEENTH: Contractual Address for the Parties: Any notices and communication regarding this contract shall be in writing and delivered to the parties to the following address:
SELLER: At the property which is the object of this contract.
BUYER: 2122 N. Alameda Drive, Los Angeles, CA.

NINETEENTH: Public Instrument and Translation: Both parties have requested that the following contract be drafted in the English language since this is the language they read and understand. Either party may have this agreement elevated to a Public Instrument by having it translated into Spanish by either an official translator of the Ministry of Foreign Relations or a Notary Public of their choice pursuant to the regulations of the Costa Rican Notary Code. In the event that this contract is recorded as a Public Instrument, the party that orders its recording shall provide a true copy of the recording to the other party.
Signed in the city of SAN JOSE ON THIS 30 day of JANUARY OF the year 2009.

_____

JOHN WHITE
BUYER

_____

JOHN DOE as President of
Costa Rica International, S.A.

Appendix 15

Sale of Property to a Corporation

NUMERO TREINTA Y SIETE: Ante mí, Pedro Mendez Mendez, Notario Publico con oficina en San José, comparece **JOHN SMITH**, único apellido en razón de su nacionalidad Estadounidense, mayor, casado una vez, empresario, vecino de Heredia, Urbanización Ciudad Cariari, con pasaporte de su país numero uno dos dos tres cuatro nueve uno dos, en su condición de Presidente con facultades de Apoderado Generalísimo sin Límite de Suma para este acto de **PROPIEDAD AZUL, SOCIEDAD ANONIMA**, cedula jurídica numero Tres- ciento uno- doscientos veintitrés mil ochocientos treinta y cinco, con domicilio en San José Barrio Escalante, personería inscrita en la sección Mercantil del Registro Publico al Tomo: Mil cuarenta y uno, Folio: Veintidós, Asiento: Ciento once la cual se encuentra vigente y de lo cual el suscrito Notario da fe y PETER DOE, único apellido en razón de su nacionalidad Canadiense, mayor, soltero, empresario, vecino de San José, con pasaporte de su país numero VN siete siete siete cuatro cuatro cuatro, en su condición de Presidente con facultades de Apoderado Generalísimo sin Límite de Suma de la Compañía EMPRESAS VERDE, SOCIEDAD ANONIMA, cedula jurídica numero Tres- ciento uno- doscientos noventa y nueve mil trescientos treinta y tres, con domicilio en San José, personería inscrita en la Sección Mercantil del Registro Publico al Tomo: Mil uno, Folio: Ciento doce, Asiento Ciento veintiuno, la cual se encuentra vigente y de lo cual el suscrito Notario da fe y DICEN: Que la Sociedad representada por el primero le VENDE a la sociedad representada por el segundo, quien acepta la venta libre de anotaciones y gravámenes hipotecarios y con los Impuestos Municipales al día y por la suma de cuatro millones doscientos mil colones, recibidos a entera satisfacción por la sociedad vendedora, la finca inscrita en el Registro Publico de la Propiedad **PARTIDO DE HEREDIA**, MATRICULA DE FOLIO REAL **NUMERO_ CIENTO SESENTA Y OCO MIL QUINIENTOS OCHENTA Y CINCO- CERO CERO CERO**, que según el Registro Publico de la Propiedad es de Naturaleza: Terreno para construir con una casa, Situado en: Distrito Cuatro- Ulloa, Cantón: Primero- Heredia, de la Provincia de Heredia, con los siguientes Linderos: Norte: Calle Publica, Sur: Calle Publica, Este: Lote Ciento seis, Oeste: Lotes cien, ciento uno, y con una Medida: de MIL DOSCIENTOS CUARENTA Y DOS METROS CON SESENTA Y SEIS DECIMETROS CUADRADOS. **Plano Catastrado**: Corresponde a dicha finca el plano catastrado inscrito en el Catastro Nacional bajo el numero H- UNO SEIS CINCO UNO DOS UNO- NOVENTA Y NUEVE y de lo cual el suscrito

Notario da fe copia del mismo que conservo en mi protocolo de referencia. ES TODO. Expido un primer testimonio. Manifiestan los comparecientes su total conformidad y firmamos en la ciudad de San José a las catorce horas del cuatro de marzo del dos mil nueve. JOHN SMITH- PETER DOE- PEDRO MENDEZ M-
LO ANTERIOR ES COPIA EXACTA DE LA ESCRITURA NUMERO TREINTA Y SIETE INICIADA AL FOLIO TREINTA Y TRES FRENTE DEL TOMO CUATRO DE MI PROTOCOLO. CONFRONTADA CON SU ORIGINAL RESULTO CONFORME Y LA EXPIDO COMO PRIMER TESTIMONIO, EN EL MISMO ACTO DE FIRMARSE LA MATRIZ.

ENGLISH TRANSLATION
SALE OF PROPERTY FROM ONE CORPORATION TO ANOTHER

NUMBER THIRTY SEVEN: Before me, Pedro Mendez Mendez, Notary Public with office in San Jose personally appeared JOHN SMITH, no second surname on account of his United States nationality, of legal age, married once, business person, resident of Heredia, Urbanizacion Cariari with passport number 12234912 in his capacity as Presidente with unlimited Power of Attorney for PROPIEDAD AZUL, SOCIEDAD ANONIMA, corporate identity card number 3-101-223835 with legal domicile in San Jose, Barrio Escalante, and authorization to bind the corporation duly recorded in the Mercantile Section of the National Registry at Book: 1041, Page: 22, Entry: 111 which is current and to which is current and to which the undersigned Notary hereby attests to and PETER DOE, no second surname on account of his Canadian nationality, of legal age, single, business person, resident of San Jose, with passport number VN 777444 in his capacity as President with unlimited Power of Attorney for his act for EMPRESAS VERDE, SOCIEDAD ANONIMA, corporate identity card number 3-101-299333, domiciled in San Jose, and authorization to bind the corporation duly recorded in the Mercantile Section of the National Registry at Book: 1001, Page 112, Entry 121, which is current and to which the undersigned Notary hereby attests and STATE: That the corporation represented by the first party in the capacity previously indicated sells to the corporation represented by the second party whom accepts the sale free from any mortgage liens and annotations and with the property and municipal taxes paid to date for the sum of four million two hundred thousand colones received to the entire satisfaction of the seller for the property title number 168585-000 which according to the National Registry is described as follows: Description: a residence with one house, Locates: in District Four- Ulloa, Canton One- Heredia- of the Province of Heredia and with the following boundaries North: Public Street, South: Public Street, East: Lot 100

West: Lot 101, Size: 1.243.66 m2. The corresponding property survey map is recorded in the National Registry under number H-135121-99 and of which the undersigned Notary hereby attests to copy of which I retain for reference. THAT IS ALL. I issue one original testimony of this act. The parties to this transaction manifest their acceptance and conformity with the content herein and we sign in the city of San Jose at 14:00 hours on the 4th day of March, 2009.

Appendix 16

Maritime Zone Concession Application

CARRILLO

Municipalidad de Carrillo
Departamento de Zona Maritimo Terrestre
SOLICITUD DE CONCESION

N° Expediente

USO DE LA MUNICIPALIDAD DE CARRILLO	
Fecha:	/ /
Hora:	
Funcionario:	
Nombre:	
Firma:	

TIMBRES

1. DATOS DEL SOLICITANTE:

1.1 SOLICITANTE (Nombre o Razón Social)

Primer Apellido	Segundo Apellido		Nombre
1.1 CEDULA IDENTIDAD, JURIDICA, RESIDENCIAL	1.3 ESTADO CIVIL	1.4 PROFESION U OFICIO	

1.5 DOMICILIO EXACTO   1.6 TELEFONO

1.7 DATOS DEL CONYUGE

Primer Apellido	Segundo Apellido	Nombre

2. DATOS DE LA PARCELA

2.1 LUGAR	2.2 DISTRITO	2.3 CANTON	2.4 PROVINCIA
	SARDINAL	CARRILLO	GUANACASTE

2.5 LINDEROS

Norte
Sur
Este
Oeste

2.6 SUPERFICIE	2.7 FRENTE	2.8 FONDO	2.9 CONSTRUCCION
m²	m	m	m²

2.10 TIEMPO OCUPACION

2.11 MEJORAS EXIXTENTES

2.12 USO QUE SE LE DARA A LA PARCELA (Marque con una X)

Agropecuario		Recreativo		Industrial	
Habitacional		Comercial		Minero	
Hotelero		Extractivo		Otros	

3. SOLAMENTE PARA PERSONAS JURIDICAS		
3.1 REPRESENTANTE LEGAL		
Primer Apellido	Segundo Apellido	Nombre
3.2 CEDULA IDENTIDAD O RESIDENCIA	3.3 CALIDAD	3.4 TELEFONO

4. DOCUMENTOS QUE SE ACOMPAÑAN	
Documentos de adquisición.	
Plano Catastrado o Croquis.	
Certificación Migración (solo extranjeros).	
Certificado Notarial de Personeria Juridica.	
Certificación Notarial de Capital con Vista a Libro de Acciones.	
Otros	

El suscrito manifiesta conocer u acepta en todos sus externos las limitaciones, condiciones y obligaciones establecida en la ley N° 6043 del 2 de Marzo de1977 y su Reglamento aprobado por decreto Ejecutivo N° 7841-P del 16 de Diciembre de 1977

Así mismo faculta a la MUNICIPALIDAD DE CARRILLO y al Instituto Costarricense de Turismo, a dar por denegada la presente solicitud si algunos de los datos son omisos.

_____   _____

Firma del solicitante o representante legal   *Firma Lic:*

USO EXCLUSIVO DE LA MUNICIPALIDAD DE CARRILLO			
	SI	NO	FECHA
DECLARATORIA APTITUD TURISTICA			/ /
DEMARCACION DE LA ZONA PUBLICA			/ /
AVALUO TRIBUTARIO DIRECTA			/ /
PLAN REGULADOR O ESQUEMA DEL USO DE SUELO			/ /

Appendix 17

Mortgage Deed Instrument

NUMERO CIENTO DOS: Ante mi Juan Pérez Perea, Notario Publico con oficina en San José, comparece RICHARD DOE, único apellido en razón de su nacionalidad Estadounidense, mayor, divorciado, comerciante, con cedula de residencia numero ciento setenta y cinco- ciento veintiséis mil doscientos ochenta y dos – once mil diecinueve y vecino de Sabana Larga de Atenas, Urbanización Vista Atenas, lote cincuenta y ocho en su condición de PRESIDENTE CON FACULTADES DE APODERADO GENERALISIMO, Sin límite de suma de la compañía VISTA GRANDE, SOCIEDAD ANONIMA, con igual domicilio que su representante, cedula jurídica Tres- ciento uno- ciento sesenta y cinco mil setecientos cuarenta y ocho, personería inscrita en el Registro Publico, Sección Mercantil al Tomo: mil doscientos siete, Folio ciento sesenta y dos, Asiento: ciento cincuenta y seis, la cual se encuentra vigente y de la cual el suscrito notario da fe y DIJO: Que INVERSIONES HIPOTECARIAS, SOCIEDAD ANONIMA, con domicilio en San José, Calle treinta y seis y Paseo Colon, cedula jurídica Tres- ciento uno- ciento noventa mil novecientos, e inscrita en el Registro Publico, Sección Mercantil al Tomo: mil ciento ocho, Folio: ciento once, Asiento: ciento doce, le ha dado en préstamo mercantil la suma de SESENTA MIL DOLARES, moneda de los Estados Unidos de América, por lo cual se constituye deudor de esa entidad. Que el préstamo devenga intereses corrientes del DOCE por ciento anual. Que se obliga a reintegrar esa suma mediante sesenta cuotas semanales, sucesivas y vencidas de UN MIL TRESCIENTOS TREINTA Y CUATRO DOLARES CON SESENTA Y SIETE CENTIMOS cada una de ellas. Las cuotas comprenden amortización e intereses, debiendo hacerse el pago de la primera el día quince de marzo del dos mil nueve. Que todos los pagos los hará en el domicilio del acreedor libres y netos, sin deducciones de ninguna clase, en dólares de los Estados Unidos de América inmediatamente disponibles. Y que estipula para el evento de demora de intereses moratorios al mismo tipo de que los corrientes más cuatro puntos porcentuales. Si el creedor pagare alguna suma de dinero por cuenta del deudor por impuestos, tasas, o para mantener en vigencia de garantías o para asegurar pagos u obligaciones del deudor este reembolsara inmediatamente su importe al acreedor en la moneda que indique el recibo, reconociéndole intereses sobre la suma pagada al tipo señalado por los intereses moratorios en este documento, desde la fecha del pago y hasta la fecha de su efectivo reembolso. Que las construcciones que existan en la finca garante deberán mantenerse cubiertas por un seguro contra los riesgos usuales a juicio del acreedor, mientras exista la deuda, por un monto no menor a su valor, siendo beneficiario del mismo INVERSIONES HIPOTECARIAS, SOCIEDAD ANONIMA: que anualmente el deudor deberá entregar al acreedor evidencia de haber pagado los impuestos que soporta la finca gravada y los recibos de las primas de la póliza de seguro; y que no podrá constituir hipotecas posteriores sin autorización del acreedor, la cual podrá tener vencida anticipadamente y por exigible la deuda si dejare de pagar oportunamente una cuota de amortización o intereses, o si incumpliere cualesquiera otras condiciones de esta hipoteca. Si el inmueble hipotecado es vendido o exista contrato para su venta, se tendrá por vencido el plazo de la deuda, y deberá el deudor cancelar al día de la venta la totalidad del saldo adeudado, salvo consentimiento por escrito en contrato por el acreedor. Que en garantía del pago del capital adeudado, los intereses corrientes y moratorios dichos, y ambas costas de la eventual ejecución, el deudor impone a favor del acreedor INVERSIONES HIPOTECARIAS, SOCIEDAD ANONIMA, HIPOTECA DE PRIMER GRADO sobre la finca del PARTIDO DE ALAJUELA, Matricula de Folio Real numero DOSCIENTOS NOVENTA Y CINCO MIL DOSCIENTOS QUINCE- CERO CERO CERO de Naturaleza: Terreno de solar, Lote cincuenta y cinco, Situado: en el Distrito Dos- Jesús, Cantón Cinco- Atenas, de la provincia de Alajuela, Mide: diez mil cuatrocientos treinta y seis metros con ochenta y ocho decímetros cuadrados, Linderos: Norte: Lote Sesenta, Sur: Lote cincuenta y siete, Este: Lote cincuenta y nueve, Oeste: Calle Publica; Plano Catastrado: A- cero dos cuatro cuatro ocho uno ocho- mil novecientos noventa y cinco, inscrito en el Catastro Nacional y de lo cual el suscrito notario da fe. Los gravámenes hipotecarios cubren todo exceso de cabida, así como las mejoras presentes o futuras. Y que para el caso de ejecución renuncia a su domicilio, los trámites del juicio ejecutivo y requerimientos de pago y deja valorada la finca hipotecada para el evento de remate en la suma de capital por la cual responde. Que si por cualquier causa imputable al deudor o propietario de la finca que se da en garantía no pudiera inscribirse esta hipoteca en el Registro Nacional dentro de un plazo de tres meses a partir de la presentación del documento en ese Registro, el acreedor también quedara facultado para tener por vencido anticipadamente el plazo de la obligación y exigible totalmente lo adeudado sin previo requerimiento. Extiendo un primer testimonio. Advertí al representante de la sociedad deudora el valor y transcendencia legales de sus renuncias y estipulaciones. Manifiesta el compareciente su total conformidad. Leo la presente escritura al compareciente haciendo traducción simultánea al idioma Ingles para el señor Doe quien manifiesta su aceptación. Firmamos en la ciudad de San José a las doce horas del quince de febrero del dos mil nueve. RICHARD DOE- JUAN PEREZ P.-

ENGLISH TRANSLATION OF
MORTAGE INSTRUMENTS

NUMBER ONE HUNDRED AND TWO: Before me, **JUAN PEREZ PEREZ**, Notary Public with office in San Jose, personally appeared **RICHARD DOE,** no second surname on account of his United States nationality, of legal age, divorce, business person, with residency card number 175-126281-1120 resident of Sabana Larga, Atenas, Urbanization Vista Atenas lot number sixty in his capacity as PRESIDENT with unlimited Power of Attorney and without monetary limit of VISTA GRANDE, SOCIEDAD ANONIMA, with the same domicile as it's representative, corporate identity card number 3-101-165748 authority to bind the corporation recorded in the Public Registry, Mercantile Section at Book: 1008 Page:111, Entry: 112 has given a loan in the amount of SIXTY THOUSAND DOLLARS, United States currency and for which the corporation now becomes the debtor of that entity. That the loan earns interest at the rate of 12% per year. That the corporation agrees to repay the loan amount to the Lender by way of 60monthly payments of $ 1.334.67 each one. The payments represent amortization of principal and interest and the first payment is due on the 15th of March of 2009. That all payments shall be made at the legal domicile of the Lender in US dollars which are immediately available funds. That he agrees that in the event of late payment the late interest payment will be calculated by adding an additional four points to the stipulated interest rate. If the Lender advances funds on behalf of the Borrower to pay taxes, assessments, o to maintain current any guarantees or insurance payments of the Borrower then the Borrower must immediately reimburse the Lender in the currency indicated in the receipt and shall recognize an inters on the amount paid at the late inters rate payment set forth herein from the date the disbursement was made until the reimbursement. That all buildings or structures which exist on the property must be covered by an insurance policy to cover all risk specified by the Lender and which shall remain in full force and effect during the existence of this debt. The insurance amount may not be less than its value and the beneficiary of said insurance policy must be listed as Inversiones Hipotecarias, S.A. On an annual basis, the Borrower must deliver to the Lender proof that the property taxes an insurance premium have been paid. The Borrower may not confer subsequent mortgages without the authorization of the Lender who may accelerate the due date of this mortgage loan if the Borrower fails to comply with the conditions set forth in this mortgage loan document. In order to guarantee the payment of the loan principal, interest payments, late interest payments and both cost of an eventual foreclosure suit, the Borrower hereby liens in favor of the Lender **INVERSIONES HIPOTECARIAS, SOCIEDAD ANONIMA,**

a FIRST MORTGAGE on the parcel registered in the ALAJUELA SECTION, property title number 295215-000 with the following registry information: Description: Lot number fifty five, Located: District- Two Jesus, Canton-Five, Atenas of the Province of Alajuela. Measure: 10.436.88 m2, Boundaries: North: Lot 54, South: Lot 56, East: Lot 57, West Public Road: Survey Map: Recorded in the Registry Section with number A-0244818-1995. The mortgage lien includes the current boundaries and any excess as well any present or future improvements to the property. That in the event of a mortgage foreclosure suit, the Borrower waives his legal domicile, waives executory trial procedures and waives any demand for payment and this act values the property for foreclosure purposes in the principal amount of the loan. That if for any reason attributable to the Borrower or the property owner this mortgage document cannot be registered within the next three months then the Lender is authorized to accelerate the mortgage and make it due and payable without prior notice. I have advised the Borrower of the value and legal consequences of waivers and stipulations set forth herein. He manifests his acceptance total conformity with the content herein. The following document is being read by the undersigned Notary simultaneously in the English language which is the language spoken by Mr. Doe. We sign in the city of San Jose at 12:00 hours on the February of 2009.

Appendix 18

Mortgage Bond

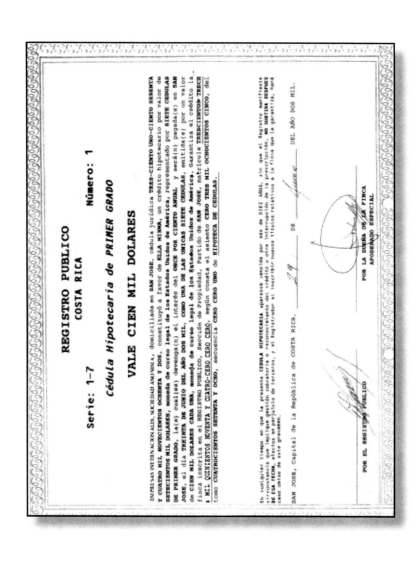

Appendix 19

Residential Lease Agreement

RESIDENTIAL LEASE AGREEMENT

THIS CONTRACT IS ENTERED INTO BETWEEN. **COSTA RICA INTER-NATIONAL, S.A.** with corporate identity card number 3-101- 0000 who us represented in this act by Sharon Perez Zuñiga, of legal age, Attorney, married once, resident of San José, with cédula number 1-111-111, as President and whom shall hereinafter be referred to as the LANDLORD AND **JOHN SMITH**, no second surname on account of his United States of legal age, married once, business person with passport number 10222000 and whom shall hereinafter be referred to as the TENANT.

WHEREAS, The parties indicated above have agreed to enter into this Residential Lease Agreement which shall be governed by the following clauses and by the Costa Rican General Law of Urban and Suburban Rental (Ley General de Arrendamientos Urbanos y Suburbanos)

NOW, THEREFORE, the parties hereto hereby agree as follows

1. **THE OBJECT.** The object of this rental contract is the rental of a residential home located within the Condominium "Eco Real" and property which is duly recorded in the Costa Rica National Registry, SAN JOSE SECTION pursuant to computerized registry title number FIVE THOUSAND SEVENTY SIX – F- ZERO ZERO ZERO [5076-F-000] and identified as located on Block M – Property A (finca filial) within the "Eco Real" Condominium in District 3 – Pozos, Canton- 9 Santa Ana of the Province of San Jose and property which measures 1,000 m2.
The home located upon the property has an approximate measurement of 230 m2 and has 3 bedrooms and 2 bathrooms on the main floor. A living room, dining room, kitchen with its furniture and appliances; The second floor is finished with wood moldings and all the items contained in the home are in good working order and condition and the TENANT agrees in this act to return the home in the same condition it is received when this contract term ends.
2. **USE OF PREMISES.** The Premises shall be used and occupied by Tenant and Tenant's immediate family, exclusively, as a private single family dwelling, and no part of the Premises shall be used at any time during the term of

this Agreement by Tenant for the purpose of carrying on any business, profession, or trade of any kind, or for any purpose other than as a private single family dwelling. TENANT may not vary the use of the Premises in any way without express written permission of the LANDLORD.

3. **TERM.** This Agreement is for a TERM of TWO YEARS [2]. The term shall commence on FEBRUARY 1ST, 2009 and the termination shall be on JANUARY 31ST of 2011 at 11:59 PM. Upon termination date, Tenant shall be required to vacate the Premises unless Landlord and Tenant formally extend this Agreement in writing or create and execute a new, written, and signed agreement. If the TENANT wishes to extend the lease term he shall notify the LANDLORD in writing with at least THREE MONTHS (3) prior notice. If the LANDLORD does not wish to renew the lease term they shall provide the TENANT with three month (3) notice prior to the expiration of the lease of their intent not to extend the lease term. During this notice period the TENANT agrees to allow the entry of third parties that may be interested in renting the property to enter within reasonable hours.

4. **RENT.** Under the terms of this Agreement, Tenant shall pay to Landlord the sum of ONE THOUSAND TWO HUNDRED DOLLARS, Currency of the United States of America (USD$1,200.00) in funds immediately available per month as Rent for the Term of the Agreement. Due date for Rent payment shall be the 1st day of each calendar month and shall be considered advance payment for that month. If not remitted on the 1st, Rent shall be considered overdue and delinquent on the 2nd day of each calendar month and shall under no circumstance be considered as tolerance by the LANDLORD nor may tolerance be the basis of any defense in an eviction proceeding. As such it is expressly agreed that the TENANT waives and resigns to any tolerance term and that the rental payments shall be paid no later that the due date set out in this contract.

5. **SECURITY DEPOSIT.** Upon the execution of this Agreement, Tenant shall deposit with Landlord the sum of ONE THOUSAND TWO HUNDRED DOLLARS, Currency of the United States of America (USD$1,200.00) which is the equivalent of one month's rent as security deposit for any damage caused to the Premises during the term hereof. The deposit shall be held to guarantee and cover any repairs for damages to the premises or for un paid utility services that would have to be paid once the house has been vacated. Such deposit shall be returned to Tenant, without interest, and less any set off for damages to the Premises upon the termination of this Agreement. It is understood that in the event the cost of repairs or utility and services exceeds the amount of the deposit then the TENANT shall be liable for the difference.

It is further agreed by the parties that in the event that the TENANT decides to vacate the premises and terminate the contract prior to the completion of at least (1) one year of occupancy they shall loose the earnest money deposit.

6. **CONDITION OF PREMISES**. Tenant stipulates, represents and warrants that Tenant has examined the Premises, and that they are at the time of this Lease in good order, repair, and in a safe, clean and tenantable condition with all appliances properly functioning. The TENANT agrees to return the premises to the LANDLORD at the termination of the lease term in the same condition in which it was received with the exception of normal wear and tear caused by normal use.

The TENANT shall be responsible for the replacement or repair of any glass, mirrors, lamps, ballasts, fluorescent tubes and light bulbs located within the premises. In the event the TENANT places nails or screws on the walls he shall remove them prior to vacating the premises and repair and repaint those walls.

7. **ALTERATIONS AND IMPROVEMENTS**. Tenant shall make no alterations to the buildings or improvements on the Premises or construct any building or make any other improvements on the Premises without the prior written consent of Landlord. Any and all alterations, changes, and/or improvements built, constructed or placed on the Premises by Tenant shall, unless otherwise provided by written agreement between Landlord and Tenant, be and become the property of Landlord and remain on the Premises at the expiration or earlier termination of this Agreement.

8. **PAYMENT OF SERVICES AND PROPERTY TAXES**. The TENANT shall pay for the Electrical Services as per electrical meter 11111 of the C.N.F.L. and water consumption as per water meter 22222 o the consumption reported by the Condominium Administration of "Eco Real". The telephone number for the property is 2000-000 and the TENANT shall be responsible for payment of the telephone services.

It is the obligation of the TENANT to insure that all utilities above are paid when due. If the TENANT fails to pay the utilities when due although not obligated to do so the LANDLORD may to mitigate any damages or loss of service pay for the services and the TENANT shall immediately reimburse the LANDLORD and failure to due so gives the LANDLORD the right to pursue an eviction for lack of payment.

The LANDLORD shall pay the property taxes on the property as well as the condominium fee which is imposed by "Condominio Eco Real" which includes security, garbage collection and use of the common areas of the condominium.

9. **LIABILITY AND INDEMNIFICATION**. LANDORD shall not be liable for any damage or injury of or to the TENANT, tenant's family, guests, invitees, agents or employees or to any other person entering the premises, or to

goods, personal belongings or equipment which belongs to the TENANT due to accidents, acts of nature, fire, earthquake or any other catastrophe that could occur and cause damage. The TENANT waives any and all claims or assertions of every kind and nature against the LANDLORD this indemnification includes, but is not limited to, any damage or injury which may be incurred by tenant, tenant's family, guests, invitees, agents or employees or to any other person for damage or injuries that arise from natural disasters, acts of good, negligence of the Tenant, their guests or invitees or actions of any third parties.

10. **ASSIGNMENT AND SUB-LETTING.** Tenant shall not assign this Agreement, or sub-let or grant any license to use the Premises or any part thereof without the prior written consent of Landlord. An assignment, sub-letting or license without the prior written consent of Landlord or an assignment or sub-letting by operation of law shall be absolutely null and void and shall, at Landlord's option, terminate this Agreement.

11. **CONTRACT TERMINATION AND DEFAULT.** The TENANT shall be in default of the contract for (a) for the failure to pay rent when due, (b) for activities in contravention of this Agreement. The TENANT may voluntarily terminate this agreement at any time by providing written notice to the LANDLORD of the intent to vacate with no less than TWO MONTHS (2) notice to the LANDLORD. Failure to provide the adequate notice shall require the TENANT to pay two months' rent as the equivalent. If the TENANT wishes to terminate during the first year of the lease in addition to the required notice he will forfeit the rental deposit to the LANDLORD.

12. **LATE INTEREST.** Without waiving any rights authorized by law in case of breach of this agreement, if the TENANT is in default for failure to pay rent he must pay late interest at a rate of 3% per month from the date on which the payment obligation was due and up and until payment is made to the LANDLORD. The same rate of interest will apply for any funds advanced by the LANDLORD to pay past due utilities owed by the TENANT as set forth in Clause 7 of this contract.

13. **MAINTENANCE AND REPAIR; RULES.** Tenant will, at its sole expense, keep and maintain the Premises and appurtenances in good and sanitary condition and repair during the term of this Agreement and any renewal thereof. Without limiting the generality of the foregoing, Tenant shall: (a) Keep all windows, glass, window coverings, doors, locks and hardware in good, clean order and repair; (b)   Keep all lavatories, sinks, toilets, and all other water and plumbing apparatus in good order. Any damage to any such apparatus and the cost of clearing stopped plumbing resulting from misuse shall be borne by Tenant; (c) Abide by and be bound by any and all rules and regulations affecting the Premises or the common area which may be adopted

or promulgated by the Home Owners Association of Condominio Eco Residencial Villa Real. (d) Under no circumstance may the TENANT deduct any repairs from the monthly rental payment.

14. **INSPECTION OF PREMISES.** Landlord and Landlord's agents shall have the right at all reasonable times during the term of this Agreement and any renewal thereof to enter the Premises for the purpose of inspecting the Premises and all buildings and improvements thereon as stipulated by the Costa Rican Tenancy Law. Landlord and its agents shall further have the right to exhibit the Premises and to display the usual "for sale", "for rent" signs on the Premises at any time within forty-five (45) days before the expiration of this Lease.

15. **ABANDONMENT.** If at any time during the term of this Agreement Tenant abandons the Premises, Landlord may, at Landlord's option, obtain possession of the Premises in the manner provided by law, and without becoming liable to Tenant for damages or for any payment of any kind whatever.

16. **NOTICE.** Any notice required or permitted under this Lease shall be deemed sufficiently given or served as stipulated by Article 4 of the Costa Rican Law of Notices and Citations and Other Judicial Communications if sent via Courier to the following address:

Landlord and Tenant shall each have the right from time to time to change the place notice is to be given under this paragraph by written notice thereof to the other party.

17. **Translation and Elevation to Public Instrument.** This rental agreement was drafted in the English language at the request of the TENANT since this is the language they read and understand. A translation of this contract into Spanish by an official translator that is authorized by the Ministry of Foreign Relations may be done by either party should the need arise. Likewise, either party may elevate this contract to public instrument by appearing before a Notary Public to request it.

In agreement with each and every clause of this contract we sign in the city of San Jose on this 1st day of February, 2009.

Appendix 20

Municipal Construction Permit

MUNICIPALIDAD DE ESCAZU
Proceso Desarrollo Territorial
SOLICITUD DE PERMISO DE CONSTRUCCIÓN

N° PERMISO

PROPIETARIO
DIRECCION EXACTA DE LA PROPIEDAD

INSCRIPCIÓN DE LA PROPIEDAD

PLANO DE CATASTRO   No. FOLIO REAL:

PERMISO DE (X):
Construccion   ☐ Ampliación ☐ Remodelación ☐ Demolición ☐ Mov. de Tierras ☐
Otros (especifique):

PARA USO (X):
Vivienda   ☐ Industria ☐ Comercial ☐ Condominio ☐ Urbanizacion ☐
Otros (especifique):

OBSERVACIONES:

AREA DE CONSTRUCCION | VALOR DE LA OBRA | FECHA ESTIMADA DE FINALIZACION

Nombre del Propietario o Apoderado | Firma | No. cedula | No teléfono
Correo electrónico

Nombre del Profesional Responsable | Firma | No. cedula | No teléfono
Correo electrónico

ESPACIO EXCLUSIVO DE PROCESO CATASTRO, TOPOGRAFIA Y VALORACION
REGISTRO CATASTRO MUNICIPAL | CONTROL No. | FIRMA Y SELLO

ESPACIO EXCLUSIVO DE PROCESO PLATAFORMA DE SERVICIOS, FISCALIZACION Y TARIFAS
SERVICIOS Y IMPUESTOS | SI | NO | FIRMA Y SELLO
MUNICIPALES AL DIA

ESPACIO PARA USO DEL PROCESO DE DESARROLLO TERRITORIAL
VALOR TASADO SEGUN PROCESO DE DESARROLLO TERRITORIAL ¢
Derecho de construcción | ¢ | Firma:
Multa segun avance obra ( ) | ¢
Total impuesto de construcción | ¢ | Autorizado por:
Alineamiento municipal | | Fecha: /

Observaciones generales

sello
de
caja

Original: Municipalidad Copia: Cliente   Tel. 208-7557 - 208-7548 Fax: 208-7594 E-mail: mofflar@municescazu.go.cr

Appendix 21

Municipal Zoning Request

MUNICIPALIDAD DE SANTA ANA
DIRECCION DE DESARROLLO Y CONTROL URBANO
TELEFONOS 203-3344 FAX. 282-5347

BOLETA DE SOLICITUD
CERTIFICADO DE USO DE SUELO

Nombre del solicitante:_____

Teléfono:_____

Nombre del Propietario:_____

No. de plano catastrado: SJ-_____ Folio Real:_____

Área de terreno: _____M2.
Frente a calle: _____M.

Ubicación: _____   Urbanización: _____
Distrito: _____   Barrio: _____

Otras señas (Dirección): _____

Uso solicitado: _____

Construcciones y usos existentes: _____

Doy fe de que todos los datos que aquí se consignan son fieles y exactos.

_____   _____
Nombre del solicitante   Firma del solicitante

Fecha: _____

NOTA: ADJUNTAR UNA FOTOCOPIA DEL PLANO CATASTRADO Y
       UN JUEGO DE TIMBRES DE ¢ 100.00

Appendix 22

Zoning Information for Selected Municipalities

Municipal Government	Zoning Plan	Date Orignally Passed	Published in
PROVINCE OF SAN JOSE			
	Yes	1995	Gaceta # 17 01-24-95
Canton 1 San Jose	Yes	2005	Gaceta # 54 3-17-2005
Canton 2 Escazu	Pending Approval	NA	NA
Canton 3 Desamparados	None	NA	NA
Canton 4 Puriscal	None	NA	NA
Canton 5 Tarrazu	None	NA	NA
Canton 6 Aserri	Yes	1993	Gaceta # 205 10-27-1993
Canton 7 Mora	Yes	2000	Gaceta # 65 3-31-2000
Canton 8 Goicoechea	Yes	1991	Gaceta # 174 04-19-1991
Canton 9 Santa Ana	None	NA	NA
Canton 10 Alajuelita	Yes	1998	Gaceta #78 04-09-1998
Canton 11 Vazquez Coronado	None	NA	NA
Canton 12 Acosta	None	NA	NA
Canton 13 Tibas	Yes	2000	Gaceta # 162 8-24-2000
Canton 14 Moravia	Yes	1972	Partial 04-10-1972
Canton 15 Montes de Oca	None	NA	NA
Canton 16 Turrubares	None	NA	NA
Canton 17 Dota	Yes	1991	Gaceta #190 10-08-1991
Canton 18 Curridabat	Yes	1984	#070 04-09-1984
Canton 19 Perez Zeledon	None	NA	NA
Canton 20 Leon Cortes			
PROVINCE OF ALAJUELA			
	Yes	1994	#63 03-30-1994
Canton 1 Alajuela	Pending Approval	NA	NA
Canton 2 San Ramon	Yes	2006	Gaceta # 116 06-16-2006
Canton 3 Grecia	None	NA	NA
Canton 4 San Mateo	None	NA	NA
Canton 5 Atenas	None	NA	NA
Canton 6 Naranjo	None	NA	NA
Canton 7 Palmares	NA	NA	NA
Canton 8 Poas	None	NA	NA
Canton 9 Orotina	Yes	1982	Gaceta # 81 01-21-1982
Canton 10 San Carlos	None	NA	NA
Canton 11 Alfaro Ruiz	Yes	2004	Gaceta #05 01-08-2004
Canton 12 Valverde Vega	None	NA	NA
Canton 13 Upala	None	NA	NA
Canton 14 Los Chiles	None	NA	NA
Canton 15 Guatuso			
PROVINCE OF CARTAGO			
	GAM	NA	NA
Canton 1 Cartago	None	NA	NA
Canton 2 Paraiso	Yes	2003	Gaceta # 91 05-14-2003
Canton 3 La Union			

Canton 4 Jimenez	None	NA	NA
Canton 5 Turrialba	None	NA	NA
Canton 6 Alvarado	None	NA	NA
Canton 7 Oreamuno	GAM	NA	NA
Canton 8 El Guarco	GAM	NA	NA
PROVINCE OF HEREDIA			
Canton 1 Heredia	None	NA	NA
Canton 2 Barva	None	NA	NA
Canton 3 Santa Barbara	None	NA	NA
Canton 4 Santo Domingo	None	NA	NA
Canton 5 San Rafael	None	NA	NA
Canton 6 San Isidro	Yes	2005	Gaceta #242 12-15-2005
Canton 7 Belen	None	NA	NA
Canton 8 Flores	NA	NA	NA
Canton 9 San Pablo	None	NA	NA
Canton 10 Sarapiqui			
PROVINCE OF GUANACASTE			
Canton 1 Liberia	Yes	2002	Gaceta #200 10-17-2002
Canton 2 Nicoya	Yes	1983	Gaceta #18 01-26-1983
Canton 3 Santa Cruz	Yes	1983	Gaceta #29 01-10-1983
Canton 4 Bagaces	None	NA	NA
Canton 5 Carrillo	None	NA	NA
Canton 6 Canas	Yes	2006	Gaceta #2001 10-20-2006
Canton 7 Abangares	None	NA	NA
Canton 8 Tilaran	None	NA	NA
Canton 9 Nandayure	None	NA	NA
Canton 10 La Cruz	None	NA	NA
Canton 11 Hojancha	None	NA	NA
PUNTARENAS			
Canton 1 Puntarenas	None	NA	NA
Canton 2 Esparza	Yes	2007	Gaceta #32 02-14-2007
Canton 3 Buenos Aires	Yes	2004	Gaceta #46 03-05-2004
Canton 4 Montes de Oro	None	NA	NA
Canton 5 Osa	Yes	1997	Gaceta #90 05-13-1997
Canton 6 Aguirre	Yes	2002	Gaceta #116 06-18-2002
Canton 7 Golfito	Yes	1992	Gaceta #237 12-10-1992
Canton 8 Coto Brus	None	NA	NA
Canton 9 Parrita	NA	NA	NA
Canton 10 Corredores	None	NA	NA
Canton 11 Garabito	None	NA	NA
PROVINCE OF LIMON			
Canton 1 Limon	Yes	1994	Gaceta # 171 09-08-1994
Canton 2 Poccoci	Yes		
Canton 3 Siquirres	None	NA	NA
Canton 4 Talamanca	None	NA	NA
Canton 5 Matina	NA	NA	NA
Canton 6 Guacimo	None	NA	NA

Appendix 23

CFIA Standard Consulting Contract

COLEGIO FEDERADO DE INGENIEROS Y DE ARQUITECTOS DE C.R.
CONTRATO DE SERVICIOS PROFESIONALES PARA CONSULTORIA

(Para uso de la oficina de tasación)FECHA _____   CONTRATO No. _____

Entre nosotros _____
_____ — y
Propietario   No. Cédula
Consultor o empresa   No. Cédula   No. Registro ___ suscribimos el presente

contrato de consultoria que se regirá por las siguientes cláusulas:

1. Ambas partes declaran que tienen capacidad jurídica para suscribir el presente contrato, que conocen y acogen en todos sus extremos las condiciones que establecen el Reglamento para la Contratación de Servicios de Consultoría en Ingeniería y Arquitectura, y el arancel para Edificaciones respectivo, que regirá como documento base esta relación contractual.

2. El propietario contrata con el consultor, los servicios de consultoria indicados en la tabla que se presenta a continuación, para la ejecución de un proyecto de

Ubicado en el distrito _____ del Cantón _____ de la Provincia _____ Dirección exacta _____

El valor estimado preliminar de las obras es de ¢ _____
(_____ colones) para los fines de la estimación preliminar de los honorarios profesionales.

	FASE	SERVICIOS	TARIFA MINIMA VIGENTE	TARIFA CONTRATADA
P R O Y E C T O S	(1) PLANOS Y DOCUMENTOS	Estudios Preliminares	(a) 0.5 %	
		Anteproyecto	1.00 ó 1.5	
		Planos de Construcción y especificaciones técnicas	4.00 %	
		Presupuesto	0.5 % Global ó 1.0 % Detallado	
		Licitación y adjudicación	0.5 %	
	(2) CONTROL Y EJECUCION	Inspección	3.00 %	
		Dirección Técnica	5.00 %	
		Administración	12. 0 %	
		Total Contratado		%

Tarifa aplicable   ☐ Repetitiva   ☐ Prototipo

	SERVICIOS	TARIFA MINIMA VIGENTE	TARIFA CONTRATADA
O T R O S	Estudios Básicos	(b)	
	Fiscalización de inversiones	1.5 %	
	Supervisión		
	Otros Servicios	(c)	
	Total Contratado		%

Tarifa aplicable   ☐ Reintegro de costo más porcentaje   ☐ Precio global o suma alzada

Notas:
a-) Se calculará bajo la modalidad de precio global o suma alzada, pero no será inferior al 0.5 % del valor estimado de las obras
b-) Se calculará con base en el sistema de reintegro de costos, más una suma fija o porcentaje de esos costos.
c-) Se calculará por cualquiera de los sistemas: precio global o suma alzada, o bien mediante el reintegro de costos más porcentaje o suma fija.

3.- El monto de los honorarios provisionales, según los porcentajes y el valor estimado del proyecto pactados en la cláusula anterior, es de ¢ _____
(_____ colones)
Los honorarios definitivos se determinarán según lo establece el Reglamento y el Arancel mencionados en la cláusula primera de este contrato.

4.- La forma de pago de los servicios de consultoria será la siguiente:
a - Adelanto contra firma de contrato ¢ _____
b - Pagos parciales según etapa:
_____
_____
_____

5.- Los plazos para entrega y aprobación de los informes, estudios, planos, en sus distintas etapas serán los siguientes:
_____
_____

6.- También serán aplicables dentro de los términos de esta contratación las siguientes disposiciones especiales, según lo establecen el Reglamento y el Arancel mencionados en la cláusula primera:
a -) En caso de que el proyecto se contrate por etapas, las partes contratantes declaran que se ha cumplido lo establecido en el artículo 39 del reglamento, bajo pena de las sanciones que se establecen al respecto, en caso de que los requisitos establecidos no se hayan cumplido.
b -) Los alcances de los servicios contratados, en caso de ser aplicables, son los establecidos en el Reglamento y en el Arancel. En caso de ser necesario podrán ampliarse como adendum al presente contrato
c -) En el caso de que durante la etapa constructiva la obra sea realizada por una empresa inscrita en el CFIA, se podrán variar los honorarios profesionales, cambiando la dirección técnica por la inspección; y el profesional responsable de la empresa constructora asumirá para todos los fines legales, la dirección de obra y la responsabilidad civil de la misma en cuanto a esta etapa. Estos cambios deberán ser incluidos en la fórmula especial diseñada por el CFIA, para tener validez y la misma constituirá un adendum al presente contrato.

7.- Quedan autorizadas ambas partes para Protocolizar ante Notario el presente contrato y así consignarle fecha cierta notarial, si es de su interes sin que sea necesario la presencia de la otra parte.

8.- En el cumplimiento del artículo 53 de la Ley Orgánica y del artículo 64 del Reglamento Interior del CFIA, firmamos en la ciudad de
_____ a los _____ días del mes de _____ de 19 _____

Propietario _____ Céd. _____   Consultor o Representante Legal de la Empresa _____

Firma del Profesional Responsable _____ No. Carné _____   Céd. _____

No. Registro _____

Appendix 24

Civil Marriage Document

CIVIL MARRIAGE DOCUMENT

NUMERO CIENTO OCHENTA Y NUEVE: Ante mí, **ROXANA RO-DRIGUEZ PEREZ**, Notario Publico con oficina en San José, comparecen **JAMES HANSEN**, único apellido en razón de su nacionalidad Estadounidense, mayor, soltero, pensionado, vecino de San José, con carne de residente rentista número once mil cien, y **MARIA CASTRO FERNANDEZ**, mayor, soltera, secretaria, vecina de Heredia, con cedula de identidad número cuatro- uno cinco cinco-ocho ocho ocho, hijos de **RICHAR HANSEN, Y JENNIFER JONES**, ambos de nacionalidad estadounidense y de **JUAN CASTRO PEREZ Y MARIA FERNANDEZ RAMIREZ**, ambos de nacionalidad costarricense, respectivamente. DICEN: Que desean unirse en Matrimonio Civil de conformidad con lo que autorizan los artículos veinticuatro y siguientes del Código de Familia y que encontrándose ambos en Libertad de Estado y libre uso y disfrute de sus facultades mentales para este acto, ofrecen para este acto el Testimonio de los señores **PATRICIA ROJAS SEGURA**, mayor, divorciada, empresaria, vecina de San Rafael de Heredia, con cedula de identidad numero uno- nueve seis tres- cinco uno siete y **ROGER CAMPOS BROWN**, mayor, casado una vez. Empresario, vecino de San José, con cedula de identidad numero uno- cinco seis seis- cinco cinco seis, quienes manifiestan que conocen a los contrayentes y que saben de su libertad de estado y del libre disfrute de sus facultades mentales para este acto. Aporta **JAMES HANSEN** Declaración Jurada en la que consta su Libertad de Estado y **MARIA CASTRO FERNANDEZ** Certificación de Estado Civil emitida por el Registro Civil en la que consta su Libertad de Estado. Por encontrarse autorizada la suscrita Notario y reunidos los requisitos que contempla al efecto el articulo veintiocho del Código de Familia doy por comprobada la Libertad de Estado de ambos comparecientes para contraer matrimonio. Pregunto a los contrayentes si es su libre y expresa voluntad el unirse en matrimonio y contestaron afirmativamente. Leo a los otorgantes los artículos once, trece, treinta y cuatro y treinta y cinco del Código de Familia. Habiendo los contrayentes expresado su voluntad de unirse en matrimonio, la suscrita Notario bajo su responsabilidad y conocimiento personal que tiene de los contrayentes, prescinde de la publicación de Edicto de la ley que se refiere el articulo veinticinco del Código de Familia, los declaro marido y mujer de acuerdo con las facultades que me otorga el articulo treinta y dos de dicho Código, por cuanto el conocimiento de los testigos y los documentos presentados por

los otorgantes no tienen ningún impedimento para contraer matrimonio. ES TODO. Expido un primer testimonio. Leído lo escrito a los comparecientes ante los testigos, lo aprobaron y firmamos en San José, a las quince horas del treinta de enero del año dos mil nueve. JAMES HANSEN.- MARIA FERNANDEZ.- ILEGIBLE.- ILEGIBLE.- R. RODRIGUEZ.-
LO ANTERIOR ES COPIA EXACTA DE LA ESCRITURA NUMERO CIENTO OCHENTA Y NUEVE INICIADA AL FOLIO CIENTO CINCUENTA Y NUEVE VUELTO DEL TOMO DECIMO DE MI PROTOCOLO. CONFRONTADA CON SU ORIGINAL RESULTO CONFORME Y LA EXPIDO COMO PRIMER TESTIMONIO. EN EL MISMO ACTO DE FIRMARSE LA MATRIZ.

ENGLISH TRASNLATION OF MARRIAGE BEFORE NOTARY PUBLIC

NUMBER ONE HUNDRED EIGHT NINE: Before me, **ROXANA RODRIGUEZ PEREZ**, Notary Public with office in San Jose, personally appeared **JAMES HANSEN**, no second surname on account of his United States nationality, of legal age, retired, resident of San Jose, with residency card number 11100 and **MARIA CASTRO FERNANDEZ**, of legal age, single, secretary, resident of Heredia, with identity card number 4-155- 888, son and daughter of **RICHARD HANSEN** and **JENNIFER JONES**, both of United States nationality and of **JUAN CASTRO PEREZ** and **MARIA FERNANDEZ RAMIREZ**, both Costa Rican citizens respectively and they STATE as follows: That they wish to unite in Matrimony as set forth in Article 24 of the Family Code and that both are single as with the mental capacity to carry out this act. The parties offer the statements of **PATRICIA ROJAS SEGURA**, of legal age, divorced, business person, resident of San Rafael de Heredia with identity card number 1- 963-517 and ROGER CAMPOS BROWN, of legal age, married once, business person, resident of San Jose with identity card number 1- 566- 556 whom manifest that they personally known the contracting parties and have personal knowledge as to their marital status and their mental faculties for this act. Mr. **JAMES HANSEN.** Submits in this act a sworn statement as to his marital status and **MARIA CASTRO FERNANDEZ** submits a certification from the Costa Rican Civil Registry demonstrating here marital status. Therefore, the undersigned Notary being duly authorized by law to carry out this act by Article 28 of the family Code and having verified their marital status and capacity to enter in to marriage. The parties manifest that they do not have any children outside of marriage. I ask each of the parties to freely express their willingness to enter into matrimony the undersigned Notary under her personal responsibility and due to the fact that both parties are personally know to her she waive the publication requirement referred to in Article 25 of the Family Code and there being no impediments to his marriage. I hereby declare them as husband and wife as authorized by Article 32 of the Family Code. THAT IS ALL. I issue on testimony. Having read the foregoing to the parties before the witnesses they approve it and we sign in the city of San Jose at 15:00 hours on the 30th of January of 2009. JAMES HANSEN.- MARIA FERNANDEZ.- ILEGIBLE.- ILEGIBLE.- R. RODRIGUEZ.-********

THE FOREGOING IS AN ESTRACT OF DEED NUMBER ONE HUNDRED EIGHTY NINE INITIATED AT PAGE ONE HUNDRED FIFTY NINE OF BOOK TENF OF MY PROTOCOLO. HAVING VERIFIED THE SAME WITH ITS ORIGINAL I ISSUE THIS EXTRACT SIMULTANEOUSLY UPON SIGNING THE ORIGINAL.

Appendix 25

Marital Dissolution Agreement

NUMERO CIENTO VEINTICUATRO: Ante mil, **FRANCISCO SALA-ZAR PEREZ,** Notario Publico con oficina en San José, comparecen **ROBERT DOE,** único apellido en razón de su nacionalidad Estadounidense, mayor, casado una vez, empresario, vecino de San Rafael de Escazu, con pasaporte de su país numero uno cinco cinco cuatro cuatro nueve nueve, y **PATRICIA SEVILLA ROSALES,** mayor, casada una vez, empresaria, vecina de San José, con cedula de identidad numero uno- trescientos once- trescientos doce y DICEN: Que conforme a los artículos cuarenta y ocho inciso siete del Código de Familia y ochocientos dieciséis del Código Procesal Civil, han convenido en divorciarse por mutuo consentimiento y al efecto toman los siguientes acuerdos: **PRIMERO:** Que han convenido divorciarse por mutuo consentimiento del matrimonio que los une, contraído en el estado de California, Estados Unidos de America, el día cinco de enero de mil novecientos noventa y cinco, según consta en certificación debidamente legalizada expedida por el Departamento de datos Vitales del Estado de California, Estados Unidos de América. **SEGUNDO:** De nuestro matrimonio no nacieron hijos. **TERCERO:** El compareciente **ROBERT DOE** pagara a favor de su esposa por concepto de pensión alimenticia la suma de trescientos dólares mensuales. El dinero será entregado los primeros días de cada mes mediante depósito en una cuenta de Banco a elección de la compareciente. **CUARTO:** No hay bienes gananciales dentro de nuestro matrimonio. ES TODO. Expido un primer testimonio. Leído lo escrito a los comparecientes, lo aprobaron y firmamos en San José, a las diez horas del seis de marzo del año dos mil nueve.

ENGLISH TRASLATION OF MARITAL DISSOLUTION AGREEMENT

NUMBER ONE HUNDRED TWENTY FOUR: Before me, **FRANCISCO SALAZAR PEREZ,** Notary Public with office in San Jose, personally appeared ROBERT DOE, no second surname on account of his United States nationality, of legal age, married once, business person, resident of San Rafael de Escazu, with passport from his country number 15554499 and **PATRICIA SEVILLA ROSALES**, of legal age, married once, business person, resident of San Jose with identity card number 1- 311- 312 an the **STATE:** That pursuant to Article 48 (7) of the Family Code and 816 of the Code of

Civil Procedure they have agreed to enter into this dissolution of marriage by mutual consent and as such they enter into the following agreement: **FIRST**: That they have mutually agreed to dissolve the marriage which was entered into the State of California, United States of America on the 5th day January of 1995 as is evidenced by the Certificate of Marriage issued by the Department of Vital Statistics of the State of California. **SECOND**: There are no children to this marriage. **THIRD**: Mr. Robert Doe: agrees to pay to Patricia Sevilla Rojas, the sum of three hundred dollars per month as spousal support. The money shall be paid on the first of each month by way of direct deposit to the account of Patricia Sevilla Rojas. **FOURTH:** There are no other assets to this marriage. THAT IS ALL. I issue on extract of this agreement. Having read the foregoing in the presence of both parties they approve it and we sign in the City of San Jose at 10:00 hours on the 6th day of March of 2009.

Appendix 26

Last Will and Testament

NUMERO CIENTO CUARENTA Y OCHO: Ante mí, **MARIA SAN-CHEZ PEREZ,** Notario Publico con oficina en San José, comparece **WAL-TER HARRISON**, único apellido en razón de su nacionalidad Canadiense, mayor, divorciado, empresario, vecino de Escazu, Urbanización Bello Horizonte, de la primera entrada cien metros al sur, y quinientos al oeste, con pasaporte de su país numero BR uno seis cuatro seis cuatro seis cuatro tres dos, y **DICE:** Que viene a ordenar como a efecto ordena su Testamento y última voluntad, conforme a la legislación costarricense y a las siguientes cláusulas: **PRIMERA:** Que nombra a **ANNE O'BRIEN,** único apellido en razón de su nacionalidad Canadiense, mayor, casada una vez, empresaria, vecina de la ciudad de Vancouver Canadá, nacida el veintitrés de Diciembre de mil novecientos setenta y uno como única y universal heredera de todos los bienes, propiedades, certificados accionarios y cuentas bancarias ubicados dentro o fuera del territorio costarricense que tuviera al momento de su fallecimiento. **SEGUNDA:** Que designa a **ANNE O'BRIEN**, de calidades antes indicadas como Albacea Testamentaria de su sucesión para todos los efectos indicados por ley y como suplente al señor **RONALD JONES**, único apellido en razón de su nacionalidad Canadiense, mayor, casado, empresario, vecino de Vancouver, doscientos Calle Real, Canadá, **TERCERA:** Que para prever el caso de que el compareciente y el heredero universal fallecieran en un mismo acto o accidente, otorga al compareciente que la totalidad de sus bienes que tuviera en ese momento pasaran a ser propiedad en partes iguales de los hijos de **ANNE O'BRIEN. CUARTA:** Que revoca y deja sin ningún efecto y valor cualquier otra disposición testamentaria que hubiera otorgado anteriormente en Costa Rica o en el extranjero. ES TODO. Expido un primer Testimonio al que se le agrega un timbre del Colegio de Abogados de un mil colones. Lo anterior es leído al testador en vos alta a su expresa solicitud y en vos alta es traducido al idioma ingles para el compareciente por ser tal idioma el que habla y entiende, por los siguientes interpretes quienes hablan y entienden dicho idioma: **JUAN FERNANDEZ RODRIGUEZ** , mayor, casado una vez, abogado, cedula de identidad numero uno- cinco cinco cinco-seis seis seis, vecino de San José, de la Pops setecientos metros al oeste y diez al sur y **PRISCILLA SANTOS MAYOR**, mayor, soltera, abogada, cedula de identidad numero uno- seiscientos cincuenta- setecientos, vecina de Ciudad Cariari, Bosques de doña Rosa y ante los siguientes testigos instrumentales, **JUAN GUTIERREZ GUTIERREZ**, mayor soltero. Comerciante, vecino de

San José, Barrio Don Bosco, veinticinco metros al sur de Purdy Motors Paseo Colon, con cedula de identidad numero uno- ochocientos uno- ochocientos dos, **MARIA ESQUIVEL SANTIAGO**, mayor, casada una vez, profesora, vecina de Sabana Oeste, de la Pops setecientos metros al oeste y diez metros al sur, con cedula de identidad numero uno- cuatro cuatro cuatro, cinco cinco cinco, y **GILBERT GONZALEZ ICASA**, mayor, casado una vez, Asistente Legal, vecino de Llorente de Tibas, ciento cincuenta metros al este de La Nación, con cedula de identidad número seis- dos dos dos- tres tres tres, y precede el compareciente testador a aceptarlo. La suscrita Notario de fe, según la información que poseo de la capacidad legal para este acto de los testigos dichos, y de conocer al otorgante, así como de la capacidad legal y moral de estos para este acto. Todos procedemos a firmar en San José, a las diez horas del dieciséis de abril del dos mil nueve. WALTER HARRISON.- JUAN FR.- PRISCILLA SANTOS.- JUAN GG.- MARIA ESQUIVEL.- GILBERT GONZALEZ.- MARIA SANCHEZ**********LO ANTERIOR ES COPIA EXACTA DE LA ESCRITURA NUMERO CIENTO CUARENTA Y OCHO INICIADA AL FOLIO CIENTO VEINTICUATRO VUELTO DEL TOMO CUATRO DE MI PROTOCOLO. CONFRONTADA CON SU ORIGINAL RESULTO CONFORME Y LA EXPIDO COMO PRIMER TESTIMONIO, EN EL MISMO ACTO DE FIRMARSE LA MATRIZ.

ENGLISH TRANSLATION OF LAST WILL AND TESTAMENT

NUMBER ONE HUNDRED FOUTY EIGHT: Before me, **MARIA SANCHEZ PEREZ**, Notary Public with office in San Jose, personally appeared WALTER HARRISON, of legal age, divorced, businessman, resident of Escazu, Urbanization Bello Horizonte from the first entrance one hundred meters south and five hundred west with passport number BR 1646432 and STATES: That he appears in this act to state this Last Will and Testament according to the laws of Costa Rica and the following clauses: **FIRST**: That he names **ANNE O'BRIEN**, no second surname on account of her Canadian nationality, of legal age, married, businessperson, resident of Vancouver, Canada and born on December 23, of 1971, only heir of all my assets, property, share certificates, bank accounts which are located in or outside of Costa Rica which I may have at the time of me death. **SECOND**: That he designates **ANNE O'BRIEN** as the Executor of the estates for all purposes as required by law. In her absence I name a substitute, Mr. **RONALD JONES**, no second surname on account of his Canadian nationality, of legal age, married, businessperson, resident of 200 Royal Street Vancouver, Canada, **THIRD**: In the event the testator and the beneficiary die in the same act he confers his entire estate to the children of **ANNE O'BRIEN** which may living. **FOURTH:** That in this act he revokes and leaves without legal effect any prior wills which he may have granted either in Costa Rica or abroad. THAT IS ALL. I have read this document to Mr. Harrison and making a simultaneously translation to the English language by the following two interpreters which are also present in this act: **JUAN FERNANDEZ RODRIGUEZ**, of legal age, married once, Attorney, with identity card number 1- 555- 666, resident of San José, from Pops 700 meters west and 10 south; **PRISCILLA SANTOS MAYOR**, of legal age, single, Attorney, with identity card number 1- 650- 700, resident of Ciudad Cariari, Bosques de Doña Rosa, and in presence of the following witnesses: **JUAN GUTIERREZ GUTIERREZ**, of legal age, business person, resident of San Jose, Barrio don Bosco, 25 meters south of Purdy Motors on Paseo Colon, with identity card number 1-801-802; **MARIA ES-QUIVEL SANTIAGO**, of legal age, married, professor, resident of Pops 700 meters west and 10 south. With identity card number 1- 444- 555, and **GILBERT GONZALEZ ICASA**, of legal age, married, Legal Assistant, resident of Llorente de Tibas, 125 meters east of La Nacion, with identity card number 6- 222- 333. The Testator accepts the dispositions made herein. The undersigned Notary Public hereby swears that based upon the information provided and based upon her personal knowledge of the testator she manifests his capacity to enter in to this act. We sign in the City of San Jose at 10:00 hours on the 16 of April, 2009. WALTER HARRISON.- GILBERT GONZALEZ.- MARIA SANCHEZ

THE PRECEDING IS AN EXACT TRU COPY OF DEED NUMBER ONE HUNDRED FORTY EIGHT INITIATED AT PAGE NUMBER ONE HUNDRED TWENTY FOUR OF BOOK FOUR OF MY PROTOCOL BOOK. HAVING CONFRONTED THIS WITH ITS ORIGINAL I ISSUE THIS TESTIMONY IN AS WE SIGN THE ORIGINAL DEED.

Appendix 27

Sample Income Letter for Residency

COSTA RICA BANK

San José,

Señores
Migración General de Migración y Extranjería
Departamento de Residentes Rentistas

Estimados señores:

Por medio de la presente COSTA RICA BANK, S.A.   , entidad con cédula de persona jurídica número 3-101-46536-02, hace constar que nuestros clientes, el Sr. **John Smith Jones**   , posee una inversión con el Banco que genera un ingreso mensual mínimo de US$ 1,000.00 (mil dólares estadounidenses) por un periodo no menor a 5 (cinco) años, por lo que de acuerdo con las instrucciones que al día de hoy ha recibido por parte de los **Sres. Jones** , el Banco garantiza al Gobierno de la República de Costa Rica y a la Dirección General de Migración y Extranjería que dicho señor recibirá una suma anual mínima en forma estable y permanente de US$ 12,000.00 (Doce mil dólares estadounidenses).   **COSTA RICA BANK** expresamente se compromete a notificar a la Dirección General de Migración y Extranjería cualquier cambio de destino o revocación que los señores **Jones** le den a su inversión o a las instrucciones dadas al Banco, para lo que corresponda.

Se extiende la presente a solicitud del interesado para cumplir con las exigencias de la Dirección General de Migración y Extranjería en cuanto al otorgamiento del status de residente rentista al

Atentamente.

Jaime Rodríguez Zapatero
Gerente General
Sucursal de San Jose

Appendix 28

Immigration – Pensionado Apllication Form

> **SOLICITUD DE RESIDENTE PENSIONADO**

> **SOLICITANTE:** JOHN DOE

Señores (a)
DEPARTAMENTO DE MIGRACIÓN
Y EXTRANJERIA
PRESENTE.-

El que suscribe, **JOHN DOE**, civil status, occupation, home address, Passport number 1256988, emitido por la autoridad de pasaportes de Washington, D.C, el día 15 de abril de 2009, y el cual expira el día 15 de abril del 2020

FECHA DE NACIMIENTO: 12 de Agosto de 1948

DIRECCION TEMPORAL EN COSTA RICA:
San Jose, Costa Rica

PUESTO MIGRATORIO DE ENTRADA: Aeropuerto Juan Santamaría

FECHA DE INGRESO A COSTA RICA: 12 de Octubre del 2008

ORIGEN DE LA PENSION: Pensión del Seguro Social de Estados Unidos
MONTO DE LA PENSION: US$ 1,250 dólares mensuales

NOMBRE DEL PADRE: **FRED DOE**

NOMBRE DE LA MADRE: **ROSALINDA SMITH**

Por este medio manifiesto expresamente mi deseo de obtener la Residencia Temporal de Residente Pensionado y por lo tanto respetuosamente solicito se me apruebe la solicitud yse me otorgue el estatus de **RESIDENTE PENSIONADO**

DOCUMENTACION

Aporto a mí solicitud los siguientes documentos:

1. Certificado de carencia de antecedentes penales, y su traducción.

2. Certificado de nacimiento de y su traducción;

3. Fotocopia certificada del pasaporte;

4. Traducción de la primer página del pasaporte

5. Carta de comprobante de Ingresos económicos y su traducción

6. Huellas Digitales del Archivo Policial de Costa Rica

7. 3 Fotografías tamaño pasaporte, de frente y recientes

8. Certificación de no residencia de la solicitante;

NOTIFICACIONES:

Señalo para recibir notificaciones, el FAX 2200-0000 o a la oficina del autenticante, cita en Escazú.

San José, 15 de marzo del 2009.-

JOHN DOE
El suscrito Notario Público de San José doy fe que la firma que antecede fue estampada en mi presencia, por lo que he procedido a autenticarla en el mismo acto con mi firma, plasmada de mi puño y letra y con mi sello, que corresponden a los inscritos en el Registro Nacional de Notariado.

Appendix 29

Trademark Application Form

REGISTRO NACIONAL REPUBLICA DE COSTA RICA
REGISTRO DE LA PROPIEDAD INDUSTRIAL
DEPARTAMENTO DE RECEPCIÓN DE DOCUMENTOS

RPI-01

No. Expediente _____

SOLICITUD DE INSCRIPCIÓN DE MARCA

El suscrito (1) _____

_____

_____

_____

En concepto de apoderado (2) _____

Según:

_____Certificación o Poder adjunta (3)

_____Certificación o Poder adjunta al Expediente (4)

de la sociedad (5) _____

_____

_____

organizada y existente bajo las leyes de (6) _____

domiciliada en (7) _____

Hace constar que el solicitante de esta marca   es titular de una empresa o establecimiento ubicado en
(8) _____

_____

_____

Se aporta el comprobante de pago (art.9 inc. j) y art.10 inc.e)) de la Ley de Marcas) (9)

UPH - Desarrollo Creativo 12

Solicito la inscripción de la: **marca de fábrica ( )**, **marca de comercio ( )**, **marca de servicio ( )**
(nombre del signo distintivo, con o sin logotipo) (10)

Descripción del logotipo: (11) _____
_____
_____
_____
_____

_____Adjunto 3 facsímiles del diseño solicitado (12)

_____Reservas: (13)

Clase _____ internacional (14), para proteger y distinguir (15) _____
_____
_____
_____
_____

País de Origen: (16) _____

Señalo para atender Notificaciones sobre esta gestión en el siguiente domicilio, fax, apartado postal o
cualquier otro medio electrónico: (17) _____
_____
_____

Declaro bajo Fe de Juramento que toda la información contenida en esta solicitud es cierta y de conformidad
firmo en la ciudad de _____
El día _____ (18)

(19) Se autoriza a (indicar nombre completo y número de cédula): _____
_____

para que retire todo lo relacionado con este expediente.

_____   _____
     Firma (20)   Autentica:
                                              (Abogado o Notario) (21)
                                       Sello:

Timbres:
¢ 20 Archivo Nacional (22)
¢ 250 Abogado (23)

Appendix 30

Income Tax D-101 Form

Appendix 31

Tax Registration Application Form

Appendix 32

Municipal Property Declaration Form

MUNICIPALIDAD DE ESCAZÚ DEPARTAMENTO DE BIENES INMUEBLES	DECLARACIÓN DE BIENES INMUEBLES (LEY 7509, ARTICULO 14, JUNIO 19 DE 1995)	Nº 82273

CUADRO 1.- DATOS DEL PROPIETARIO

NOMBRE: (FISICO O JURÍDICO) _____

CÉDULA FISICA O JURÍDICA: _____

DIRECCIÓN: _____

PROVINCIA: _____ CANTON: _____ DISTRITO: _____

TELEFONO: _____ FAX: _____ APARTADO: _____

Llenar solamente si se trata de una sociedad anónima o un poder especial de persona física

APODERADO LEGAL: _____

IDENTIFICACIÓN: _____ DIRECCIÓN: _____

CUADRO 2.- DATOS DEL INMUEBLE

No DE FINCA	SUB-MATRICULA	DUPLICADA	DOMINIO	USUFRUCTO	% POSESIÓN
HORIZONTAL	SCONDOMINIO CATASTRO SI		AREA(M2)		FRENTE(ML)

CARACTERÍSTICAS DEL LOTE — **SERVICIOS PUBLICOS DE LA ZONA**

PLANO	ONDULADO	QUEBRADO	CAÑERÍA	ALCANTARILLADO	ELECTRICIDAD
MUY QUEBRADO	REGULAR	IRREGULAR	TELEFONO	CORDON Y CAÑO	ACERA

TIPO DE VIA O ACCESO PRINCIPAL

ASFALTO	LASTRE	TIERRA	SERVIDUMBRE	ALAMEDA
VALOR UNITARIO POR m² ₡		VALOR TOTAL DEL TERRENO ₡		

CUADRO 3.- CONSTRUCCIONES E INSTALACIONES

USOS DE LAS CONSTRUCCIONES E INSTALACIONES

HABITACIONAL	COMERCIAL	INDUSTRIAL	EDUCATIVO	RECREATIVO	RELIGIOSO

CARACTERÍSTICAS DE LA CONSTRUCCIÓN E INSTALACIONES

CLASE	EDAD	MATERIALES PREDOMINANTES				No DE APOSENTOS		No DE PISOS	AREA TOTAL m²	VALOR X m² ₡	VALOR TOTAL ₡
		PAREDES	ESTRUCTURA TECHO	CIELOS	PISOS	ESTRUCTURA TECHO	DORMITORIOS BAÑOS				

VALOR TOTAL DE LAS CONSTRUCCIONES E INSTALACIONES: ₡

CUADRO 4.- DECLARACIÓN DEL PROPIETARIO

VALORES

TERRENO ₡ _____

CONSTRUCCIONES E INSTALACIONES ₡ _____

MONTO TOTAL ₡ _____

DECLARO QUE LA INFORMACIÓN AQUÍ PROPORCIONADA ES VERAZ

FIRMO EN: _____ EL _____ DE _____ DEL _____

FUNCIONARIO
QUE RECIBE - CALCULA: _____ FECHA: _____

CUADRO 5.- USO DEL DEPARTAMENTO DE BIENES INMUEBLES

MAPA	PARCELA	PREDIO	BLOQUE	No CONTROL

ZONA DE VALOR	VALOR X m² LOTE TIPO ₡	VALOR ACTUALIZADO DE TERRENO ₡	VALOR ANTERIOR ₡
TIPOLOGIA CONSTRUCTIVA	VALOR X m² DE CONSTRUCCIÓN ₡	VALOR TOTAL DE LA CONSTRUCCIÓN E INSTALACIONES ₡	

MONTO A PAGAR TRIMESTRAL ₡ _____ MONTO A PAGAR ANUAL ₡ _____

REVISO: _____ FECHA: _____	FISCALIZO: _____ FECHA: _____

Appendix 33

Notary Security Ticket

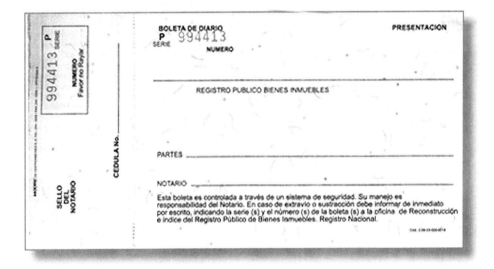

Appendix 34

General Power of Attorney

GENERAL POWER OF ATTORNEY

NUMERO CIENTO VEINTISIETE: Ante mí, **JUAN FERNANDEZ RO-DRIGUEZ**, Notario Publico con oficina en San José, comparece el señor **ROBERT DOE**, único apellido en razón de su nacionalidad Estadounidense, mayor, soltero, empresario, vecino de San Rafael de Escazú, carretera vieja a Santa Ana, de TVA cien al norte, con pasaporte de su país numero uno tres cinco cinco nueve dos cuatro siete seis y DICE: Que **CONFIERE PODER GENERALISIMO SIN LIMITE DE SUMA** al señor **ROGER CAMPOS GAMBOA,** mayor casado una vez, empresario, vecino de San José, con cedula de identidad numero uno- seiscientos cincuenta- quinientos cuarenta y seis, confiriéndole al efecto las facultades que determina el articulo mil doscientos cincuenta y tres del Código Civil y además le otorga las facultades de sustituir ese poder en todo o en parte, revocar sustituciones y hacer otras de nuevo. Presente en este acto el apoderado, manifiesta que acepta el poder que se le ha conferido. Leída esta escritura al otorgante, resulta conforme, manifiesta que lo aprueba y ambos firmamos en la ciudad de San José, a las once horas del día cinco de marzo del dos mil nueve. ROBERT DOE.- ROGER CAMPOS GAMBOA. JUAN FR.*** ******************

LO ANTERIOR ES COPIA EXACTA DE LA ESCRITURA NUMERO CIENTO VEINTISIETE INICIADA AL FOLIO OCHENTA Y SEIS FRENTE DEL TOMO CATORCE DE MI PROTOCOLO. CONFRONTADA CON SU ORIGINAL RESULTO CONFORME Y LA EXPIDO COMO PRIMER TESTIMONIO A SOLICITUD DEL INTERESADO A QUIEN LO ENTREGO EN EL MISMO ACTO DE FIRMARSE LA MATRIZ.

ENGLISH TRANSLATION OF GENERAL POWER OF ATTORNEY

NUMBER ONE HUNDRED TWENTY SEVEN: Before me, **JUAN FERNANDEZ RODRIGUEZ**, Notary Public with office in San Jose personally appeared ROBERT DOE no second surname on account of his United States nationality, of legal age, single, business person, resident of San Rafael de Escazu on the old road to Santa Ana, from TVA one hundred meters north and with passport number 135592476 and he states that: He confers an **UNLIM-ITED GENERAL POWER OF ATTORNEY WITHOU MONETARY LIMITATION** to Mr. **ROGER CAMPOS GAMBOA**, of legal age, married once, business person, resident of San Jose, with identity card number 1-650-546, conferring upon said person the mandate which are established in Article 1256 of the Civil Code. The Attorney in fact may subrogate this power in whole or in part. May revoke and sub rogations made and make new ones as necessary. Present in this act is the Attorney in Fact who manifests his acceptance of the Power of Attorney herein conferred. Having read this instrument to the person conferring the Power of Attorney he manifests his acceptance and we sign in the city of San Jose at 11:00 hours on the 5th day of March of 2009. S/ ROBERT DOE.- ROGER CAMPOS GAMBOA.- JUAN FR.******************

THE FOLLOWIN IS AN EXACT COPY OF DEED NUMBER ONE HUNDRES TENTY SEVEN INITIATED AT PAGE EIGHT SIX OF BOOL FOURTEEN OF MY PROTOCOLO. HAVING CONFRONTED ITS CONTENT WITH THE ORIGINAL I ISSUE THIS FIRST TESTIMONY AT THE REQUEST OF THE INTERESTED PARTY TO WHOM I DELIVER SIMULTANEOUSLÑY UPON SIGNING THE ORIGINAL.

Appendix 35

Special Power of Attorney to Sell an Automobile

JOHN HANSEN

Confiere Poder Especial sin Límite de Suma a Francisco Gamboa Pérez Escritura Otorgada en San José a las 9:00 horas del 15 de abril del 2009

NOTARIO: PATRICIA SEVILLA CASTRO

NUMERO SESENTA Y UNO: Ante mí, **PATRICIA SEVILLA CASTRO,** Notario Publico con oficina en San José, comparece **JOHN HANSEN**, único apellido en razón de su nacionalidad Estadounidense, mayor, casado dos veces, pensionado, vecino de Brasil de Mora, con carnet de residente pensionado número nueve nueve nueve uno y DICE: **Que CONFIERE Y OTORGA PODER ESPECIAL** Sin Límite de Suma de conformidad con el articulo mil doscientos cincuenta y seis del Código Civil **FRANCISCO GAMBOA PEREZ**, mayor, casado una vez, Abogado, vecino de San José, con cedula de identidad numero uno-nueve dos nueve- cinco cinco seis, para que en mi nombre comparezca ante Notario Publico con el fin de otorgar escritura de traspaso del vehículo de mi propiedad con las siguientes características y por el precio que el apoderado estime conveniente MARCA: JEEP, ESTILO: CHEROKEE, CATEGORIA: AUTOMOVIL, CARROCERIA: FAMILIAR STATION WAGON, CAPACIDAD: CINCO PERSONAS, COLOR: NEGRO, MODELO: DOS MIL OCHO, CILINDROS: SEIS, CILINDRADA: DOS MIL OCHOCIENTOS CENTIMETROS CUBICOS, COMBUSTIBLE: GASOLINA, TRACCION: DOBLE, MOTOR NUMERO: K CERO OCHO OCHO SEIS UCH, CHASIS: UNO JCWL SIETE OCHO DOS SEIS FT UNO CINCO CINCO CINCO CINCO SIETE, TIPO: UNO JCWL SIETE OCHO, PLACA NUMERO: TRES CUATRO CINCO TRES NUEVE CUATRO. El apoderado podrá firmar documentos o escrituras adicionales con el fin de inscribir en el Registro Nacional el vehículo a favor del comprador quedando facultada dicha persona para dar ante las autoridades que sean necesarias todos los pasos necesarios al objeto indicado, elevar solicitudes, formular descripciones, declaraciones, recibir documentos, girar instrucciones, recibir y hacer pagos, hacer solicitudes, en fin de la manera más amplia llevar a cabo todas las gestiones que considere pertinentes con el objeto de cumplir el mandato que mediante este documento se le otorga. ES TODO. Leída esta escritura al compareciente lo aprueba y firmamos en

la ciudad de San José a las nueve horas del quince de abril del dos mil dos..-
JOHN HANSEN.- PATRICIA SEVILLA C.
LO ANTERIOR ES COPIA EXACTA DE LA ESCRITURA NUMERO SESEN-
TA Y UNO INICIADA AL FOLIO CINCUENTA Y TRES FRENTE DEL TOMO
PRIMERO DE MI PROTOCOLO. CONFRONTADA CON SU ORIGINAL
RESULTO CONFORME Y LA EXPIDO COM PRIMER TESTIMONIO EN EL
MISMO ACTO DE FIRMARSE LA MATRIZ.

ENGLISH TRANSLATION OF
SPECIAL POWER OF ATTORNEY TO SELL AUTOMOBILE

JOHN HANSEN

**Confers a SPECIAL POER OF ATTORNEY without monetary limi-
tation to
FRANCISCO GAMBOA PEREZ**

**Deed conferred in San Jose at 9:00 hours on the 15th of April of
2009.**

NOTARY PUBLIC: PATRICIA SEVILLA CASTRO.

NUMBER SIXTY ONE: Before me, Patricia Sevilla Castro, Notary Public
with office in San Jose personally appeared **JOHN HANSEN,** no second
surname on account of his United States nationality, citizen of the United
States, of legal age, married on two occasions, retired, resident of Brasil de
Mora with Pensionado Rentista number 9991 an he states that: He confers a
SPECIAL POWER OF ATTORNEY without monetary limitation pursuant to Article 1256 of the Civil Code to Mr Francisco Gamboa Perez, of legal
age, married once, Attorney, resident of San Jose, with card number 1- 929-
556 so that in his name he can appear before a Notary Public with the specific
purpose of appearing before a Notary Public to sell, for the price the Attorney
in fact deems convenient, the vehicle titled in his name and which has the
following characteristics: MAKE: JEEP, STYLE: CHEROKEE, CATEGORY:
AUTOMOBILE, BODY TYPES: STATION WAGON, CAPACITY: FIVE PER-
SONS, COLOR: BLACK, YEAR: TWO THOUSAND EIGHT, CYLINDERS:
SIX, DISPLACEMENT: TWO THOUSAND EIGHT HUNDRED CUBIC CEN-
TIMETERS, FUEL: GASOLINA, TRACTION: FOUR X FOUR, ENGINE
NUMBER: K ZERO EIGHT SIX UCH, VIN NUMBER: ONE JCWL SEVEN
EIGHT, PLATE NUMBER: THREE FOUR FIVE THREE NINE FOUR. The

Attorney in fact may sign any document including public instruments that are necessary to have the sale of the vehicle recorded in the National Registry in the name of the Buyer. He is authorized to carry out all tasks before the registry offices that are necessary comply with his mandate. He may make requests, receive documents, issue instructions, make and receive payments and carry out any tasks in the most ample manner possible to carry out the task established herein. THAT IS ALL. Having read the foregoing to the grantor he accepts it and we sign in the City of San Jose at 9:00 hours on the 15th April of 2009. S/ JOHN HANSEN.- PATRICIA SEVILLA C.**

THE FOLLOWING IS AN EXACT COPY OF DEED NUMBER SIXTY ONE INITIATED AT PAGE FIFTY THREE OF BOOK ONE OF MY PROTOCOL. HAVING CONFRONTED ITS CONTENT WITH THE ORIGINAL ISSUE THIS FIRST TESTIMONY AT THE REQUEST OF THE INTERESTED PARTY TO WHOM I DELIVER SIMULTANEOUSLY UPON SIGNING THE ORIGINAL.

Appendix 36

List of Costa Rican Consulates

CONSULATE	LOCATED IN	JURISDICTION FOR
Argentina		Av. Callao 1769 7° B (1024) Ciudad Autónoma de Buenos Aires Republica Argentina Tel: (005411) 4815-007 conrica@fibertel.com.ar
Aruba		Savaneta 235- B Aruba Tel: (297) 523-3246 consuladodecostaricaaruba@ hotmail.com
Australia, Sydney		PO Box 205 Spit Junction NSW 2088 Australia Tel: (00612) 99694050 congenrica@gmail.com
Austria, Salzburg		Hagenaustrasse 5, A- 5020 Salzburgo, Austria Tel: (0043) 66-244-1386 zeilinger@salzburg.co.at
Belgium, Brussels		489 Ave. Louise, Boite 13, 1050 Bruselas Tel: (00322) 640-5541 info@costaricaembassy.be
Brasil		SRTVN 701 Conjunto C, Ala A Salas 308/ 310 Edificio Centro Empresarial Norte 70.710.200. Asa Norte, Brasilia D F. Brasil Tel: (0055) 61-328-2219 concrbr@solar.com.br

Brasil	Andar Curitiba, PR 80240-140 Tel: (0055) 41-322-6030
Brasil	Avenida Río Branco, N° 387 4to piso Espaco Mercosul Centro Florianapolis SC Brasil CEP88015-200 Santa Catarina, Brasil CEP88015-201 Tel: (0055) 483-223-2437 conscostarica1sc@zipmail.com.br
Brasil	Av. N.Sra. de Copacabana, 1.417 loja 120 Copacabana Río de Janeiro, Brasil Cep: 22070- 011 Tel: (0055) 21-2267-9513 congericario@oi.com.br
Brasil	Rua Canadá, N° 107 Jardim America- Sao Paulo Cep: 01436-000 Tel: (0055) 11-3062-5348 consulcostarica@ig.com.br / mvabbud@terra.com.br
Canada	325 Dalhouise Street, Suite 407 Ottawa, ON, K1N 7G2, Canadá Tel: (001) 613-562-0842
Canada (Toronto)	Provisional: 325 Dalhouise Street, Suite 407 Ottawa, ON, K1N 7G2, Canadá
Canada (Vancouver)	Vancouver, British Columbia, V7J- 3S9, Canadá Tel: (001) 604-983-2152 consulado@can.rogers.com /

arreaga@axionet.com

Chile   Máximo Reyes N° 1590
                                Depto 601, Temuco, Chile
                                Tel: (0056) 45 23-5568
                                notariht@ctcinternet.cl

China (Beijing)   Jianguomenwai Jiao Gong Yu

                                1- 5- 41 CP 100 600 Beijing
                                consuladocrchina@gmail.com

Germany   Dessauerstr. 28-29
                                D- 10963 Berlin, Germany
                                emb@botschaft-costarica.de
                                Tel: (0049) 30 2639 8990

Germany   Nieder Kirchweb 22
                                65934 Frankfurt/ main
                                Tel: 00 49-69-39 04 36 56
                                DrJDressler@t-online.de

Germany   Meyerhofstrasse 8 22609
                                Hamburgo, Germany
                                Tel: (0049) 408-01395
                                rica@congenricahh.de

Germany   Marienstrasse 8
                                30171 Hannover, Germany
                                Tel: (0049) 51-128-1127
                                consulrica-hannover@telesonmail.de

Germany   Lutzowstr. 34, 04157
                                Leipzig
                                Tel: 0049 341 909 6732
                                leipzig@konsulat-costa-rica.de

Korea	ILJIN Bldg. N° #7, 50-1 Dohwa- Dong, Mapo- Gu, Seoul, 121- 040, Korea Tel: (00822) 707-9249 rsolano@ecostarica.or.kr
Denmark	Landemarket 10 1119 Copenhague K, Denmark Tel: (00945) 33433100
France	4 Square Rapp 75007, Paris France Tel: 00-331- 45789696 consulat.cr@gmail.com
India	D-388 Defence Colony, New Delhi 110024, Indian Tel: 00 (911) 1-233 1 0212
Israel	Abba Hillel Silver Street- 14 Mail Box. 38 Beit Oz, 15th Floor Ramat Gan, 52506 Tel: 00 (972) 3-613-5061 emcri@netvision.net.il
Italy (Bologna)	Via A. Righi 13, 40126 Bologna Tel: 00 (39) 051 23 20 97
Italy (Florence)	Via Giambologna 10, Florencia 50312 Tel: 00 (395) 557-36-02
Italy (Milan)	Via Dante 4 20121 Milán Tel: 00 (39)02-8645-4585 consmil.cr@interlaw.biz
Italy (Rome)	Viale Liegi 2, INT 8, Roma

	Tel: 00 (3906) 84242853 concostarica@yahoo.it
Italy (Turin)	Via Susa 31 10138 Torino Italy Tel: 00 (39) 011 433 7218 corica@aerre.it
Italy (Venice)	Sestriere Di Santa Corce N° 312- A=30135 Venezia Tel: (0039) 041-243-25-90 consolatocostarica.ve@gmail.com
México DF, México	Calle Río Poo #113 Colonia, Cuactemoc entre Río Panuco y Lerma, Tel: 00 (525) 55-208-3361 embajada@embajada.decostaricae nmexico.org
Moscow, Russian Federation	121615 Moscow, Rublyovskoye Chaussee 26, Building 1, Apartment 23-24 Tel: 7 (495) 415-4014 conscr@rol.ru
Managua, Nicaragua	Reparto Serrano, de la Policía de Plaza del Sol 4 cuadras al Lago, casa esquinera, Managua Tel : (00505) 251-04-29
Rivas, Nicaragua	Frente Hospital Gaspar García Laviana, Rivas Tel: (00505) 563-5353 ichaves@rree.go.cr, sduncan@rree.go.cr
Panamá	Calle Samuel Lewin, Edificio Plaza Omega 3 Piso, costado Santuario Nacional, Ciudad de

	Panamá Tel: (00507) 264-2980 conscr.panama@gmail.com
Portugal (Lisbon)	Casa Escondida, Travessa das Rolas N° 25- 2705-333 Alto do Rodizio Colares, Sintra, Portugal Tel : (00 351) 21-929-0581 consulado-costarica@wondertur.com
Puerto Rico (San Juanj)	1413 Avenida Fernández Juncos San Juan, Puerto Rico 00909 Tel: (001) 787-723-6227 consuladopr@yunque.net
Spain, Barcelona	Avda. Sarria, N° 2 08029 Barcelona Cataluña Tel: (0034) 933.632.257 junca@comunired.com
Spain (Canarias)	Edificio Mercurio, Torre 2-5° A 35100 Playa del Ingles Tel: (0034) 92-876-1509 welt-immbilien@pa-servicom.es
Spain (Madrid)	Paseo de la Castellana 164 17- A, 28046 Madrid, España Tel: (0034) 913-459-622 consul@embcr.org
Spain (Tarragona)	Calle Rambla Nova 75, Principal 43003, Tarragona, España Tel: (0034) 97-723-7513
Spain (Valencia)	Calle Conde de Altea 3 Valencia Tel: 003496-3747542/963-642135 manelajej@hotmail.com

Sweden (Stockholm)

Pilgatan 3 SE- 11223
Stockholm, Sweden
Tel: (00 468) 646-00-00
gc.costarica@franchisekollegiet.se

Sweden (Goteborg)

Embajada Concurrente:
Olof Wijkosgatan 4, S-402-24
Goteborg, Sweden
Tel: (0046) 3-183-2165

Switzerland (Bern)

Schawarztortr 11, 3007, Berna
Tel: (0041) 31 372-7887
costa.rica@bluewin.ch /
embcr.suiza@gmail.com

Switzerland (Geneva)
Geneva

Chemin de Mormex 1001

Tel: (0041) 21-312-7764

Trinidad y Tobago (Port of Spain)

Mutual Building, 3 Floor,
16 Queen's Park West,
Woodford Street Entrance,
Port Spain
Tel: (001) 868-628-0652
emticatt@trinidad.net

United States of America

Atlanta

1870 The Exchange, Suite 100,
Atlanta Georgia
Tel: 001 (770) 951-702
consulate_ga@costarica-embassy.org

Jurisdiction: Kentucky, Tennessee, Alabama, Atlanta, Georgia California,
South Carolina, North Carolina.

Chicago

203 N Wabash Ave. Suite 702

Chicago, ILL, 60601-
Tel: 001-312- 2632772
crchi@sbcglobal.net

Jurisdiction: Michigan, Ohio, Minnesota,Iowa, Missouri, Dakota del Norte, Dakota del Sur, Indiana, Wisconsin.

Dallas

7777 Forest Lane B- 445,
Dallas, Texas 75230
Tel: 001 (972) 566-7020

Denver, Colorado

3356 South Xenia Street,
Denver, Colorado 80231
Tel: 001(303) 696-8211
cronsul@msn.com

Houston
Texas 77042

3000 Wilcrest Suite 112, Houston,

Tel: 001 (713) 266-0484
consulatecr@sbcglobal.net

Jurisdiction: Louisiana, Mississipi, texas, Nuevo México, Colorado, Nebraska, Kansas y Oklahoma

Los Ángeles

1605 West Olympic Blvd. Suite 400, Los Angeles, Ca. 90015.
Tel: 001-213- 3806031
costaricaconsulatela@hotmail.com

Jurisdiction: Estados de California, Nevada, Utah, Alaska, Hawai, Arizona, Washington, Oregón, Idaho, Montana, Wyoming,

Miami

2730 SW 3rd Avenue, Suite 401 Miami, FL 33129
Tel: 001 (305) 871-7485
consulate_mia@costarica-embassy.org

New York

Edificio 14 Penn Plaza, oficina
1202, localizado en el número 225
West 34 Street, Nueva York,
NY 10122. Tel: 001(212) 509-3066
/ 001(212) 509-3067
costaricaconsul@yahoo.com
conscr.nuevayork@gmail.com

Jurisdiction: Maine, New Hampsire, Vermon, Massachussets, Rhode, Island, Conneticcut, Pennsylvania, New Jersey.

Phoenix

Gainey Ranch Financial Center
Ste 200 7373 East Double Tree
Rancho Road Scottsdale, Arizona
85258
Tel: 001 (480) 951-2264
burkeap@aol.com

Saint Paul, Minnesota

6 West 5th Street, Suite 201 Saint
Paul, MN 55102.
Tel: 001 (651) 293-1816
CNicholson@CRConsulateMN.com

Tucson

3567 E Sunrise Drive, Suite 235
Tucson, AZ 85718
Tel: 001(520) 529-7068
costarica@missiontrust.com

Washington

2114- S Street, North West,
Washington, DC. 20008
Tel: 001 (202) 328-6628
consulate@costarica-embassy.org

Jurisdiction: D.C., Delaware, Maryland, Virginia y West Virginia

United Kingdom (London)

Flat1, 14 Lancaster Gate, London

W2 3LH United Kingdom
Tel: (0044) 207 706 -8844
crconsulate@btconnect.com

Uruguay (Montevideo)   Roque Graseras 740 entre
                                     Juan Maria Perez y Solano
                                     Antuña Montevideo, Uruguay
                                     Tel: (0059) 82-7116408
                                     consuladocr@adinet.com.uy

Venezuela (Caracas)   Av. San Juan Bosco de Altamira
                                     Entre 1 y 2, Transversales, Edificio
                                     For You PH,
                                     Urbanización Altamira.
                                     Caracas, Venezuela.
                                     Tel: (0058) 212-267-1104
                                     consulgralcrvene@yahoo.com.mx

Appendix 37

Automobile Transfer Deed

JEFFREY JONES, VENDE VEHICULO A
TIERRA AUTO, SOCIEDAD ANONIMA
Escritura otorgada en
San José a las once horas del ocho de febrero del dos mil nueve.
NOTARIO: FEDERICO PEREZ PEREZ.

NUMERO NOVENTA Y CUATRO: Ante mí, **FEDERICO PEREZ PEREZ**, Notario Publico con oficina en San José, comparecen **JEFFREY JONES,** único apellido en razón de su nacionalidad Canadiense, mayor, casado una vez, pensionado, vecino de Grecia, Barrio San José, cien metros al este de la Pulpería Plus, con carne de residente rentista número nueve nueve nueve, y **JUAN GUTIERREZ RODRIGUEZ,** mayor, soltero, comerciante, vecino de San José, Barrio Don Bosco, veinticinco metros al sur de Purdy Motors, Paseo Colon, con cedula de identidad numero cinco- dos dos dos- tres tres tres, en su condición de **PRESIDENTE** con facultades de Apoderado Generalísimo son Limite de Suma de la compañía **TIERRA AUTO, SOCIE-DAD ANONIMA**, con domicilio en San José, calle treinta y seis entre Avenida Central y Avenida Segunda, casa numero treinta y nueve S, con cedula jurídica numero Tres- ciento uno- doscientos catorce mil ochocientos diez, personería inscrita en la Sección Mercantil del Registro Publico al Tomo: Mil sesenta y uno. Folio: Ochenta y uno, Asiento: Noventa y uno, la cual se encuentra vigente y de la cual el suscrito Notario da Fe, y DICEN: Que el primero le vende a la sociedad representada por el segundo compareciente por la suma de NUEVE MILLONES QUINIENTOS MIL COLONES que confiesa recibidos el vendedor del comprador en dinero efectivo y a entera satisfacción, el vehículo que tiene las siguientes características: **MARCA:** Nissan, **CARROCERIA:** Familiar Station Wagon, **ESTILO:** Pathfinder, **CATEGORIA:** Automóvil, **AÑO:** dos mil seis, **MOTOR NUMERO:** CR ocho tres tres tres siete D cero cero uno cinco cero A, **COMBUSTIBLE:** Gasolina, **CILINDRADA:** Tres mil novecientos centímetros cúbicos, **CILINDROS:** seis, **TRACCION:** Doble, **COLOR:** Blanco, **CAPACIDAD:** Cinco personas, PESO BRUTO: Dos mil quinientos diez kilogramos, **PESO NETO:** Mil novecientos veintisiete kilogramos, **CHASIS NUMERO:** SALLHAM nueve GA cuatro cuatro cuatro ocho ocho siete, **PLACA NUMERO:** Trescientos veintiún mil quinientos uno, libre de gravámenes, anotación e infracciones.

ES TODO. Expido un primer testimonio. Leído lo escrito a los otorgantes, lo aprobaron y firmamos en la ciudad de San José a las once horas del ocho de febrero del dos mil nueve. ILEGIBLE.- JUAN GUTIERREZ RODRIGUEZ.- FEDERICO PP.- ** ***********************************

LO ANTERIOR ES COPIA EXACTA DE LA ESCRITURA NUMERO NOVENTA Y CUATRO INICIADA AL FOLIO OCHENTA FRENTE DEL TOMO DECIMO DE MI PROTOCOLO. CONFRONTADA CON SU ORIGINAL RESULTO CONFORME Y LA EXPIDO COMO PRIMER TESTIMONIO EN EL MISMO ACTO DE FIRMARSE LA MATRIZ.

JEFFREY JONES, SELLS AN AUTOMOBILE TO TIERRA AUTO, SOCIEDAD ANONIMA.
Deed granted in San Jose
on the 11th hour of the 8th of February 2009.
NOTARY PUBLIC: FEDERICO PEREZ PEREZ.

NUMBER NINETY FOUR: Before me, **FEDERICO PEREZ PEREZ,** Notary Public with office in San Jose, personally appeared **JEFFREY JONES,** no second surname on account of his Canadian nationality, of legal age, married once, retired, resident of Grecia, Barrio San Jose, 100 meters east of the Plus store with resident card number 999 and **JUAN GUTIERREZ RODRIGUEZ,** of legal age, single, business person, resident of San Jose Barrio Don Bosco, 25meters south of Purdy Motors, Paseo Colon, with identity card number 5- 222- 333, in his capacity as President with Power of Attorney of **TIERRA AUTO, SOCIEDAD ANONIMA,** domiciled in San Jose, Street 36 between Central avenue and 2nd Avenue and with corporate identity card number 3-101- 241810, and recorded in the Mercantile Section of the Public Registry at Volume: 1061, Page: 81, Entry: 91, which is current and to which the undersigned Notary hereby attests to and they state as follows: That the first party sells to the corporation represented by the second party for the sum of NINE MILLION FIVE HUNDRED THOUSAND COLONES which the seller acknowledge receipt of in cash and to his entire satisfaction for the sale of the vehicle which has the following characteristics: **MAKE:** Nissan, **CHASIS:** Station Wagon, **STYLE:** Pathfinder, **CATEGORY:** Automobile, **YEAR:** 2005, **ENGINE NUMBER:** CR 83333D00150A, **FUEL:** Gasoline, **DISPLACEMENT:** 3900, **CILINDERS:** six, **TRACTION:** 4X4, **COLOR:** White, **CAPACITY:** Five persons, **GROSS WEIGHT:** 2,510 Kg, **NET WEIGHT:** 1,927 Kg, **VIN NUMBER:** SALHAMM9GA444887, **TAG NUMBER:** 321501; free from any liens, annotations or traffic infractions.

THAT IS ALL. I issue one extract. Having read the foregoing to the parties they manifest their acceptance and we sign in the city of San Jose at 11 hours on the 8th of December of 2001. ILEGIBLE.- JUAN GUTIERREZ RODRI-GUEZ.- FEDERICO PP.- ***T HE FOLLOWIN EXTRACT IS A TRUE AND ACCURATE COPY OF DEED NUMBER 94 INITIATED AT PAGE 83 OF PROTOCOL BOOK NUMBER TEN. HAVING COMPARED THE SAME WITH THE ORIGINAL I ISSUED IT AS FIRST EXTRACT.

Appendix 38

Automobile Certificate of Title

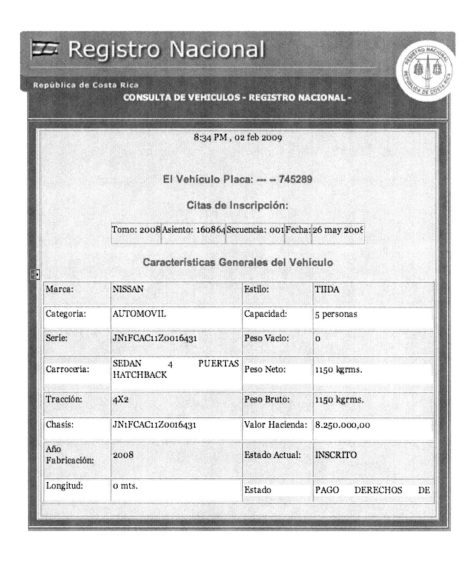

Registro Nacional

República de Costa Rica

CONSULTA DE VEHICULOS - REGISTRO NACIONAL -

8:34 PM , 02 feb 2009

El Vehículo Placa: --- -- 745289

Citas de Inscripción:

Tomo: 2008 | Asiento: 160864 | Secuencia: 001 | Fecha: 26 may 2008

Características Generales del Vehículo

Marca:	NISSAN	Estilo:	TIIDA
Categoria:	AUTOMOVIL	Capacidad:	5 personas
Serie:	JN1FCAC11Z0016431	Peso Vacio:	0
Carroceria:	SEDAN 4 PUERTAS HATCHBACK	Peso Neto:	1150 kgrms.
Tracción:	4X2	Peso Bruto:	1150 kgrms.
Chasis:	JN1FCAC11Z0016431	Valor Hacienda:	8.250.000,00
Año Fabricación:	2008	Estado Actual:	INSCRITO
Longitud:	0 mts.	Estado	PAGO DERECHOS DE

		Tributario:	ADUANA
Cabina:	DESCONOCIDO	Clase Tributaria:	2282987
Techo:	NO APLICA	Uso:	PARTICULAR
Peso Remolque:	0	Valor Contrato:	9.176.476,00
Color:	DORADO	Numero registral:	1
Convertido:	N	Moneda:	COLONES
VIN:	JN1FCAC11Z0016431		

Motor:	HR16384624A	Serie:	NO INDICADO	Marca:	NISSAN
Modelo:	FDTALAFC11EYADAH-B	Combustible:	GASOLINA	Fabricante:	NO INDICADO
Procedencia:	DESCONOCIDA	Cilindrada:	1.598 c.c.	Potencia:	80 kw.
Cilindros:	4				

Calidad(es) del(os) Propietario(s)

Detalle	Tipo Identificación	Número Identificación	Nombre
ver persona	CEDULA DE IDENTIDAD	100-291-999	JOHN DOE

No Posee Gravamen(es)

No Posee Anotación(es)

No Posee Infracción(es) / Colisión(es)

rNo Posee Levantamiento

Appendix 39

Automobile Registration

Appendix 40

Free Trade Zone Application

FORMULA 01

SOLICITUD DE INGRESO AL RÉGIMEN DE ZONAS FRANCAS Y DE AUTORIZACIÓN DE AUXILIAR DE LA FUNCIÓN PUBLICA ADUANERA

DATOS GENERALES DE LA EMPRESA

1. Nombre del Solicitante: _____

2. Documento de Identificación: _____ Número de Identificación: _____

3. Tipo de empresa:

   3.1 Clasificación: ☐ Procesadora ☐ Servicios ☐ Comercializadora ☐ Administradora

   3.2 Realizará actividades productivas fuera del área: ☐ SI ☐ NO

   Requerirá internamiento temporal de maquinaria, equipo, materias y mercancías al territorio aduanero nacional: ☐ SI ☐ NO

   3.3 Solicita Código Provisional de Auxiliar de la Función Pública Aduanera: ☐ SI ☐ NO

4. Nombre del Representante Legal: _____

   4.1 Documento de Identificación: _____ Número de Identificación: _____

5. Estado de la Empresa: ☐ Empresa en operación ☐ Proyecto

6. Ubicación de la empresa: ☐ Dentro de Parque de Zona Franca ☐ Fuera de Parque de Zona Franca

   6.1 Dirección: _____

   Provincia: _____ Cantón: _____ Distrito: _____

   6.2 Teléfono: _____ Fax: _____ Correo electrónico: _____

   6.3 Se ubicará en las instalaciones de otra empresa beneficiaria del Régimen ☐ SI ☐ No

   Nombre de la empresa donde se ubicará: _____

7. Detalle de las instalaciones: ☐ Propio ☐ Arrendado Por construir: ☐ SI ☐ No

   7.1 Áreas de producción industrial (excluir zonas verdes, parqueos, áreas de recreación, bienestar social y salud): _____ m2

   7.2 Área inicial para proyectos: _____ m2

   7.3 Área total: _____ m2

8. Compromisos de la empresa:

   8.1 Fecha de inicio de operaciones productivas: _____

   8.2 Monto de la inversión nueva inicial: _____ US$

   8.3 Fecha de cumplimiento de la inversión nueva inicial: _____

   8.4 Monto de la inversión mínima total: _____ US$

8.5 Fecha de cumplimiento de la inversión mínima total: _____

8.6 Nivel de empleo mínimo requerido en plena producción: _____

8.7 Fecha de cumplimiento del empleo en plena producción: _____

9. Lugar para recibir notificaciones en la ciudad de San José: _____

_____

Provincia: _____ Cantón: _____ Distrito: _____

DECLARACIÓN JURADA

DECLARO BAJO LA FE DEL JURAMENTO LO SIGUIENTE: Primero. Que la empresa por mí representada no se dedicará a la fabricación o comercialización de ningún tipo de armas (ni permitidas ni prohibidas) ni componentes, ensambles, ni subensambles de uso exclusivo en la industria militar. Segundo. Que mi representada se encuentra inscrita en el Registro de Contribuyentes del Ministerio de Hacienda. Tercero. Que mi representada se encuentra al día en todas sus obligaciones obrero-patronales con la Caja Costarricense del Seguro Social. Cuarto. Que mi representada, sus accionistas, directores, empleados o personeros, no han sido sancionados en relación con las actividades de la empresa, mediante resolución firme en vía administrativa, por haber incurrido en infracciones administrativas, aduaneras, tributarias o tributario-aduaneras. Quinto. Que mi representada, sus accionistas, directores, empleados o personeros, no han sido condenados en relación con las actividades de la empresa, mediante resolución firme en la vía judicial, por haber incurrido en delitos aduaneros o tributarios. Sexto. Que mi representada y el proyecto de inversión a desarrollar no son beneficiarios de ningún régimen de incentivos. Séptimo. Que mi representada y el proyecto de inversión a desarrollar no se han beneficiado con anterioridad de los incentivos del Régimen de Zonas Francas, ni siquiera al amparo de una persona física o jurídica distinta. Octavo. Que mi representada, sus accionistas o cualquier beneficiario potencial no puede descontar, en su país de origen, los impuestos exonerados en Costa Rica. Noveno. Que mi representada no es una entidad bancaria, financiera o aseguradora y tampoco se dedica a prestar servicios profesionales. Asimismo, hago constar que conozco que de acuerdo a lo establecido en la Ley de Régimen de Zonas Francas, dichas actividades no pueden ser desarrolladas al amparo de dicho régimen. Décimo. Que mi representada se compromete a adquirir un software apto para la transmisión electrónica de datos al sistema de información del Servicio Nacional de Aduanas. Decimoprimero. Que mi representada se compromete a cumplir con las disposiciones legales, reglamentarias y procedimentales relativas al control y seguridad de las mercancías que deben observarse en las instalaciones. Decimosegundo. Que el propietario registral del inmueble donde se ubican las instalaciones de la empresa, otorgó la correspondiente autorización para permitir a ésta, realizar sus operaciones en dicho inmueble dentro del Régimen de Zonas Francas. Decimotercero. Que conozco que el suministro de información falsa en la solicitud del Régimen de Zonas Francas podría implicar la revocatoria del régimen, de conformidad con el artículo treinta y dos inciso s) de la Ley número 7210, Ley de Régimen de Zonas Francas y sus reformas. Hago la presente declaración y reconozco que se de las penas previstas en el Código Penal por los delitos de falso testimonio y de perjurio, consciente de ello, reitero que los datos otorgados en este documento son legítimos y verdaderos y que los he rendido bajo la fe del juramento.

La firma que de seguido se estampa, avala la información contenida en la totalidad de los folios que integran este formulario.

_____   _____   _____

Nombre del representante legal   Firma   Número de documento de identificación

Autenticación
(firma, sello y timbre)

Nota: La empresa debe presentar documentos adicionales a este formulario: Ver Instructivo

Appendix 41

Municipal Business License Application

Index

Breinigsville, PA USA
22 November 2009
227991BV00004B/74/P

9 780971 581548